The Better Angels

The Better Angels

Five Women Who Changed Civil War America

ROBERT C. PLUMB

Foreword by Elisabeth Griffith

Potomac Books

AN IMPRINT OF THE UNIVERSITY OF NEBRASKA PRESS

For
Louise Kittell Plumb
Sarah Plumb DiGioia
Janet Needham Plumb
Judy Plumb Panico
Marjorie Ewing Kittell

The five better angels in my life

For he will give his angels
charge of you to guard you
in all your ways. On their hands
they will bear you up, lest you
dash your foot against a stone.

—PSALM 91:11,12

The mystic chords of memory, stretching from
every battlefield and patriot grave to every living heart
and hearthstone all over this broad land, will yet swell the
chorus of the Union, when again touched, as surely they
will be, by the better angels of our nature.

—ABRAHAM LINCOLN, first inaugural address, March 4, 1861

CONTENTS

ILLUSTRATIONS

Following page 118

FOREWORD

ELISABETH GRIFFITH

As I came over, the next day, I met Doctor Rivers at the door of [the] ward.

"Really," said he, "that little Mrs. Addison is a true heroine!"

As I smiled assent to him, I said inwardly to myself—"Really, she is a true woman!"

—ROSE TERRY COOKE, "A Woman," *Atlantic Monthly*, December 1862

Historians have long faced the challenge of recognizing and reassessing the role of women in our history. Did any women have major roles, or were all of them supporting actors? Do we even know the names of the ensemble players? Indeed, there were starring roles, but many women were in the chorus, nameless rather than notable: enslaved blacks, homesteaders, factory workers, immigrants, farm wives. It's hard to write about the lives of women who were illiterate or impoverished, who left no diaries or whose correspondence was not valued enough to be saved, and who appear nowhere but on ship manifests, slave inventories, or the census.

The Civil War tore the American union in half, presented a constitutional crisis, freed enslaved African Americans, killed 620,000 soldiers, devastated whole sections of the country, destroyed an economy based on slave labor, and sowed seeds of racism and hatred that still fester. Yet the war also increased American manufacturing capacity, drove the intercontinental railroad, and opened educational opportunities with the Morrill Land-Grant Act. It inspired the Fourteenth Amendment. And it created unexpected opportunities for women, as every war has.

Until recently women have been underrepresented in accounts

of the Civil War period. As abolitionist Maria Weston Chapman wrote, women "leaped from their spheres" to participate. She was referring to the "separate sphere" of domesticity that confined upper- and middle-class, mostly urban white women to limited roles. This sphere was defined by social custom, Judeo-Christian teaching, and common law, all of which saw women as secondary and subservient. At the time of the Civil War, married women had no rights to earned wages, did not inherit property or the custody of their children, and had no recourse to divorce. (There were a few exceptions in a small number of Northern states.) Access to education and employment opportunities was limited. While men were free to pursue enterprise, politics, warfare, and public roles, privileged women were confined to a private peaceful sphere of domesticity, of home, children, morality, and virtue. They were expected to be pious, pure, domestic, and submissive. Less privileged women, mill workers or field hands or frontier wives, could only aspire to be "true ladies."

This book's title, *The Better Angels*, is an artful choice, with its dual references to Lincoln's first inaugural address and to the roles nineteenth-century women were expected to play within their domestic spheres. Clara Barton, Sarah Josepha Hale, Julia Ward Howe, Harriet Beecher Stowe, and Harriet Tubman challenged those confining limits to expand women's traditional roles to encompass petitioning, organizing, educating, writing, and reforming as part of their assigned spheres. In addition, Harriet Tubman escaped that confinement both literally and figuratively as she fled enslavement and helped others on their paths to liberty. While these women maintained the outward appearance of ladylike modesty and manners, they became fierce warriors in their own right. Clara Barton's belief was that when the Civil War ended, "woman was at least fifty years in advance of the normal position which continued peace would have assigned her." Barton's contemporary, Julia Ward Howe, also a witness to the effect of the war on the nation's women, wrote that women "found a new scope for their activities and developed activities hitherto unsuspected by themselves."

They were notable women, subjects of past biographies with stories known to many schoolchildren. But this work, *The Better Angels*, expands our understanding of how slavery and civil war provoked, inspired, and energized these capable women. It helps us understand the power of chaos to stimulate creative enterprise and to inspire lives of promise and purpose. The book chronicles the achievements of these five women, whose legacies surround us today: the American Red Cross, the national Thanksgiving holiday, "The Battle Hymn of the Republic," the novel *Uncle Tom's Cabin*, and the liberation narrative associated with the Underground Railroad.

These legacies have been a platform from which future generations of women could benefit. As Elizabeth Cady Stanton commented about her own contemporaries' accomplishments: "I never forgot that we are sowing winter wheat, which the coming spring will see sprout, and other hands will reap."

ACKNOWLEDGMENTS

Every book starts with the seed of an idea, and then the real work begins. The author has to steer the idea through a series of creative stages of execution. Each step along this path, people help in ways that cannot be imagined at the start of the process. My idea for *The Better Angels* was helped at the beginning by the patient and insightful Elisabeth "Betsy" Griffith. She challenged and guided me at the same time. Her career as an educator was evident as she encouraged me to expand my idea. Betsy's knowledge of women's history made her the kind of mentor and muse all authors hope will play a major role at the start of their projects. I am deeply indebted to her.

Ideas are essential, but crafting the language to tell the story in a compelling way is something that every author works hard to achieve. M. G. Lord and my classmates at the Yale Writing Workshops were candid and constructive as they commented on my early drafts of *The Better Angels*. I am thankful for their wise counsel at a critical juncture for the project. Adding spice to our group—lest we become too serious and overlook the joys of writing—was our instructor, the ever-witty and inspiring Ms. Lord.

Both original and secondary research sources played an essential part of developing my narrative. I was helped countless times over the years by the superb staffs at the National Archives and the Library of Congress. Additionally, a number of excellent recent biographies of the five better angels gave me valuable insights that became part of my manuscript as secondary research or gave me a starting point for further primary research. The work of Nancy Koestor, Kate Clifford Larson, the late Elizabeth Brown Pryor, and Elaine Showalter are among the giants on whose shoulders my work humbly stands. I was pleased to have the opportunity to speak to Ms. Larson and Ms. Showalter as I worked on this project.

Roger Williams, my literary agent, was always persistent, optimistic, and tireless in finding the appropriate home for my manuscript. I am delighted that he was in my corner during the entire process. I appreciate the excellent work done on my behalf at Potomac Books by Tom Swanson, acquisition editor; Abby Stryker, acquisitions assistant; and Elizabeth Zaleski, project editor, as well as the diligent work done by copyeditor Vicki Chamlee. They are an all-star team.

This book is dedicated to the five "better angels" of my life: my wife, Louise Kittell Plumb; my daughter, Sarah Plumb DiGioia; my mother, Janet Needham Plumb; my sister, Judy Plumb Panico; and my mother-in-law, Marjorie Ewing Kittell. They have been the epitome of independent, talented, and strong women from whom I have learned so much. I am forever grateful for the part each has played in my life. I am also indebted to the gifted historian the late professor James O. Horton, my undergraduate classmate, whose incisive works on slavery gave me a deeper understanding of the subject that is so central to *The Better Angels'* narrative.

I owe thanks to my friends who helped me focus on the task of writing. Their continuing interest in my project and periodic questions as to how the book was going kept me researching and writing with diligence and dedication. I will always be thankful that this Greek chorus watched over me and had my best interests in mind.

I am also appreciative for the years I have been immersed in the *Better Angels* project. It has been an illuminating and rewarding experience. As historian David McCullough has written in *The American Spirit*: "To a large degree, history is a lesson in proportion. History reminds us that nothing counterfeit has any staying power. . . . History teaches us that character counts. Character above all." The five better angels confirm McCullough's observation. Their characters shine brightly through the centuries of the American past, and I am honored to be their admiring narrator.

1

The Better Angels of Our Nature

Prior to and during the Civil War, women stepped forward to take roles previously denied them in antebellum America. Roles that some thought only a man could fulfill. Roles that were too dangerous, too rigorous, too daring for women to attempt. But women did attempt them, and their successes were extraordinary at the time. Many of these accomplishments were so important that they reverberate today, over 150 years later.

On a starlit early September evening, a woman and her two brothers set out from the Eastern Shore of Maryland to escape enslavement and find freedom in the North. Frightened by the potential consequences of their flight, her two brothers turned back. The woman did not. She continued on to free herself and later returned to help guide other enslaved people to freedom. She was a liberator.

So enraged by the passage of the Fugitive Slave Act by Congress, she began writing a story that would bring the ugliness of slavery to the bookshelves of America. Her writing was compelling and fanned the sparks of abolition in the North to a fiery cause. She was a literary provocateur.

In a Washington DC hotel, she tossed and turned in her bed. Images of marching soldiers paraded through her subconscious. The men seemed to call out for inspiration amid a time of defeats, a lackluster military leadership, and a motivated and successful enemy. The woman rose from her bed and began writing verses on scraps of U.S. Sanitary Commission letterhead: "He hath loosed the fateful lightning of His terrible swift sword. . . . Let the Hero, born of woman, crush the serpent with his heel. . . . He has sounded from the trumpet that shall never call retreat. . . . As he died to make men holy, let us die to make men free."[1] When completed, the verses would be set to music and become a hymn. She was the inspirer of a noble cause.

With a teamster and a male helper, she crossed the mountainous Maryland terrain in a wagon filled with medical supplies. When she reached the battlefield at Antietam near Sharpsburg, Maryland, doctors there had been reduced to binding men's wounds with corn husks. One of the doctors treating the wounded was so impressed with her courage, resourcefulness, and sheer grit, he called the woman "the angel of the battlefield" in a letter to his wife.[2] Through her transportation of essential medical supplies and with her compassionate service to the wounded, she was a healer.

As the editor of one of the most successful magazines in mid-nineteenth-century America, she used her considerable publishing resources to urge government leaders to issue proclamations for a national day of thanksgiving. Most ignored her, but in 1863 she succeeded in her longtime quest. Abraham Lincoln declared Thursday, November 26, 1863, a national day of thanksgiving for the entire nation. Her success came after a twenty-year campaign and was an important first step in bringing the North and the South back together. She was a reconciler.

The "better angels of our nature" that Lincoln referenced in his first inaugural address is an apt description of five women who made singularly important contributions to the nation leading up to the Civil War and continuing during the conflict where countrymen fought countrymen: Harriet Tubman, Harriet Beecher Stowe, Julia Ward Howe, Clara Barton, and Sarah Josepha Hale. Amid this tragic time of death and destruction, these five women came forward to take on noble causes that were exceptional because of the ambitiousness of their goals and their lasting impact on the United States. Justly honored in their time, the five continue to be recognized today.

These five "angels" were every bit as human as the rest of their fellow citizens at the time. They had pervasive human foibles—jealousy, impatience, resentment, pride—that all, both male and female, share as mortal beings. Yet, many times, their perceived shortcomings, such as impatience and a reckless disregard of authority, allowed them to succeed where other more reticent or submissive behavior would have been a barrier to success.

The five are exceptional examples of how gifted and courageous women championed causes in mid-nineteenth-century America, finding inspiration amid the chaos and gloom of a war that left little room for anything but suffering and loss. They remain powerful reminders of the human spirit that manifests itself in acts of freedom, truth, inspiration, compassion, and reconciliation.

The Five Angels

Harriet Ross Tubman: Liberator

In early September 1849, twenty-seven-year-old enslaved Harriet Ross Tubman had borne enough misery and threats to her freedom and well-being. Along with her two brothers, Henry and Ben, she "self-liberated" by fleeing her bondage in Dorchester County, Maryland, on the state's Eastern Shore. It was a bold and dangerous step to flee slavery and evade the long arm of the slave masters and law enforcement officials. Being caught would likely result in severe beatings or sometimes being sold to slave owners in the Deep South, where conditions were often even harsher for enslaved people than in the border state Maryland.

Tubman and her brothers, employing a sophisticated, multi-layered communications network of free blacks, enslaved people, and abolitionist whites, began traveling the path to freedom through Dorchester County. Fearing the consequences of being caught, Harriet Tubman's brothers abandoned their flight and turned back to their owners. Alone, she continued traveling north to freedom guided by the North Star and with directions offered by supportive black and white friends and other antislavery sympathizers. Her escape was a success. She reached the "promised land" of freedom in New York State and continued to Canada.

Over the succeeding years, Harriet Tubman was not content to bask in her own freedom from slavery. Again and again, she returned to the Eastern Shore of Maryland to help family and friends escape slavery, guiding them over a trail that wound from safe haven to safe house through Maryland and Delaware to Philadelphia, then to New York State, and, in some cases, on to sanctuary in Canada. Each time she succeeded leading enslaved people to freedom, but with each passing year, the risk and complexity of escape grew. Maryland slave owners became increasingly frustrated with the growing numbers of escaped slaves; they were not about to let their slave assets slip away from their control with impunity.

By 1860 Tubman had led scores of enslaved people to freedom and new lives in the North. In early December of that year, she began yet another freedom mission into Maryland, this time to free her sister Rachel and her sister's small children, Angerine and Ben. As she approached the neighborhood where her relatives lived, Tubman discovered that Rachel had died, and the location of the two children was unknown. Tubman had to give up the idea of freeing her orphaned niece and nephew for the time being. Despite this setback, Tubman was unwilling to forgo an opportunity to liberate other slaves while she was in the area. She took the Ennals family under her wing and began leading them to freedom from enslavement in Dorchester County. The Ennals family consisted of Stephen; his wife, Maria; and their children: Harriet, Amanda, and a three-month-old baby. The Ennals were accompanied by a man known only as John and later were joined by a female runaway slave in Baltimore.

Using her network of safe houses and agents on the Underground Railroad, Tubman took the Ennals' group to the home of a known Underground Railroad "stationmaster," a black friend whom Tubman trusted. Using a coded knock on the friend's door, Tubman sought refuge for the party during the early morning hours. Rather than the friend whom Tubman had relied on during previous trips, an agitated white man came to the window of the house and demanded that the group identify itself.

Tubman had been exceptionally successful in her efforts to guide others to freedom over the past ten years, but her efforts had also resulted in slave owners clamping down on escape attempts throughout the Eastern Shore. Tubman's communications and safe house networks were being compromised as slave owners became more vigilant and aggressive in penetrating the escape structure. Underground Railroad agents in the area had been ferreted out and some jailed.

Despite this seeming setback in guiding her group to safety and freedom, Tubman rebounded quickly. She led them away from the populated area to a nearby swamp, where the potential for being discovered by roving gangs of slave catchers was greatly reduced. There she located a suitable hiding place, a small island covered with long grasses that could conceal the fleeing group. Everyone remained hidden as search parties combed the area, looking for runaways. The cold December weather and lack of food began to take its toll on them as the swamp became a prison as well as a sanctuary. The infant in the party could only be calmed with a dose of a paregoric.

Their presence did not go undetected. Fortunately, an antislavery Quaker, who had a previous role in helping runaway slaves, discovered them and offered directions to his barn. There they found a horse and wagon along with food that had been left for them. Once refreshed, the group traveled to another nearby Quaker safe house known by Tubman. The runaways continued on, inching their way north to freedom. Along the way, Tubman served as their guide, sought food for them, and provided needed encouragement when their hope began to waver. She never questioned a successful outcome for her mission. Tubman was convinced they were being guided and guarded by God.

As they made their way north, Tubman left the Ennals and John in a safe hiding place while she scouted the area and foraged for food. She communicated with them in their hiding places by singing spirituals with verses coded to announce danger or the all clear. It is reported that in some cases, she sang songs through twice to signal an all clear to her hidden party of six. Other times she would sing selected verses of "Go Down, Moses" to confirm that the danger had passed.

Let my people go!
Oh go down, Moses,
Way down to Egypt's land.
Tell old Pharaoh,
Let my people go.[3]

Tubman reasoned that slave catchers and Maryland authorities, fulfilling their responsibilities in returning escaped slaves under the Fugitive Slave Act, would not be suspicious of a black woman singing spirituals to herself as she walked alone on a country road, presumably conducting errands for her owners.

By the end of December 1860, Tubman and her seven charges (joined now by the female runaway slave in Baltimore) reached Canada. Reports on her latest safe and successful journey to bring slaves to freedom were rapidly communicated among the abolitionists in Pennsylvania, Delaware, and New York. Weary, hungry, and footsore (and touched by frostbite), Tubman had successfully executed another slave liberation. She accomplished this with minimal financial resources and maximum personal courage.

Harriet Beecher Stowe: Literary Provocateur

When Harriet Beecher Stowe's antislavery novel was published, she knew that her candid and detailed descriptions in the narrative would provoke many who had vested interests in denying the facts of slavery. They would dispute her accounts of human suffering. Some would claim that *Uncle Tom's Cabin* was pure fiction with no basis in the real world, the fantasy of a vivid imagination. Others had more nuanced accusations. What she described, some claimed in letters to the *New York Observer*, were evils no different than the occasional evils that accompany all human interactions throughout history. Some thought her novel "anti-ministerial," which the critics found contradictory in a writer whose father, husband, and brothers were in the ministry. Still others challenged the temerity of a woman to create literature—even if what she wrote was accurate—that was not a fitting subject for a woman to read or write about. It was, they wrote, a pollution of literature and of the heart and mind of a woman author.

One commentator took the criticism to a personal and repugnant level: "[She] betrays a malignity so remarkable that the petticoat lifts itself and we see the hoof of the beast under the table."[4] Yet Stowe did not retreat an inch from the intent and specifics of her novel. To shrink from bullies and outright lies was not in her character. In a letter to the *New York Observer* in May 1852, she wrote: "We women are naturally retiring, fearful, shrinking from the coarse abuse of life, but when we once truly believe in the honor & worth of man or cause we follow them thru good report & evil report, into prison & unto death."[5]

She was resolute, buoyed by her strong belief in the cause that undergirded her work and by the support of her family. Her sister-in-law wrote her: "Now Hattie, if I could use a pen as you can, I would write something that would make the whole nation feel what an accursed thing slavery is."[6] And Harriet Beecher Stowe did just that. She wrote the most compelling and persuasive anti-slavery narrative the world has ever seen. Her novel *Uncle Tom's Cabin* sold over one million copies and was translated into two dozen languages.

To confront her critics with logic and facts, she set about to publish a response to her challengers, primarily those Southern critics who were confounded both by her attack on a core economic institution and by the fact that a woman had thrown down the gauntlet. In 1853—a year after *Uncle Tom's Cabin* was released— she published a book that was a head-on counterattack to her pro-slavery critics. *A Key to Uncle Tom's Cabin* was a book, according to Harriet, that did not begin to "measure the depth of the abyss of slavery" as depicted in *Uncle Tom's Cabin*.[7]

Harriet Beecher Stowe had the creative and literary skills to produce a successful fictional narrative with well-developed characters and a compelling story line. She also possessed a logical, precise mind that could construct a defense of her work as brilliantly reasoned as a skilled lawyer's brief. Even so, she consulted "legal gentlemen who have given . . . their assistance and support in the legal part of the discussion."[8] She set up her approach in the beginning paragraphs of *A Key* to show how her fictional account is supported side by side with real-life examples: "The author will now proceed along the course of the story, from the first page onward, and develop, as far as possible, the incidents by which different parts were suggested."[9]

Stowe used a variety of firsthand and documented secondary sources to build her argument in *A Key*. She drew on her experiences living in Cincinnati, Ohio, where both Harriet and her husband, Calvin, had frequent contacts with runaway slaves as the couple fulfilled their duties supporting the Underground Railroad. She drew on the experiences of a runaway slave who was hired by the Stowes as a domestic worker. Stowe also relied on the documented writings of Theodore Weld's book *American Slavery as It Is*, published in 1839, that contained unimpeachable evidence of slavery's cruelties.

In the beginning of *A Key*, Harriet set out her proposition for the authenticity of *Uncle Tom's Cabin*:

> At different times, doubt has been expressed whether the representations of "Uncle Tom's Cabin" are a fair representation of slavery as it presently exists. This work, more, perhaps, than any other work of fiction that ever was written, has been a collection and arrangement of real incidents—of actions really performed, of words really uttered—grouped together with reference to a general result, in the same manner that the mosaic artist groups his fragments of various stones into one general picture. His is a mosaic of gems—this is a mosaic of facts.[10]

While she envisioned her defense of *Uncle Tom's Cabin* to be a document of about 100 pages, the completed publication was over 250 pages packed with evidential prose. When she finished *A Key*, she reported that "it may be truly said that I wrote with my heart's blood."[11] Her writing travail was rewarded by the response the publication received from the public: ninety thousand copies sold in the first month it was in print. Eventually, some 150,000 copies of *A Key* were purchased in the United States.

The issue of slavery had now been dragged out into the sunlight for all to see, and a resolute female author and her book had earned a place in the pantheon of the world's most significant literature. Stowe's substantiation of the facts in *Uncle Tom's Cabin* through her publication of *A Key* only strengthened an already-strong story of human indignity and suffering. In less than a decade after *Uncle Tom's Cabin* and *A Key* were published, the slavery issue would be settled on the fields of fire.

Julia Ward Howe: Inspirer of the "Terrible Swift Sword"

In the early morning of November 19, 1861, Julia Ward Howe tossed and turned in her bed in Willard's City Hotel in Washington City. Images, then verses, flooded her brain, making it impossible for her to fall back asleep. As a published poet, she was frequently distracted by verses flitting through her head as she performed her daily tasks. Iambic pentameter, usually of a romantic nature, was a pleasant escape from her responsibility of caring for her six children. But these early morning verses came with images that were profound and disturbing as she lay in the dark at the Willard.

She and her husband, Samuel Gridley Howe, a physician, visited Washington City as he fulfilled his duties as a newly assigned member of the U.S. Sanitary Commission, an organization charged with both caring for the wounded and maintaining healthy living conditions for the Federal Army. Samuel and Julia were accompanied to the capital city by John Andrew, governor of their home state of Massachusetts, and Mrs. Eliza Andrew. Also joining the group were Edwin Whipple; his wife, Charlotte; and the pastor of the Howe's church, Rev. James Freeman Clarke.

During the day leading up to her restless night's sleep, Julia Ward Howe, the Whipples, and Reverend Clarke crossed the Potomac River and visited a troop encampment in Virginia to observe a Union troop review. The review had just begun when Confederate skirmishers interrupted the proceedings with musket fire. The federal troops quickly took positions to disperse the rebels; once the enemy had been repulsed, the leadership sent the troops back to their quarters and canceled the review for the day.

When the four headed their carriage back to Washington, they found themselves surrounded by Union foot soldiers on the march. Now, for the first time, Howe saw close up the instruments that would accomplish the battle to end slavery. The tempo of men marching, the sound of their battle gear thumping together in time with their cadence, and the sight of bayonets glinting in the sun created a tableau of the senses that immediately resonated

with her and haunted her throughout the day. These soldiers—
many seemed mere boys—had in Julia's mind a divine purpose.
Their commitment, courage, and sacrifice were the means by
which a war would be won and slavery ended for all time in the
United States.

As their carriage moved slowly along the crowded road of marching men, the four civilians "began to sing some of the well-known
songs of the war," according to Howe.[12] The soldiers soon joined them:

> John Brown's body lies a moldering in the grave;
> His soul's marching on!
> Glory, glory, hallelujah! Glory, glory, hallelujah!
> Glory, glory, hallelujah, his soul is marching on!
>
> He's gone to be a soldier in the army of the Lord!
> His soul is marching on!
> John Brown's knapsack is strapped upon his back!
> His soul is marching on!
> Now, three rousing cheers for the Union,
> As we are marching on![13]

The origins of the "John Brown's Body" lyrics are murky. Some
said that the song was to remember and honor the abolitionist
martyr John Brown who was hanged in December 1859 after his
Harpers Ferry raid. Others had a more prosaic attribution for
the song. They said it came from Union soldiers who were singing about John Brown, a sergeant in their unit. The melody had its
origins in camp meeting songs from the late eighteenth and early
nineteenth centuries. Regardless of the derivation of the words
and music, many found the tune well suited for marching, but the
lyrics were thought to be common, perhaps even disrespectful to
abolitionist Brown.

Sometime later in the day when Howe and her traveling companions reflected on the events in the Union camp and on the
road, someone suggested that she, an accomplished poet, could
write more suitable lyrics for the men as they marched. Perhaps something more inspirational. More noble. Better fitting

the cause for which they were marching and fighting. (Who specifically made the suggestion is unclear. Some have suggested it was Reverend Clarke.)

The four returned to the Willard's City Hotel after a long day in the field. Exhausted from the day's activities, Howe retired to her hotel room and fell into a restless sleep. In the early morning hours, she awoke brimming with inspiration. She found a pen and paper and, by candlelight, began to write down stanzas as they flowed from her mind. Howe, a devout Christian who was intimately familiar with the Old and New Testaments of the Bible, drew on the apocalyptic images from Revelations. In this book the expected millennium is preceded by the grapes of man's unrighteousness being crushed in God's wine press of wrath. Other biblical and literary allusions are found throughout Howe's verses, which came to be known as "The Battle Hymn of the Republic."

Once Howe completed writing down her stanzas on the back of U.S. Sanitary Commission letterhead, she went back to bed. There is no evidence that she spent any significant time editing or rewriting her initial work. She considered the verses to be inspired; therefore, further editing was not required. She later wrote of her experience: "Because of my sincere desire, a word was given me to say which did strengthen the hearts of those who fought in the field and those who languished in prison."[14]

Three months after writing the stanzas down on paper in her hotel room, Julia Ward Howe's "The Battle Hymn of the Republic" was published in the *Atlantic Monthly*. The publication paid her a mere five dollars for her efforts but did give her front-page placement. Following its appearance in February 1862 in the *Atlantic Monthly*, Howe's words were picked up by numerous other publications, and "Battle Hymn" quickly found its way to Union troops in the field (and in Confederate prisons), where it was beloved as an anthem of the Union cause. The forty-two-year-old wife, mother of six, and poet had captured a cause and national purpose so well that her hymn quickly became a favorite of Northern military and civilian singers.

Clara Barton: Compassionate Healer

The large covered wagon drawn by a team of mules lurched over the road through South Mountain, Maryland, on its way to a small farming community near the Potomac River. In addition to the army teamster handling the wagon filled with medical supplies were Clara Barton and her faithful helper, Cornelius Welles, who had accompanied her on similar missions to aid the wounded. Barton's iron resolve in dangerous situations left little sympathy for those of faint heart. "If my countrymen are to suffer my place is with them, my northern brothers are here in arms danger and death staring them in the face and I cannot leave them."[15]

As the wagon wound its way over South Mountain, the evidence of a recent battle became obvious. Union soldiers straggled past, going in the opposite direction. The road on which Barton's wagon rumbled along was a scene of devastation. The detritus of military equipment mixed with dead men and horses was scattered along their route. She later wrote about the "blood and carnage" she saw along the way: "A mingled mass of stiffened, blackened men, horses, muskets, bayonets, knapsacks, haversacks, blankets, coats, canteens, broken wheels, and cannon balls which had done this deadly work—the very earth plowed with shot." Undaunted, the wagon and its occupants proceeded onward with brief pauses for Barton and Welles to treat wounded men who were not beyond help. It made her "shocked and sick at heart" at what she saw. She called it "that field of death" with a "hideous pile of mangled and dismembered bodies."[16] She did not know a horror of even greater magnitude lay ahead.

Soon Barton's wagon joined a ten-mile-long train of the Union Army as it sluggishly headed west to the next expected battle near Sharpsburg. Barton, impatient with the pace, urged her wagon's teamster to pass the larger Union wagon train loaded with ammunition, food, and other military supplies on its way to the Army of the Potomac. The matériel of war abounded, but only Clara Barton's wagon held the materials to treat the aftermath of war. Union officers in charge of the large wagon train, however, ordered the medical supply wagon stopped. There would be no leapfrogging the supply train by Barton's wagon. Pleading and threats of using her connections with high-ranking officers were to no avail. Seeing that neither reason nor "pulling rank" would succeed, she used subterfuge. After a few hours of sleep, Barton, Welles, and her teamster awoke in the middle of the night, harnessed their mules, and got underway, passing the sleeping officers and teamsters of the large wagon train.

The medical supply wagon traveled along the Boonsboro Road until it reached the vicinity of Sharpsburg in the early morning. As they drew closer to the town, a cacophony of artillery and musket fire greeted them. The ground trembled as Union field pieces— brass Napoleons and huge twenty-pound Parrott guns—fired round after round into the Confederate lines. To do her job properly, Barton reasoned, she wanted to be just behind the cannons so that the wounded could be treated as quickly as possible. Proximity and speed could make the difference between saving or losing a wounded soldier's life.

By mid-morning on September 17, the battle that was later known as Antietam (for the small creek that ran along the battlefield) saw casualties beginning to mount at an alarming rate. Barton surveyed the battlefield and determined that a barn on the farm owned by the Poffenberger family would serve as a good field hospital. Once on the property, mules were unhitched and supplies unloaded. Standing in the doorway of the Poffenberger farmhouse, Dr. James L. Dunn saw a familiar face as the large covered wagon was unloaded by the teamster, a second man, and a lone woman. Recognizing Clara Barton amid the unloading, Dr. Dunn rushed up to her. "God has indeed remembered us. How did you get from Virginia to here? So soon? And again to supply our necessities."[17] Dr. Dunn remembered her from their service together tending the wounded at Fairfax Station, Virginia, where the casualties were taken following the Second Battle of Bull Run just a month earlier.

Dr. Dunn's need for supplies was critical. He and his fellow surgeons had resorted to using corn leaves to bandage gunshot wounds and to cover the remaining parts of limbs following amputation. The situation was catastrophic, Dr. Dunn told Barton. "We have nothing but our instruments and the little chloroform we brought in our pockets. I have torn up the last sheets we could find in this house . . . and all those wounded men bleeding to death."[18] With her medical supplies now available, corn husks were replaced with linen bandages. Barton went about, one eye witness reported, "staunching wounds . . . administering cordials to the fainting soldier, cheering those destined to undergo amputation, moistening lips parched with thirst."[19]

She moved among the wounded in the farmhouse and then went outside to help the casualties who had not yet been brought inside for examination and treatment. The closeness of the battlefield was apparent as Confederate artillery rounds dropped on the Poffenberger farmyard and as minié balls riddled the farmhouse and nearby barn. A wounded soldier lying on the ground beckoned to her, asking for a drink of water. She knelt beside him, lifted his head, and held a cup to his lips. As he sipped the water, she heard a whizzing sound, and at the same time the soldier stiffened and fell back from the cradle of her arm. A stray bullet had passed through the sleeve of Barton's dress and struck the soldier in the chest. "The poor fellow sprang from my hands and fell back quivering in the agonies of death," she later reported.[20] Clara Barton was spared from any injury, but there was a bullet hole in the sleeve of her dress. It was an incident she would remember and retell for the rest of her life.

She was called upon to treat scores of wounded soldiers at Antietam, even using her pocketknife to remove a bullet from a soldier's face when a surgeon was not available. "I do not think a surgeon would have pronounced it a scientific operation," she recalled, "but that it was successful I dared to hope from the gratitude of the patient."[21]

Clara Barton continued to treat soldiers at the Poffenberger farm during and after the Battle of Antietam, even at one point treating a young soldier who turned out to be a female. The young girl, Mary Galloway, had dressed in a Union uniform, hoping to join her lover, a young lieutenant in a Wisconsin regiment. In the chaos of battle, she was hit by a musket ball but refused to let a male surgeon treat her. With Barton's intervention and assistance, a surgeon dressed the wound, and Mary made a full recovery. She was later reunited with her lieutenant, Harry Barnard. (Harry and Mary married and named their eldest daughter Clara, the woman Mary credited with saving her life.)

Barton worked tirelessly, helping the wounded at Antietam on a virtually around-the-clock schedule. Official accounts recorded twenty-five thousand casualties between daylight and dusk on September 17, making the Battle of Antietam the bloodiest single day in a blood-soaked war. For her, there was much work to be done amid this carnage. Her admiring coworker during most of her time at Antietam, Dr. Dunn, later wrote to his wife about his experiences at the battle, the contributions Clara Barton made, and her unceasing devotion to the wounded. "In my feeble estimation," Dunn wrote, "General [George] McClellan [commanding general of the Army of the Potomac], with all his laurels, sinks into insignificance beside the true heroine of the age, the angel of the battlefield."[22]

Sarah Josepha Hale: Seeker of Reconciliation

As the editor of the popular women's magazine *Godey's Lady's Book*, Sarah Josepha Hale walked a very narrow path when accepting content for the publication as the Civil War drew closer. Increasing dissension between the Southern states that favored slavery and the Northern states that longed to end the "peculiar institution" grew more virulent with each passing week. In her early writing, notably in her book *Northwood*, she sought to strike a balance between the two regions, praising "the great men who know no North or South."[23] The book did make a case for emancipating all slaves in the entire United States, so that "finally, every obstacle to the real freedom of America would be melted away."[24] Hale's book also promoted the idea of a national Thanksgiving Day as a celebration of the country's bountiful resources and a reconciliation between the two regions. In her writings she stopped short of advocating for the incorporation of freed slaves into American society. Rather, she proposed a program of colonization where free blacks would be sent to an African country to reestablish their lives after enslavement in the United States. These views often put her at odds with both slave owners, who refuted emancipation, and ardent abolitionists, who opposed colonization.

Sarah Josepha Hale's boss, Louis A. Godey, founder and publisher of *Lady's Book*, wanted no part of politics in his publication. She parroted her publisher's wishes by writing that *Godey's* was to avoid the controversies implicit in political subjects and be "a lodge in the wilderness . . . a quiet, cultured garden on which the burning lava had not yet breathed."[25]

The "lava" never touched *Godey's* content throughout the war. No mention was ever made of battles, emancipation, or the burning of Atlanta. It was almost as if America's hearthside—the magazine's essential core focus—was insulated from a war that otherwise turned the country upside down. The Battles of Gettysburg and Antietam, the horrors of Andersonville and Elmira Prisons, the starvation in Vicksburg, and the 1863 draft riots in New York City never intruded on the genteel environment of the *Godey's* "lodge."

Just prior to the war, Hale made a plea to her readers. She urged: "Every state join in Union Thanksgiving on the 24th of this month [November 1859]. . . . Would it not be a renewed pledge of love and loyalty to the Constitution of the United States which guarantees peace, prosperity, progress and perpetuity to our great Republic?" In 1861 she repeated her plea and added, "Shall we not, then, lay aside our enmities and strifes, and suspend our worldly cares, toils, and pursuits on one day in the year, devoting it to a public Thanksgiving for all the good gifts God has bestowed on us and on all the earth?"[26]

Despite the publisher's and her efforts to keep *Godey's* from being enmeshed in political subjects—or because of that stance— its circulation dropped by one-third during the war. Northern readers looked to *Harper's Weekly* and *Frank Leslie's Illustrated Magazine* for information and opinions about the war. Southern readers may have found that any publication coming out of Philadelphia was tainted by its Yankee location no matter how neutral the publisher and editor claimed to be.

Hale continued to keep her editorial content free from North-South bias and pursued reconciliation and politically unassailable causes such as the establishment of Vassar College for the education of women and the restoration of Mount Vernon, home of George Washington, an unimpeachable symbol of national unity. Writing about the Mount Vernon Ladies' Association in 1857, she hoped "that in this Association, the North and South will meet together, and East and West unite, and all be as one in this work of love."[27]

Sarah Josepha Hale may have been averse to conflict over North-South issues because it would have a negative effect on readership, hence a threat to her own livelihood. She had been a widow since age thirty-four with the responsibility of raising five children. The troubling thought of losing her position as the editor or having her only source of income diminished may never have been very far from her mind. Maintaining a loyal reader base was essential for any publication. No magazine, regardless of its success, was immune to circulation loss or collapse.

Another reason for Hale's reluctance to wade into the turbulent waters of the South's secession and the North's reaction to disunion was her love of country and its unity of purpose since 1776. Much as a relative who sees family members embroiled in an acrimonious divorce, the separation of America into two parts broke her heart. Rather than take sides with either party, she continually sought reconciliation and acts that would reunify the separated parties. Honor those things that unite rather than focus on those things that separate was her guiding principle.

The most significant tangible action to foster unification in Hale's mind was to celebrate a national day of thanksgiving. To realize her dream of a Thanksgiving Day, she wrote scores of editorials in *Godey's* and sent hundreds of letters to politicians and civic leaders throughout the country. Her extensive efforts began to have an effect. States initiated days of thanksgiving commemoration, and the practice started to spread. Her goal, however, was bolder, more comprehensive. She wanted the entire country—every state—to celebrate a national day of thanksgiving at the same time.

Sarah Josepha Hale put her considerable persuasive writing skills to the test and tried to convince the president of the United States of the need for a national day of thanksgiving. First, she wrote to

Zachary Taylor. No response. Then Millard Fillmore. No response. Franklin Pierce. No response. James Buchanan. No response.

On Monday, September 28, 1863, Hale sat at her desk at the *Lady's Book* in Philadelphia and wrote another letter to the chief executive. Now, as never before, she felt the nation must establish a day set aside for giving thanks throughout the country. The nation needed a time of prayer and reflection on the bounties received. It needed a time for healing and reconciliation amid the strife. In her concluding paragraph, she asked President Abraham Lincoln to acknowledge the last Thursday in November as a national day of thanksgiving and that it be "forever secured."[28] Ending the letter, written in her elegant Spencerian handwriting, she signed her name: Sarah Josepha Hale, Editress of the *Lady's Book*.

Five days after she sent her letter, President Lincoln proclaimed Thursday, November 26, 1863, a day of national thanksgiving.

These five women, these better angels, never met face-to-face before or during the Civil War. Despite their prominence and their shared aspirations, for most their paths never crossed. (Sarah Josepha Hale did publish Harriet Beecher Stowe's writing until it became "too political" for *Godey's Lady's Book*. The two corresponded but never met.) All five operated on separate tracks within their areas of interest, but they were united in their desire to see the United States rid of slavery. While all were abolitionists in philosophy, Sarah Josepha Hale was more muted in her outward expression of that cause because of her role as the editor of a national magazine that struggled to be neutral and apolitical in content.

The stories of these five women are intertwined like a ball of string. Their narratives crisscrossed and overlapped, but they are essentially single strands running their own course. Their narratives are all influenced by social and economic currents of change that ran with increasing speeds through the antebellum United States. These currents were especially pronounced in the northeastern United States, but they became a torrent on April 12, 1861, when Confederate forces in Charleston Harbor fired upon federally held Fort Sumter. The American Civil War changed everything and everyone.

In the Northeast, industrialization had begun to open doors for women at the start of the nineteenth century. Women began moving into factory jobs that the Industrial Revolution had started to generate. Increasingly, women began filling teaching positions. They began having their poems, essays, and various works of fiction and nonfiction published in journals previously limited to the work of male authors. The growing political movements such as abolitionism had women leaders as well as active female participants. And a nascent women's rights movement was gaining traction, most notably after the Seneca Falls Convention of 1848.

Abolitionism flourished in the North and led to a vibrant Underground Railroad network instituted and staffed by many women committed to manumission. Harriet Tubman was able to employ this network to her advantage as she escaped slavery in southern Maryland and then as she helped scores of her fellow African Americans escape to freedom.

While the better angels had established leadership roles, many social and economic factors were beginning to contribute to growing roles for other women in nineteenth-century American society. The Civil War, however, fueled change for women as nothing else had done.

What Alexander Hamilton wrote about "revolution" in the eighteenth century could have just as easily applied to "war" in the nineteenth century. For all their horrors, Hamilton claimed, revolutions (and wars) "serve to bring to light, talents and virtues, which might otherwise have languished in obscurity, or only shot forth a few and scattered and wondering rays."[29] The same could be said of the five better angels and the American Civil War. As Julia Ward Howe observed: "The Civil War not only had emancipated the slaves but also had liberated women, who found a new scope for their activities, and developed abilities hitherto unsuspected by themselves."[30]

Each of these five women was building her confidence and sharpening her skills prior to the war. The conditions leading up to the armed conflict in April 1861 opened a large door through which they then could take their considerable talents and potential to new levels. As toxic as the war was for the destruction and death it caused, the war was also a tonic for women who were poised to take a new role in America. The changes wrought by the U.S. Civil War resulted in widespread recognition that women could go far beyond the restraints that had been imposed on them in the first half of the nineteenth century. While just a beginning, it proved to be an immutable path of progress. The five better angels were some of the most successful and inspirational travelers on that path. And—to a woman—they continued on that path well beyond the Civil War.

I have never studied the art of paying compliments to women; but I must say, that if all that has been said by orators and poets since the creation of the world in praise of women were applied to the women of America, it would not do them justice for their conduct during this war. I will close by saying, God bless the women of America.

—ABRAHAM LINCOLN, Sanitary Fair, Washington DC, March 18, 1864

2

Women in Antebellum America

The thirty years preceding the Civil War were marked by the nation's physical growth and expansion, economic diversification, democratic advancement, intellectual progress, and tragic sectional hostility. . . . Women were affected either directly or indirectly by the challenges and changes, but most were too busy being wives and mothers to participate actively. . . . Yet an ever-increasing number were becoming economically self-sufficient, better educated, and more demanding, and these were the women who had "leaped from their spheres." Much to the consternation of the "lords of creation."

—MARY ELIZABETH MASSEY, *Women in the Civil War*

A mong the women who "leaped from their spheres" were the five better angels. They were born and came of age in antebellum America when women's rights were just beginning to bud but were of little help in confronting the strong headwinds that the five faced as females. Each of the five women had to overcome a long history of second-class status imposed by the "lords of creation." (Harriet Tubman had the additional burden of racial discrimination.) Their successes are all the more remarkable considering the extraordinary self-reliance and resourcefulness that were required to rise above the roles to which society had relegated them. They were driven by a mighty purpose, and when self-doubt crept in—as it did on occasion—they swept it away as if it were an inconsequential but annoying insect. Their paths were filled with obstacles, but one obstacle they would never allow to impede their progress was their femaleness.

Coming out of the Revolutionary War period that brought

so many important liberties to the new nation in which they lived, American women would find their prewar status largely unchanged—with a few notable exceptions. For the most part, women had subordinate roles in both the precolonial and postcolonial society. They had limited property rights and had standing only in their roles as wives and daughters. Colonial settlers brought with them not just their skills and heritage from Europe but also the discriminatory practices of the old country that locked women into roles limited to hearth and home.

Three factors served as catalysts of change for women's roles. The principles of liberty spawned by the revolution began to have their influence, albeit slowly, throughout society. (The significant exceptions were slavery and civil rights for African Americans throughout the United States but especially in the southern states.) While women were not significantly affected by this new wave of equality in postcolonial America, an important change in the way Americans thought about social hierarchy was growing in the new republic.

Expansion into the frontier after the revolution also gave women an opportunity to employ their skills and capabilities in work where men were not available or not inclined to participate. Many of these frontier occupations were devoted to providing goods for the home (cloth, shoes, and candles) that could be sold to others. Other women performed work outside their own homes in a variety of skilled occupations (butchers, silversmiths, upholsterers), producing products and providing services in demand by those on the new frontier.

The most important factor influencing women's positions in the early 1800s was the introduction of manufacturing in the United States. Industrialization was largely concentrated in the northeastern states, but it had a profound effect on bringing women into the workforce and setting a precedent nationally for women working outside the home.

In addition to these three broad influences on women's roles in antebellum America, a smaller but important opportunity for women began to be formed in the early 1830s as women moved into nursing and teaching careers. These professions began to

expand as the country grew in geographical size and population. In conjunction with the growth of these professions, education and training to prepare workers with the necessary skills
required began to blossom. Women and society overall thought
that they had innate capabilities and an affinity for teaching and
nursing. And as in other work areas that attracted women, men
were largely unwilling or unavailable to take on the work required
by these professions.

Following the Revolutionary War, in the northeast technology
and commercial opportunities combined to offer employment
for young women. Men who were tied to agricultural work were
not available (or willing) to apply for the textile jobs springing up
across New England and in other northeastern states, so young
women were hired to operate mill machinery at attractive wages.
Respectable work located in seemingly favorable working environments made these manufacturing opportunities popular with
many female job seekers. As time passed, however, the attraction
of factory jobs began to fade in the eyes of New England's native-
born, middle-class women. By the 1830s immigrants began to
take the place of workers born in America. Factory owners found
that the immigrant job applicants were willing to work for lower
wages than their native-born American counterparts would. Unattractive pay, long hours, and stark working conditions caused non-
immigrant women to leave their jobs at the mills or not consider
manufacturing jobs if they were first entering the work force. Economics aside, middle-class women were increasingly unwilling
to diminish their status by working in factories. They found more
attractive opportunities in leisure pursuits, in church-led charity
efforts, and in employment requiring higher education.

In much the same way as their working-class sisters found
opportunities in jobs that men did not want or for which they were
unavailable, middle-class women began to gravitate to work that
drew on their education and their qualities of patience, nurturing,
and compassion—qualities that made them excellent candidates for
nursing and teaching in the eyes of many. Women were also willing to take these positions at lower pay than what men demanded.
In addition to lower pay, women were also expected to remain sin-

gle during their teaching and nursing employment. These stipulations regarding marital status as a condition for employment were not, with rare exceptions, an employment quid pro quo for men.

The Education Boom for Women

In the northern states, female academies and seminaries began to flourish in the 1820s and '30s. Young women attending these institutions found that they were educated just as well as their male counterparts were. Unlike the male students, however, the young women soon came to realize that there were few avenues to apply their talents and education after graduation. At the Young Ladies' Academy of Philadelphia, the girls reported that their excellent educational foundation received at the school "offered no vision of life beyond school."[1] While the goal of some academies was to turn their female students into "useful wives," increasingly the demand for teachers—especially in the West—led to more focused, applied education of young women at these institutions. The growth of "normal schools" to train teachers surged. Catharine Beecher's school, the Hartford Female Seminary, soon found that its graduates could fill a demand for well-trained teachers in the West. Consequently, enrollment quickly expanded.

Other female graduates, not finding the teaching profession to their liking, gravitated toward philanthropic activities. These included "Bible classes. Education Society collection tours, temperance lectures, classes in which free blacks were taught to read . . . meetings where the busy fingers of women made garments for the poor. . . . The proliferation of voluntary societies in antebellum America ensured that the loose energies of educated young women would be readily tapped."[2]

To prepare for a career in teaching, it was essential for women to be educated in the classics, languages, mathematics, and natural sciences. As the country expanded westward and the commitment to public education grew, teachers were in demand, and the ranks could not be filled without bringing women into the profession. By 1888 63 percent of all teachers were women; in the cities this number jumped to 90 percent. Regrettably, despite the need for teachers and the short supply, wages for female teachers were 30–50 percent of the wages paid to male teachers.[3]

Medical Profession Opportunities Opened and Closed to Women

Women had been active in the healing arts in eighteenth-century America, but as the colonies became the United States and the medical profession began to emerge from the disparate apprentice system of training that had been the earlier path to becoming a physician, women found themselves excluded from the profession's new educational resources. State licensing of medical practitioners further kept women from entering the ranks of educated, trained, and licensed physicians.

Women did find roles in the nursing ranks as demand increased for patient care during the Civil War. Nurses required less training than physicians, and women's having cared for family members in the home was seen as sufficient expertise to become a nurse-caregiver. The most significant exception from this minimal home care experience prerequisite was in the role of the midwife, who perform obstetric services critical and essential to a mother and her newborn's health. For the most part, only women were perceived as having the necessary expertise and comportment to serve as midwives. Trained physicians valued midwives because of their relevant and crucial skills in the birthing room.

Some women were trained as physicians during the early and mid-nineteenth century, but they were anomalies in the common practice of assigning women to nursing roles that required less training and no licensing. One missing piece of the puzzle in the delivery of nineteenth-century medical care that became apparent during the American Civil War was the logistical skill in providing medical supplies in the field where and when they were needed. The best-trained and most skilled male physicians found themselves helpless in field situations and unable to perform their work due to a lack of bandages, splints, chloroform, and other basic medical materials on a regular basis. Several women stepped in to fill this gap during the Civil War. Among the most successful were Dorothea Dix and Clara Barton.

Opportunities Abound in the West

The early nineteenth century saw American expansion gaining increasing momentum as the population headed west. Territories of Kentucky and Tennessee that had virtually no non–Native American inhabitants before the Revolutionary War now were growing more populated with each passing day. By 1870 Tennessee experienced a tenfold growth in population since 1776. Kentucky grew to 220,000 white settlers from 1790 to 1810. Ohio grew from 45,000 to 230,000 inhabitants during the same period, and by 1820 the number increased to nearly a half-million people. Historian Gordon Wood wrote: "The state [Ohio] was creating so many new towns that Ohioans complained they had run out of names for them."[4]

In addition to the explosive population growth in the West, most of the new inhabitants were living on farms. According to sociologist Gerda Lerner, "During the early 19th century nineteen out of twenty Americans continued to live in rural places." Burgeoning populations in the West and the American agricultural economy gave more opportunities for women to move outside the confines of their "proper place" as dictated by the patriarchal society in the East and South. "Where class distinctions were not so great, as on the frontier, the position of women was closer to what it had been in colonial days; their economic contribution was more highly valued, their opportunities were less restricted, and their positive participation in community life was taken for granted."[5]

The population growth in the West and that area's demand for educating children—both girls and boys—opened up numerous opportunities for female teachers educated in the North and East. As a result, the well-known aphorism of newspaperman Horace Greeley might well have advised, "Go West, young woman. Go West!"

A Consciousness of Selfhood and Rights

Women living in the American colonies before the Revolutionary War enjoyed more property rights than their British sisters did on the other side of the Atlantic. British common law held that a woman forfeited her contractual rights when she married. Women could not sign a contract, even with the consent of her spouse, in

England. Colonial authorities had a more progressive interpretation of a "wife's property rights by protecting her dower rights in her husband's property, granting her personal clothing, and upholding pre-nuptial contracts between husband and wife. In the absence of the husband, colonial courts granted women 'femme sole' rights, which enabled them to conduct their husband's business, sign contracts, and sue."[6]

Historian Gordon Wood acknowledges that no organized movement arose on behalf of women's rights immediately after the American Revolution. (Rights in the postrevolutionary period pertained to the rights of free white men, not women.) A number of male and female writers began to broach the subject of women's rights just prior to the turn of the century. "The way was prepared for the future. [Judith Sargent] Murray, writing as 'Constantia' in 1798, declared that she expected to 'see our young women forming a new era in female history.' In the decades following the Revolution, women gained a new consciousness of their selfhood and their rights."[7]

It would take another catastrophic event in American history—the Civil War and the prelude to this conflict—to advance women's rights in a consequential way in the young country. The Revolutionary War had strengthened the equalitarian view of social hierarchy in the postcolonial period, and upward mobility based on ability rather than inherited privilege led to unprecedented opportunities. Men were initially favored to be sure, but the egalitarian die had been cast that would eventually lead to the granting of rights to women.

Foot Soldiers of Piety

The revolution and its aftermath brought a strong current of avid Republicanism—or even the more radical Jacobinism—in its wake. Many Federalists feared that the democratic impulses of the revolution would expand beyond the political realm and cause "crises of social order in the early Republic." The Second Great Awakening, resulting in a reinvigorated, robust evangelical Christianity, was a consequence of the fear of "Republican infidelity."[8]

Women were seen as the logical spiritual foot soldiers in this war against impieties thought to be emanating from the American Revolution. (The French Revolution and its consequences only reinforced this fear of the collapse of social order in America.) In the mid-twentieth century, one social historian wrote: "Religion belonged to women by divine right, a gift of God and nature. This 'peculiar susceptibility' to religion was given to her for a reason: 'the vestal flame of piety, lighted up by Heaven in the breast of woman' would throw its beams into the naughty world of men."[9]

Women, it seemed, were the carriers of religious antidotes to rescue the postrevolutionary American public—especially men— from the path to social dissolution. From the time of the revolution, nearly 70 percent of the members of New England churches were women, and in the decades following the revolution, the "feminization" of American Christianity increased.[10] It was Mother Ann Lee who founded the Shakers, a celibate, pious denomination that was the first American religious group to "recognize formally the equality of the sexes at all levels of society."[11]

Medical educator Dr. Charles Meigs, while addressing a graduating class of medical students, said about women: "Hers is a pious mind. Her confiding nature leads her more readily than men to accept the proffered grace of the Gospel."[12] Dr. Meigs's pronouncement in the early 1800s to medical professionals reflected the conventional wisdom of the time. As generous and flattering as his acknowledgment of piety could be to women, it also had the effect—intentional or unintentional—of relegating women to their "proper place" as pious, submissive persons restricted from applying their skills and interests outside the home.

As the American Civil War loomed, some women realized that they could be pious and virtuous, and still venture outside the home to take on tasks that would serve a greater good in society. These tasks would permit them to be good mothers and wives while serving in consequential roles that surfaced as the country drew closer to armed conflict.

The Voice of "True Womanhood"

The "Cult of True Womanhood," as it has been labeled by one historian, flourished from 1820 to 1860 in America and was reinforced by women's publications of the time.[13] True womanhood, characterized by piety, purity, submissiveness, and domesticity, found its voice in a number of publications but never more assiduously or with greater reach than the gold standard of women's magazines, *Godey's Lady's Book*. Started as the *American Ladies' Magazine* in 1834 by Sarah Josepha Hale, a diligent, hardworking widow, the magazine was bought by publisher and arch promoter Louis A. Godey in 1837. The newly named *Godey's Lady's Book* quickly became the sine qua non vehicle of women's communications. Recognizing her editing talent and work ethic, Godey retained Hale as the magazine's editor in chief. The publication became for women in America an "arbiter of the parlor, the textbook of the kitchen." Its circulation surged to 150,000 by the mid-nineteenth century.[14]

Ostensibly confining women to the household sphere and seemingly promoting submissiveness to its female readers, the magazine did champion progressive causes including improved working conditions for women, property rights for married women, temperance, and women's education. Abolition, since it found favor—or rejection—according to where readers resided, was one nineteenth-century progressive cause that was not promoted in the publication. Rather than risk alienating some readers, *Godey's Lady's Book* avoided the subject of abolition before and during the Civil War. (Although Sarah Josepha Hale had antislavery inclinations, she favored colonization of freed slaves, a concept that was anathema to abolitionists.)

Godey's Lady's Book prided itself on using original material written by American authors who were paid for their work. (In an era where copyright laws were not observed, some magazines picked up materials from other publications without paying the author.) The back cover of the publication stated: "The Book of the Nation—The Oldest Magazine in America—Devoted to American Enterprise, American Writers, and American Artists."

Editor Hale not only bought pieces for publication from male authors but also actively solicited content from women writers. One of these writers, whose initial submission, "Trials of a Housekeeper," belied her later work for the American reading public, was Harriet Beecher Stowe. This leading abolitionist writer had eight stories published in *Godey's* from 1839 to 1842. This body of work in *Godey's* helped Stowe sharpen her literary skills and introduced her to a wide audience of readers who then followed her writing. (None of Stowe's pieces in *Godey's* dealt with slavery or abolition.) This apprenticeship at *Godey's* was an important precursor for her magnum opus that followed; *Uncle Tom's Cabin* was published a decade after her articles appeared in *Godey's*.

Godey's may appear to have reinforced the "Cult of True Womanhood" in its stated editorial platform, but the magazine opened the door for a circulation of literate women who were introduced to topics that helped sow the seeds of change that would blossom during the decade leading up to the American Civil War. The loyal readers of *Godey's* began to see a whole new world that stretched well beyond the parlor and the kitchen.

A Declaration of Independence at the Seneca Falls Convention

Seventy-two years after America declared its independence from England, a group of dedicated women organized a convention "to discuss the social, civil, and religious condition and rights of women." Lucretia Mott and Elizabeth Cady Stanton took leadership roles, assisted by a small group of Quaker women, to launch this bold step to articulate their grievances and attract sympathetic followers. Held in the Wesleyan Methodist Chapel in Seneca, New York, on July 19 and 20, 1848, the event attracted three hundred persons—men and women but primarily women—to address women's rights. It was the first convention examining women's rights held in the United States.

Using the Declaration of Independence as a guiding outline and replicating the role of Thomas Jefferson in preparing the original document, Elizabeth Cady Stanton drafted the "Declaration of Rights and Sentiments" for review and approval by the convention attendees. Replacing the tyrant George III as the focus of the document, Stanton used "man" in her draft. She described women's natural rights in the areas of legal standing, property rights, employment practices, fair pay, access to education, and—most radical at the time—the right to "elective franchise," or the right to vote.

The organizers of the convention also included in the Declaration of Rights and Sentiments the right to divorce and maintain custody of children. Stanton's chief contribution to the document was the expansion of political rights based on the eighteenth-century concept of natural rights that was the basis for the Declaration of Independence in 1776; Stanton sought to extend the rights that heretofore had been guaranteed to men only. Lucretia Mott's contribution to the declaration was to ensure that economic rights were clearly stated. Mott believed that when women were granted economic equality in the marketplace, this right would spread to other areas where women were restricted.

The Declaration of Rights and Sentiments was voted on and unanimously accepted by the convention attendees. Favorable reports from some of the press quickly followed. Frederick Douglass's *North Star*, William Lloyd Garrison's *Liberator*, and the *New York Tribune* approved of the convention's purpose and outcome. However, a vast majority of newspapers wrote unfavorably about the convention. The *Philadelphia Public Ledger and Daily Transcript* claimed that no lady would favor voting rights for women, while the *New York Herald*'s editor wrote scornfully about women in the workforce. For each negative news report, organizer Elizabeth Cady Stanton wrote responses to all the newspapers.

The years immediately following the Seneca Falls Convention did not result in a tectonic change in advancing women's rights. The right to vote, for example, was not achieved for another seventy years. However, the convention did make tangible the goals for women's rights, and these goals remained guiding principles for women through the years that followed Seneca Falls. The convention also helped with tactical needs. Women now had a model for organizing meetings, electing leadership, managing operating budgets, developing and distributing positions as petitions, and engaging the print media to communicate their work to the general public. All these skills would prove vitally important to the success of achieving women's rights as the movement grew through the second half of the nineteenth century and into the early twentieth century.

Writing about the impact of the Civil War on women in America, historian Allan Nevins observed: "It was an era of change and growth. This was especially true in the North, and Clara Barton exaggerated very little when she said that the war had left women at least fifty years in advance of the position they would have held if peace had endured."[15]

3

The Underground Railroad

arriet Tubman lost track of how many trips she made to the Eastern Shore to guide enslaved people to freedom above the Mason-Dixon line and sometimes farther north to Canada. On these trips she traveled at night with a group of rescued men, women, and children, guided by the stars and her intimate knowledge of the topography of the region. Traveling by dark and avoiding the main roads, Tubman was able to lead groups of varying sizes, according to her own description, "over mountains, through forests, across rivers, mid perils by land, perils by water, and perils from enemies."[1] Usually the groups moved on foot and kept up a grueling pace that exhausted Tubman's charges until they dropped from fatigue at dawn. Occasionally some of the group would refuse to go on because of the physically demanding routine that Tubman put them through. Not willing to sacrifice the safety of the group for a few laggards, she drew the revolver she carried with her, cocked the hammer, pointed the gun at those who wanted to give up, and said: "Dead men tell no tales. . . . Go on or die!" The recalcitrant ones always chose to go on.

During the daylight hours Tubman would leave her party in a dense woods while she visited one of the stations on the Underground Railway, as she referred to it. There she would purchase food for her group and obtain any local intelligence regarding slave catchers in the area. She would then return to her runaways, signaling her approach by singing a hymn as a method of announcing an all clear. As noted previously, singing hymns allowed Tubman to signal either an all clear or, by changing the lyrics, potential danger. The technique also gave Tubman cover for her own safety if she were approached by anyone who was a "false brethren." She would be perceived as an innocent slave singing hymns as she conducted errands for her master. One of the hymns Tubman frequently sang was

> Around him are ten thousand angels.
> Always ready to obey his command.
> They are always hovering round you,
> Till you reach the heavenly land.

Fleeing from servitude has a long history in America, first occurring early in the colonial period of the nation. One historian has cited: "The subject of 'fleeing from service' first appeared in the colonial record of 1629."[2]

In another instance, three servants escaped what may have been indentured servitude in Virginia in 1640. When caught, the two white male servants were punished by having time added to their period of voluntary service. The black servant, John Punch, was punished by being sentenced to life service.[3]

By the 1800s escapes from slavery accelerated at an astounding frequency. (Indentured, or "voluntary," service was no longer in practice.) This increase had two major contributing factors: one economic and one social. As the cotton industry grew in the Lower South (later known as the Deep South)—due in large part to the invention of the cotton gin—slave labor became crucial to meet the international market's demand for cotton. The price for slave labor jumped. Many Upper South slaveholders found it financially rewarding to sell their enslaved people to cotton plantations in the Lower South. These sales devastated enslaved families living in the Upper South. Younger members of the families were sold to slaveholders on plantations with the expectation that they would be more productive than their older family members. Family ties were never considered when members were sold to the highest bidders. This new economic dynamic awakened a desire among the enslaved in the Upper South to escape their bondage and head to freedom in the North.

At the same time, the growing social tide of abolitionism in the North led a large number of sympathetic people—both black and white—to aid escaping slaves from the South. Especially in the Upper South, where enslaved people had access to a favorable transportation network of rivers, roads, and seas lanes. And the proximity to the North made escape more feasible for those in the Upper South than for those in the Deep South.

Groups of compassionate whites, free blacks, and enslaved blacks came together to create an informal network of people willing and motivated to help fugitive enslaved people on their path to freedom. Historian Eric Foner has characterized this group as "a rare instance in antebellum America of interracial cooperation and a link between lower-class urban blacks . . . and their more affluent white allies."[4] The so-called Vigilance Committees of free blacks and whites, cooperating with enslaved African Americans who sought to gain their freedom in Northern states (and later Canada), constituted secret networks that were "shrouded in mysteries and myths." Even today, in the twenty-first century, many of the details of these networks remain unknown.

In the 1830s this coalition of persons began to be referred to as the Underground Railroad, taking its name from the physical transportation system that was growing in antebellum America. The metaphor was further expanded through the use of terms such as "agents," "conductors," "engineers," and "stationmasters" for those who participated.

"Stations" were the locations of points along the way. Notable among the stations were Baltimore; Wilmington, Delaware; Philadelphia; New York City; and Albany, Syracuse, and Rochester, New York, along with St. Catharines, Ontario, Canada.

A symbiotic relationship developed as more slaves risked escaping bondage and willing Underground Railroad agents, conductors, and stationmasters grew in numbers, boldness, and cooperation. The precise number of enslaved people who fled to the North is not known, but historian Foner estimates that one thousand to five thousand slaves per year escaped from 1830 to 1860.[5] These numbers are a small percentage of the total slave population, "which approached four million in 1860," according to Foner. Though small in comparison to the overall slave population, the growth in successful escapes brought on a series of measures to stem these losses. The new laws supporting the return of fleeing or escaped slaves, the growth in the number of slave hunters, and the court system all aligned in an attempt to derail the Underground Railroad in the United States.

Two actions—one by the Congress and one by the Supreme Court—in the 1850s represented the nadir of antislavery activity that was manifested in the actions of the Underground Railroad. In 1850 Congress passed the Fugitive Slave Law that tightened the requirement to return escaped slaves and at the same time made aiding escaping slaves a crime. The grip of slavery had reached across the Mason-Dixon line from the South into the Northern states. Now residents involved in supporting slaves who were seeking freedom were subject to criminal penalties.

The other toxic step taken to support slavery was the U.S. Supreme Court's decision in 1857 that found that Dred Scott, a black man who lived for a number of years in the free territories of Wisconsin and Illinois, never lost his status as a slave. Chief Justice Roger B. Taney read the opinion of the court that Congress had no authority to exclude slavery from U.S. territories. Taney went even further, stating that African Americans were not and never had been citizens of the United States; therefore, they had no rights under the U.S. Constitution. In his opinion, Taney wrote that African Americans "had no rights which the white man was bound to respect."[6]

The *Dred Scott* decision, at a minimum, hardened the resolve of those abolitionists—black and white—who were operating the Underground Railroad. Among the most extreme reaction, African Americans in the North began to form black military associations that were prepared to use violence to respond to Southern slave-catching actions. These groups were ready to "strike a blow for freedom, marching through the South with 'a Bible in one hand and a gun in the other.'"[7]

Frederick Douglass, who considered himself a pacifist even when it came to freeing enslaved people, wrote a laudatory letter to Harriet Tubman after the war to praise her skill and success. Douglass recognized that Tubman's "devotion to freedom and heroism" had gone largely unrecognized by the public.

Rochester, August 29, 1868

Dear Harriet [Tubman],

I am glad to know that the story of your eventful life has been
written . . . and that the same is soon to be published. You ask
for what you do not need when you call upon me for a word
of commendation. I need such words from you far more than
you need them from me. . . . The difference between us is very
marked. Most that I have done and suffered in the service of our
cause has been in public. . . . You on the other hand have labored
in a private way. I have wrought in the day—you in the night.
I have had the applause of the crowd and the satisfaction that
comes of being approved by the multitude, while the most that
you have done has been witnessed by a few trembling, scarred,
and foot-sore bondmen and women, whom you have led out of
the house of bondage, and whose heartfelt "God bless you" has
been your only reward. The midnight sky and the silent stars
have been the witness of your devotion to freedom and of your
heroism. Excepting John Brown . . . I know of no one who has
willingly encountered more perils and hardships to serve our
enslaved people than you have. . . . It is to me a great pleasure
and a great privilege to bear testimony to your character and
your works . . .

Your friend,

Frederick Douglass[5]

Dorchester County in southern Maryland is a heart-shaped,
983-square-mile jurisdiction bordered by the Chesapeake Bay to
the west and the state of Delaware on the east. It was named
after the Earl of Dorset, a family friend of the Calvert family that
founded Maryland as a sanctuary for English Catholics seeking
refuge from persecution in England. One hundred and fifty years
after its founding, Dorchester was the site of prosperous plantations growing tobacco, corn, wheat, and other cash crops. A network of waterways provided the transportation necessary to get
the crops to market cheaply. The labor force used to till the soil,
harvest the crops, and assist in the transportation of goods to

market was slave labor. Early in the county's history, white indentured servants were employed with the prospect that they would
be free to leave their employment after an agreed-upon term had
been completed. By the mid-1700s, however, indentured white
servants were replaced by captives from Africa who were purchased by white plantation families. This labor force's term of
service was lifelong. These bondsmen and women were locked
into a life of servitude.

Into one of these slave families in Dorchester County was born
Araminta "Minty" Ross, daughter of Harriet "Rit" and Ben Ross.
Both mother and father were slaves owned by different masters.
Araminta's mother was the property of Edward Brodess; her father
was enslaved by Anthony Thompson, Brodess's stepson.

It is likely that Araminta's ancestors were from West Africa's
Gold Coast (today's Ghana.) Historian Kate Clifford Larson believes
that Araminta's forbearers were "likely sold directly from the deck
of a slave ship somewhere along the Chesapeake Bay or at the
eighteenth-century slave market in Oxford, Maryland. These slaves
eventually settled with the expanding planter families who were
clearing and managing property in Dorchester County."[9]

Soon after Minty was born in 1822, Brodess split the family,
taking Rit and her five children to work on his farm. In an effort
to address financial difficulties that he was experiencing, Brodess
sold several of the Ross children to buyers in other states and hired
Minty out to "temporary masters" to increase his cash flow.[10]

During the early years she was hired out, teenage Araminta
performed fieldwork on a number of plantations. The work was
physically demanding and resulted in a muscular, five-foot-tall girl
who had extraordinary stamina and a powerful physique. These
physical attributes would be important for the type of tasks that
she would undertake in the near future.

One other impact on her physical condition during her teenage years would have a detrimental effect on her for the remainder of her life. While hired out for work and performing errands,
she was involved in a scuffle in a country store where an irate
overseer threw a two-pound iron weight at a young slave he was
trying to subdue. Missing the intended target, the weight hit Ara-

minta in the head, causing her to lose consciousness. Bleeding and passing in and out of consciousness, she received no medical attention for her wound. The consequences of this trauma would linger into her adult life. While not diagnosed during her lifetime, it is likely that young Araminta suffered from temporal lobe epilepsy based on her known symptoms of seizures, narcolepsy, and dreamlike trances.[11]

Another potent influence on Araminta's early years was her involvement in combined Methodist, Catholic, Episcopal, Baptist, and African religious practices. This theological amalgam resulted in a fervor about which abolitionist Thomas Garrett later wrote that he had "never met with any person, of any color, who has more confidence in the voice of God, as spoken direct to her soul. . . . Her faith in a Supreme Power truly was great."[12]

While working in or near Peters Neck, Maryland, Araminta met and married John Tubman, a free black man, in 1844. Due to her marriage, her religious conversion, her wish to honor her mother, or a combination of all three factors, Araminta Ross changed her name to Harriet Tubman, the name she would keep for the rest of her life. Marrying Harriet was a sacrifice for John. By Maryland law, any children born from their union would be the property of Harriet's master, Edward Brodess. John Tubman would have no legal or parental rights to his children. Furthermore, the husband and wife could not share life together without the permission of Harriet's owner. It was, therefore, an arrangement rife with uncertainty and potential heartbreak as their lives together unfolded.

As much as evangelical Protestants in the South found a scriptural basis supporting slavery, enslaved black people's religious beliefs were permeated with the concepts of bearing up under oppression, of awaiting deliverance from their oppressors, and of seeking the divine guidance of a merciful God who promised freedom. According to historian Larson, "For slaves, the spirit and meaning of biblical texts had a fluidity to them that allowed slaves to embrace a world view shaped by African and American influences."[13]

Later in life, Tubman's earliest biographer, Sarah Bradford, wrote about her puzzlement regarding her subject's faith: "I hardly know how to approach the subject of the spiritual experiences of my sable heroine. They seem to enter into the reaches of the super-natural. . . . Had I not . . . seen such remarkable instances of what seemed to be her direct intercourse with heaven, I should not dare risk my own character for veracity by making these things public."[14]

Harriet Tubman's husband, as a free black man, had significantly greater freedom of movement than his enslaved wife. It is likely through John's work and social contacts that he met other local free black men who as teamsters, watermen, and dockworkers had detailed knowledge of the transportation and communications resources on the Eastern Shore. He would likely have shared this information with his wife during their marriage. In addition to her increasing knowledge about the various transportation networks in the area, her growing religious convictions helped fuel her dreams of freedom from her bondage.

As Edward Brodess's financial picture worsened in the late 1840s, Harriet Tubman became increasingly anxious over the prospect of being sold by her financially insecure owner. Prayers for her freedom changed to more urgent prayers for her owner's death. "I prayed all night long for master, till the first of March; and all the time he was bringing people to look at me, and trying to sell me. Then I changed my prayer. . . . I began to pray 'Oh, Lord, if you ain't never going to change that man's heart, kill him, Lord, and take him out of the way.'"[15]

On March 7, 1849, Edward Brodess died at age forty-seven. Harriet Tubman was shocked, then remorseful regarding her prayers for his death. But remorse quickly gave way to fear as Brodess's widow, Eliza, had to take drastic steps to shore up the family's precarious financial state. The slaves' hopes for freedom, once implied by Brodess, were quickly dashed. Initially the Brodess family squabbled over ownership of the slaves, but the indisputable outcome was that the slaves would be put up for sale. Harriet Tubman was to be sold to settle the Brodess family debts. John Tubman's attempts to intercede on behalf of his wife were unsuccessful. It was time, in Harriet Tubman's mind, to take bolder steps toward freedom.

Dark and thorny is the desert,

Through the pilgrim makes his ways,

Yet beyond this vale of sorrow

Lies the fields of endless days.

—HARRIET TUBMAN, sung to a Methodist hymn, from Sarah Bradford, *Scenes in the Life of Harriet Tubman*

Just six months after the death of her owner and following the uncertainty surrounding the Brodess family's disposition of its slaves, Harriet Tubman, along with her brothers Henry and Ben, set out to escape enslavement and take a path north to freedom. About two weeks following their escape, Eliza Brodess placed an advertisement in the *Delaware Gazette* announcing a reward for the return of Harriet Tubman and her two brothers. (The delay between the day of their escape and the placement of the ad was most likely due to the three having been hired out to others, where their whereabouts were not closely monitored.)

THREE HUNDRED DOLLARS REWARD

Ran away from the subscriber on Monday the 17th ult., three negroes, named as follows: Harry [Henry], aged about 19 years, has on one side of his neck a wen, just under the ear, he is of a dark chestnut color, about 5 feet 8 or nine inches hight [sic]; Ben, aged aged [sic] about 25 years, is very quick to speak when spoken to, he is of chestnut color, about six feet high; Minty [Araminta/Harriet], aged about 27 years, is of a chestnut color, fine looking, and about 5 feet high. One hundred dollars reward will be given for each of the above named negroes, if taken out of State, and $50 each if taken in the State.

Eliza Ann Brodess

Near Bucktown, Dorchester county, Md

Oct. 3d, 1849

Delaware Gazette

Fearing the consequences of running away if they were caught, Henry and Ben decided to return to the Brodess plantation. A reluctant Harriet accompanied them initially but then decided that fleeing her enslavement was worth the risk. Using the North Star as a navigation point and armed with the knowledge of both local Quakers who might aid her in eluding capture and local transportation routes that she could use, Harriet Tubman began her perilous journey north to freedom.

Quakers on the Eastern Shore were strong advocates of abolition not only in word but also in deed. The sect was willing to provide runaway enslaved people with shelter, food, and support on their treks north. Quakers, along with other sympathetic whites and free blacks, became the support structure for the nascent Underground Railroad. Traveling in the chill autumn night air to avoid capture, Tubman made use of safe houses along her way, seeking shelter with a number of benevolent Quaker families.

Harriet Tubman crossed the Mason-Dixon line into Pennsylvania and freedom after an arduous journey—alone—accomplished with courage and skill. Once in Pennsylvania, Tubman later admitted to biographer Sarah Bradford, "when I found I had crossed that line, I looked at my hands to see if I was the same person. There was such a glory over everything; the sun came like gold through the trees, and over the fields, and I felt like I was in Heaven." Yet, she continued, her freedom was not without apprehension. "I had crossed the line. I was free, but there was no one to welcome me to the land of freedom. I was a stranger in a strange land."[16]

There was no second advertisement for Tubman's return to the Brodess family. Perhaps the family thought she would return of her own volition, or they recognized the growing number of slaves fleeing from the Eastern Shore was inevitable and perhaps even insoluble. Maryland recorded 259 successful runaway slaves in the 1850 census, making it the lead of all slaveholding states.[17] (And this number is low due to underreporting of runaways by slaveholders.)

The Talbot County *Eastern Star* newspaper in an August 1849 article reported on the growing runaway slave situation on the Eastern Shore and recognized the role of the Underground Railroad: "Almost every week we hear of one or more slaves making their escape and if something is not speedily done to put a stop to it, that kind of property will hardly be worth anything. There seems to be some system about this business, and we strongly suspect they are assisted in their escape by an organized band of abolitionists. . . . At present, all efforts to recover [runaway slaves] after they once made their escape appear fruitless."[18]

Harriet Tubman was not content with just liberating herself. Despite stepped-up efforts to halt escaping slaves in Dorchester County, Tubman was compelled to return to the Eastern Shore to help lead other enslaved people to freedom. Several months after her escape, she aided John Bowley, his wife, and two small children in finding sanctuary in Baltimore among abolitionist friends. Several months later, Tubman returned again to Baltimore from her safe house in the North to help her brother Moses and two other men escape to freedom.

Next Tubman decided to raise the stakes by returning to Dorchester County and help her husband escape. (John Tubman was already a free man, but Harriet wanted him to join her in the North, where they would both be free and where he would be out of a hostile proslavery environment.) Returning after a two-year absence, she made her way south along footpaths used during her escape. In anticipation of the couple's freedom together, Harriet purchased a new suit of clothes for John with her meager savings, which she had earned while performing domestic work in the North. However, her hopes and anticipated joy were dashed when she arrived at John's home. Her husband had married another woman, Caroline, in Harriet's absence, and John refused to leave Dorchester County and his new wife. Harriet was hurt, dispirited, and then furious with John Tubman. Her anger soon subsided. According to historian Kate Clifford Larson, Harriet Tubman "soon realized 'how foolish it was just for temper to make mischief' and that if her husband 'could do without her, she could do without him,' so she dropped [him] out of her heart."[19]

Tubman, now that she was in Dorchester County, turned to a group of slaves who were more amenable to seeking freedom in the North than her husband had been. She shepherded the group (four or five slaves) to Philadelphia and liberty. Harriet Tubman now had the confidence, the intimate knowledge of people and places involved in a successful liberation route, and the acute sense of divine inspiration for her cause of freeing enslaved people. Family members and friends who had been led to freedom by Tubman often spoke of her spiritual support. Speaking to William Wells Brown, a former slave and prominent African American author, they reported that Tubman had the "charm" and that the "whites can't catch Moses [Tubman] because you see she's born with the charm. The Lord has given Moses the power."[20]

During the next nine years, Tubman drew on her considerable skills as a conductor on the Underground Railroad to bring seventy to eighty enslaved people to freedom on some fourteen rescue missions from Maryland's Eastern Shore, earning her the sobriquet "Moses of her People." (Some have suggested that she acted more like Joshua, the Old Testament leader and warrior, as Moses did not enter the Promised Land to do battle.)

Over the years since Tubman's active and sustained role with the Underground Railroad, the numbers of enslaved people she helped have been greatly exaggerated. Historian Milton C. Sernett developed a matrix of Tubman's efforts, showing the events, the dates, and the numbers of persons helped according to three preeminent Tubman historians: Jean Humez, Kate Clifford Larson, and Franklin B. Sanborn. These three have done exhaustive research covering Tubman's role as liberator and are recognized as the most accurate scholars on the subject. The Sernett matrix concludes Tubman made twelve to fourteen trips, led sixty-five to eighty enslaved people to freedom, and gave instructions and guidance to fifty to sixty runaway slaves on their escapes.[21]

While these numbers do not match the mythical accounts of past claims, they represent a well-documented number of persons taken from bondage to freedom under difficult and dangerous circumstances. Far from being diminished by the fewer numbers, these results are all the more compelling and credible because they have been substantiated by rigorous research. Harriet Tubman returned again and again to guide enslaved people out of bondage. While these multiple trips were daunting and became increasingly riskier over time, she never was unsuccessful. She never lost a single one of her charges.

With the passage of the Fugitive Slave Act in 1850 regarding the enforcement of returning runaway slaves and punishing those who aided them, Tubman and others working the Underground Railroad network had to extend the concept of "Promised Land." Now the escape networks went beyond Philadelphia, New York City, and upstate New York to include Canada. Slaves escaping from the Eastern Shore were taken through the well-established stations— Baltimore, Wilmington, Philadelphia, New York City, Albany, Syracuse, and Rochester—and continued to St. Catharines, Ontario, because of the Fugitive Slave Law. The Canadian government gave sanctuary to the slavery escapees from the States and refused to honor extraditions for their return. St. Catharines, located twelve miles from the U.S. border, began to host a flourishing free black community. In Canada blacks had the same rights as whites; they could vote, serve as jurors, testify in court, and run for political office unlike their counterparts south of the Canadian border.

Again and again Tubman returned to Dorchester County to bring additional enslaved people to freedom in the North. During this time, she formed friendships with the leading antislavery advocates at key stops along the path of the Underground Railroad. In Philadelphia, for example, William Still provided consistent support. Thomas Garrett was an active agent in Wilmington, Delaware. Lucretia Mott, a Quaker living in Philadelphia, also helped Tubman on numerous occasions. Mott provided logistical support and many times offered financial aid to the woman who was chronically short of the financial resources required for the transit of fugitive slaves.

In many instances, Tubman relied upon the same network that Frederick Douglass had used when he escaped from slavery in 1838. At one point, Tubman brought a group of eleven slaves along the railroad, stopping at Douglass's house in Rochester, New York, before leading them to Canada.

In addition to helping escape enslaved persons with whom she was not related, in the spring of 1857 she believed it was time to guide her parents, Ben and Rit Ross, out of Caroline County, Maryland, to a new home with her in the North. They had been granted manumission earlier, but Tubman feared for their safety and free status in an environment that was becoming increasingly uncertain and hostile south of the Mason Dixon line. Because her parents were in their seventies, Tubman took care to make the journey one that was safe and comfortable. They arrived at Thomas Garrett's house in Wilmington and then traveled to William Still's home in Philadelphia. The daughter took her parents to New York City, and then they traveled to Rochester, where they stayed for two weeks before concluding their journey in St. Catharines. By June 1858 Tubman had been successful in helping her mother, father, and four brothers escape the grip of the slaveholding South.

The paths that Harriet Tubman used to guide her runaway slave charges took advantage of the timbered areas, inlets, estuaries, and swamps that made up the escape route. Along with tidal marshes and creeks, these natural features helped provide cover for small bands of runaways on their way to the North and freedom. Tubman made use of these natural features and traveled primarily at night guided by the stars. She reported that she would tell time "by the stars and find her way by natural signs as well as any hunter."[22]

In addition to using natural resources to guide and hide, Tubman often employed guile to lower suspicion and divert attention. In one situation, she encountered a group of Irish laborers working on a bridge as she guided a group of runaway slaves. Sensing that her group was arousing suspicion among the men, Tubman attempted to turn attention away from her band by talking about the upcoming Christmas season. Quickly realizing that the conversation was not working as a diversion as the men began pressing her for the reason why this group of unaccompanied blacks was traveling and where they were headed, Tubman changed her approach. She redirected the conversation to her matrimonial prospects. In seeking a new husband, Tubman said, "she had one colored husband and she meant to marry a white gentleman next time." Whether the subject of matrimony was of general or prurient interest to the men, the approach worked, and Tubman's group crossed the bridge without incident, leaving the bemused laborers behind.[23]

Along with her knowledge of nature and having an ingenious mind, Tubman was also willing to use force—if called for—to achieve her goals. She routinely carried a pistol with her and was prepared to use it against slave catchers or any runaway who would give up to slave catchers or turn back. Knowing that a runaway slave who was caught could be forced to reveal escape routes and those who helped them, Tubman was ready to sacrifice a reluctant runaway for the good of the group. Dead fugitives would tell no tales.[24] There are no recorded instances of Tubman's having fired her sidearm at either slave catchers or reluctant runaway slaves.

Tubman's remarkable endeavors over the years to guide enslaved people to freedom and thereby further the cause of liberation while risking her own health and safety are without equal in the nineteenth century. At the same time, she was blazing a trail for gender equality. These strong drivers would be at the core of her interests and accomplishments all her life.

As the decade of the 1850s was coming to a close, Harriet Tubman's reputation as a fearless and effective member of the Underground Railroad had spread among the abolitionist community. One of the most daring and radical of those abolitionists was forming a bold plan. And he wanted Tubman's help.

Some of Harriet Tubman's most loyal friends had urged her to meet with "Captain" John Brown. He was developing an extraordinary plan that he wanted to execute in the coming months. He made it clear, through others, that he wasn't seeking financial help from Tubman; she barely had sufficient resources to support herself and her aged parents. Brown instead wanted someone who could help recruit men—strong, courageous men—and who could play a role in his planned raid. He might even want Harriet to act as a guide for the band of raiders as they passed through Maryland and Virginia on their way to their ultimate objective, the U.S. armory and arsenal at Harpers Ferry.

Brown had received glowing reports about Harriet Tubman from Frederick Douglass. She was able, Brown was told, to move undetected through the woods as if she were a deer, an elusive, silent shadow. And she had an uncanny ability to successfully guide runaway slaves over the tortuous path to freedom. She had command of intricate, clandestine networks of communications among black and white abolitionists. Many in the Northeast who financed and provided other types of support to the Underground Railroad would say that Harriet Tubman's name was synonymous with the legendary Underground Railroad.

John Brown, an antislavery zealot who claimed to be guided by apocalyptic visions, traveled to St. Catharines to meet Tubman in the spring of 1858 at her home. His hope was that Tubman would agree to help recruit his army of insurrectionists and perhaps even participate in his raid on Harpers Ferry by providing her acknowledged skills as a guide.

In answering the knock on her door that April morning, Tubman came face to face for the first time with John Brown, the fiery abolitionist whose aggressive antislavery actions went far beyond mere writing and speaking on the subject. Behind Brown was a path of violence, destruction, and bloodshed in the Kansas Territory. He must have looked to Harriet as the embodiment of an Old Testament prophet. His face was framed by a haystack of brown hair streaked with gray and a full white beard. His blue eyes burned with intensity. Quickly dispensing with the courtesies of introduction, John Brown began to explain his purpose in coming to see Tubman.

He spoke calmly and quietly, but the power of his words and the message they conveyed dominated the room. Tubman and her friends fell silent as John Brown spoke, his sentences filled with Judgment Day references and apocalyptic metaphors. He said that it was time for "God's wrath to descend," that the sin of slavery had to be expunged from the land. Turning to meet the eyes of everyone in the room, he charged everyone with becoming God's instruments in this campaign against slavery. He promised that "swift justice would be dealt to unrepentant slaveholders." Further, he said, this swift justice and the acts it required would be led by him, John Brown, God's chosen one.

In this passionate antislavery sermon about God's call to rid the land of the evil of human bondage, John Brown's "altar call" was for each person in the room to stand with him as he took up the sword in the name of freedom. For Harriet, specifically, he wanted her to help recruit an army of liberators and to employ her considerable guiding skills in reaching the U.S. armory and arsenal at Harpers Ferry. There, guns would be seized to arm the slaves who, he knew, would arise to join his growing army fighting for the liberty of all enslaved black people.

As Brown left Tubman's home and the assembled group, he took her small, muscular hand in his and shook it vigorously. "General Tubman," he said looking directly in her eyes, "you are a better officer than most. You could command an army."

Tubman pondered the meeting for several days. Her formerly enslaved black friends were moved by Brown's powerful words, but doubt lingered in their minds. During the days of their enslavement and their experiences traveling the Underground Railroad, white folks had demonstrated mercy and provided help. Yet, too, there were the nagging memories of white men who had promised much but did not honor their commitments. Some offered help only to betray them. The Fugitive Slave Act enabled many white people to profit from returning runaway slaves to their masters, who paid handsome rewards. Despite John Brown's articulate and powerful words of success in freeing slaves and his promises of liberty for black men and women, some among Tubman's friends were not convinced that Brown would succeed. Frederick Douglass, who had heard all of John Brown's visions and plans on a number of occasions, doubted that this well-meaning abolitionist would succeed at Harpers Ferry. "Doomed to fail," were Douglass's words to Tubman.

Tubman's reservations about participating in the raid with John Brown were numerous, all corroborated with a disturbing vision that came to her before Brown's visit. Among her tangible concerns were the worries expressed by her friends, the vote of no confidence in Brown's raid by Frederick Douglass, her lack of knowledge about the areas in Maryland and Virginia where she would be expected to guide, and her responsibility to care for her ailing aged parents.

The most mystical and disturbing reservation came from a vision she had one night before John Brown's visit to St. Catharines. In this dream, Tubman was in a wilderness that was covered with bushes and strewn with large rocks. From behind one of the rocks a snake rose its head. The head of the serpent changed to that of a man with a long white beard. The single head was soon joined by two additional heads that contained the visages of two young men. Then a crowd of men appeared and struck down the heads of the two young men. The head of the old man continued to stare at her with a pleading look. Tubman said that the old man seemed to want to speak to her but was silent. The dream appeared to her several times, and the sequence of events was always the same.

In the days that followed Brown's visit, Tubman decided not to accompany him during the raid on Harpers Ferry. The doubts raised by friends, her own lack of confidence in what she could contribute to the raid, and the need to stay in Canada and tend to her parents caused her to decide against participating. And then there was the dream. Perhaps an omen?

John Brown conducted his raid on Harpers Ferry on October 16, 1859, without the help of either Frederick Douglass or Harriet Tubman. When the news of the raid and its outcome reached Tubman, she realized the meaning of the dream of the three-headed serpent. During the raid, Brown's sons Oliver and Watson were killed by the U.S. Marine force sent to intercept the raiders. Their father was captured, imprisoned, tried, found guilty, and executed for treason.

4

Abolitionism in America

The movement to free enslaved people from their bondage had its roots in both secular and spiritual soil in America. James Otis, a Massachusetts lawyer and writer, held in the second half of the eighteenth-century that "the colonists, black and white, born here, are free born British subjects and entitled to all the essential civil rights of such. . . . All men . . . white or black are by the law of nature free born."[1]

The theological source of what became known as abolitionism came as a result of the Second Great Awakening, the early nineteenth-century movement that swept New England and upstate New York Protestants with a renewed zeal for evangelical thought and practice. Later spreading in the Northwest Territory above the forty-first parallel in areas populated by Yankees who migrated west, the movement had at its core the abolition of slavery. The most heinous social sin, according to the Second Great Awakening followers, was slavery. All people were equal in God's sight according to many Northern Protestants. The Society of Friends—the Quakers—also saw slavery as incompatible with their faith. Following their words with action, by the mid-1700s the Philadelphia Yearly Meeting of Friends condemned the importation, trade, purchase, or holding of slaves by their members. Quaker leaders who were slaveholders were removed from their positions.

The same moral thunderbolt, which melted the chains of allegiance that bound the colonist to his sovereign, dissolved the fetters of the slave.

—JOHN QUINCY ADAMS, 1839

In Pennsylvania, the legislature passed "An Act for the Gradual Abolition of Slavery" in 1780; New Jersey did so in 1804. Vermont, meanwhile, outlawed slavery in its constitution in 1777. In 1783 Massachusetts followed its neighboring state by abolishing slavery. The next year Rhode Island and Connecticut established emancipation laws. For the most part, New Englanders reasoned that the principles of freedom delineated in the Declaration of Independence and fought over in the Revolutionary War were applicable to all men, black and white. In her usual candid and rational language, Abigail Adams, wife of Founding Father John Adams, articulated her sentiments about slavery in a September 1774 letter to her husband: "It always seemed a most iniquitous scheme to me to fight ourselves for what we are daily robbing and plundering from those who have as good a right to freedom as we have."[2]

In the South, however, slavery was an economic consideration that was undergirded and justified by a virulent strain of white supremacy. Unlike most northern evangelicals who characterized slavery as sinful, southern theologians found justification for slavery in scripture, especially verses found in the Old Testament. Reconciling the motivations and priorities of the northern and southern colonies kept the slavery issue off the table as the newly formed states worked together on a constitutional framework. No mention of slavery can be found in the resulting Constitution of 1787.

The national dilemma of slavery did not surface again until after the completion of the Louisiana Purchase. Were the two million square miles recently acquired west of the Mississippi River to be slave holding or free as Americans migrated to new territories? A Solomon-like accord was reached in 1820: the territory north of latitude 36'30" was deemed to be free; south of the latitude would permit slavery. Missouri was the exception; despite being north of the proscribed latitude, it was granted slave-holding powers. Free Soil (antislavery) advocates were incensed that all of the newly acquired territory was not free. Free Soilers viewed slavery as not viable economically. Their contention was that free labor was significantly more efficient than slave labor and that the South, as a result, would ultimately be weakened and suffer poor economic growth. They viewed the South's reliance on cotton and its slave labor base as unsustainable over time.

Abolitionists, while sharing most of the Free Soil Party advocates' objectives, found the core issue of slavery to be a moral issue rather than an economic shortcoming. Increasingly in the early nineteenth century, politicians in the North were finding slavery was untenable for America's future on a number of important fronts: economic, social, and moral. William Seward of New York State was one of the early, articulate antislavery advocates. Historian James McPherson captured Seward's position: "Slavery undermined 'intelligence, vigor, and energy.' . . . It had produced in the South 'an exhausted soil, old and decaying towns, wretchedly-neglected roads . . . an absence of enterprise and improvement.' The institution was 'incompatible with all . . . the elements of the security, welfare, and greatness of nations.' Slavery and free labor, said Seward in his most famous speech, were 'antagonistic systems' between which raged an 'irrepressible conflict.'"[3]

As the antislavery and proslavery positions began to harden, the resolution of how to accommodate new states and territories regarding the prohibition or acceptance of slavery became a national issue. Initially, the struggle over slavery as new states were to be added to the Union was successfully—and with great difficulty—brokered by Senator Henry Clay of Kentucky. The "Compromise of 1850" was an amalgam of conflicting measures that merely delayed the inevitable rupture of the Union.

Among the citizens of the northern and eastern states, slavery was increasingly seen as a moral outrage. Women, who were playing a growing role in the religious fervor of the period, were lining up against the twin evils of slavery and alcohol abuse. Many of these women became advocates of abolition and prohibition as they sought tangible ways to express their commitment to God through action. One woman in particular was steeped in the religious antislavery expressions of the day. Additionally, she had a growing talent for writing compelling, inspiring articles that drew a large number of readers. She stepped forward to write what some would call the abolitionist manifesto that would rock the literary and political worlds in the United States. The book was

Uncle Tom's Cabin, and the author was forty-one-year-old Harriet Beecher Stowe.

But it's no kind of apology for slavery, to prove that it isn't worse than some other bad thing. . . . I'll say, besides, that ours is the more bold and palpable infringement of human rights; actually buying a man up, like a horse,—looking at his teeth, cracking his joints, and trying his paces, and then paying down for him,—having speculators, breeders, traders, and brokers in human bodies and souls,—sets the thing before the eyes of the civilized world in a more tangible form, though the thing done be . . . appropriating one set of human beings to the use and improvement of another, without any regard to their own.

—HARRIET BEECHER STOWE, *Uncle Tom's Cabin*

Litchfield, Connecticut, in the opening decade of the nineteenth century was a town infused with the colonial pride of the past and the new republic's promise of the future. Structures located around the town green were reminders of the Revolutionary War fought two decades earlier. The Tallmadge House, built about the time of the revolution, was the home of Benjamin Tallmadge, a Yale classmate of Nathan Hale's and a major in the Connecticut Dragoons who had served as Gen. George Washington's wily intelligence officer and director of the patriots' spy network in the New York–Connecticut area. On the green was the First Congregational Church, an architectural beauty with stately pillars and topped with what was considered one of the most beautiful steeples in New England. Its pastor preached the Puritan-based faith that had deep roots in the colonial experience. Near the green was a structure that housed the promise of the future—the Litchfield Female Academy, which exemplified formal education for women in postwar America.

Into this epicenter of New England culture, Harriet Beecher was born in 1811. Seventh child of the Congregational minister, Lyman Beecher, and his deeply religious wife Roxana Beecher, young Harriet grew up in a household permeated by intense religious convictions and intellectual discipline. Lyman once proclaimed that he was "harnessed to the chariot of Christ."[4]

Harriet Beecher's mother, Roxana, was the granddaughter of Gen. Andrew Ward, who had served under George Washington. Considered by her family as having an exceptional and analytical mind as a young girl, Roxana was fluent in French and well read, including novels by British and French authors. By 1816 having given birth to nine children and managed the frenetic household of a busy clergyman, she died at age forty-one. Her official cause of death was attributed to tuberculosis, but historians generally agree that her health was consistently fragile and that she just "wore out."

After her mother's death, Harriet quickly connected with her mother's family in Guilford, Connecticut. There a loving grandmother and unmarried aunts helped soften the loss of her mother and instill in the young girl a sense of compassion and awareness of the world outside the confining Calvinism of her father. Harriet returned to Litchfield with her father after he married Harriet Porter. As the pastor assigned to Litchfield Female Academy, Lyman Beecher was able to enroll his daughter at the school tuition free. Run by the formidable Miss Sarah Pierce, the academy grew in academic reputation and size with scores of female boarding students attracted to the school's scholastic offerings. Miss Pierce's nephew, John Brace, was a gifted instructor with a broad range of knowledge in subjects from astronomy to zoology who taught and had a major influence on young Harriet Beecher.

Brace introduced an expanded curriculum that included higher mathematics, Latin, science, and other subjects closely mirroring what was offered in male students' academies. Harriet joined the school at age eight in 1819, four years before the usual acceptance age of twelve. Lyman Beecher's daughter thrived in this intellectual incubator, reading across a broad range of subjects and writing compositions under Brace's demanding guidance. Harriet so excelled at writing compositions that she was selected as one of the academy's writers for its annual exhibition.

At age thirteen, Harriet graduated from the Litchfield Female Academy and elected to further her education at Hartford Female Seminary, a school started by her sister Catharine Beecher in the spring of 1823. The school sought to educate girls age twelve and older to expand their intellectual horizons and venture into an experience within a culture of "republican sisterhood." In this unique environment, Harriet evolved from student to student assistant to teacher. The school, according to biographer Joan D. Hedrick, "was one of a handful of female institutions where young women could get an education equivalent to a young man's. The curriculum . . . was essentially the same as that of the Young Ladies' Academy in Philadelphia, the Litchfield Female Academy, and Emma Willard's Troy Female Seminary. The eighteenth-century model on which they all depended was Benjamin Franklin's proposal for an 'English' school (as opposed to a 'Latin' School)."[5]

Encouraged by the religious tenor at the seminary, Harriet experienced a conversion in 1825 at age fourteen. In her letters home following this experience, she expressed her faith with such enthusiasm and clarity that her clergyman father complimented her for being an ardent Christian. This was high praise coming from a man who was frequently punctilious when it came to matters of theology.

While at Hartford Seminary, Harriet gained experience in communicating to larger audiences than that of her family letters. She served as the editor for two issues of the *School Gazette*. While the gazette's topics were pedestrian, her editorial position gave Harriet an opportunity to apply her creativity and literary skills as a journalist, albeit the editor of a school newspaper.

After graduation, Harriet remained at the Hartford Female Seminary as a teacher of rhetorical composition. In addition to her teaching duties, Harriet also found time to study French and Italian. Over time she assumed more duties from her sister and headmistress, Catharine Beecher. She even took over as acting superintendent of the school in Catharine's absence. Then, in 1832 the Beecher family made a change that had a profound effect on Harriet. Offered the position of president of the newly established Lane Theological Seminary, Lyman Beecher packed up his household and headed to "the majestic West," as he called it. The younger Beecher children—including Harriet—were expected to join the family in Cincinnati.

In 1820 Cincinnati's population was ten thousand people, or

about the same size as Hartford. By 1830 Cincinnati's population had more than doubled, making it the fastest-growing city in the United States. As the Beechers were resettling from placid Litchfield to Cincinnati, the city was booming. Not only was the population soaring compared to the small New England town they had left but also it was remarkably different in composition. German and Irish immigrants settled in increasing numbers in the city located on the Ohio River, an important trade artery that connected the farms in the West with the markets in the East.

Changes in geography and the ethnic makeup of their new hometown were not the only factors having an impact on the Beechers' lives. Calvin Ellis Stowe, a professor at the Lane Theological Seminary and a recent widower, caught the eye of the seminary president's daughter Harriet. Calvin was a gifted biblical scholar and fluent in Greek, Latin, Hebrew, French, Italian, and German. Despite his considerable intellectual stature, Calvin had some shortcomings. He was overweight, balding, given to taking to his bed when confronted with a crisis, and frequently haunted by phantoms that took various forms. He was also ten years older than Harriet. These characteristics did not, however, deter the couple from being wed in January 1836.

With a fecundity that rivaled her late mother's, Harriet Beecher Stowe gave birth to twin daughters and then four other children in close succession. The Stowes' growing family in Cincinnati put a strain on the couple's finances as well as on Harriet's ability to manage a household given the constant and considerable demands that came with raising six children younger than age twelve.

Despite a marriage filled with petty annoyances and Calvin's frequent separations from the family, Harriet shared two of her husband's strongest convictions: Calvin was an ardent abolitionist, and the family actively participated in the Underground Railroad during their time in Ohio. Calvin was also a fervent supporter of his wife's writing. In an 1844 letter to his wife, he wrote about some Pittsburgh friends: "They both told me that they devoured everything of your writing they could get hold of, and wished you would write more and oftener."[6]

On other occasions, Calvin had told Harriet she "must be a literary woman" and that it was "so written in the book of fate."[7] Calvin also had strong feelings on how Harriet should identify herself to readers: "Drop the E out of your name, which certainly only encumbers it and stops the flow and euphony, and write yourself only and always, *Harriet Beecher Stowe*, which is a name euphonious, flowing and full of meaning." Now she would be known as Harriet Beecher Stowe, rather than Mrs. Calvin Ellis Stowe.

Harriet Beecher Stowe needed little encouragement to pursue her literary interests. Initially, she wrote for and was published by the *Western Monthly Magazine*, a publication that catered to men who wanted stories about self-made males in the booming lands of the American West. The magazine satisfied Stowe's desire to be published, but the publication did limit her scope of writing because of its focused audience. In the late 1830s, she began writing for *Godey's Lady's Book* under the direction of its supportive editor, Sarah Josepha Hale. A total of eight Harriet Beecher Stowe articles appeared in *Godey's* starting in 1839. She also submitted work to the *New York Evangelist*, a weekly publication that eagerly accepted Stowe's pieces on revivals, temperance, and other religious subjects.

Writing for these three very different publications benefited Stowe in two ways for her future literary endeavors. First, the publications—reaching male pioneers in the West, appealing to women in the domestic realm, and targeting a Christian audience— helped establish Stowe in broad, essentially mutually exclusive audiences in America. Second, she positioned herself as an author who could write effectively on Western expansion, domestic issues, and moral themes. Furthermore, as a prolific writer crafting stories that appealed to receptive audiences, she honed her skills as a writer of fiction who struck responsive chords among a growing body of readers. With this literary apprenticeship, coupled with her increasing confidence, she was ready to take on a new, more challenging writing project that pulled together all the elements of her experience. Motivated by both her success in the literary world of mid-nineteenth-century America and the handsome (and welcome!) remuneration for her writing, Stowe was ready to up the ante.

Before Stowe could initiate her next literary ambition, she needed to face some challenges in her life. Harriet and Calvin's infant son Samuel Charles "Charley" died of cholera in the summer of 1849. Calvin, frustrated by his inability to increase his salary at Lane Theological Seminary and devastated by the death of Charley in Cincinnati, decided a move was necessary. Calvin accepted a professorship at Bowdoin College in Brunswick, Maine. In the spring of 1850, Harriet Beecher Stowe, grieving over the loss of her infant son, fast approaching age forty, and pregnant once again, boarded a riverboat from Cincinnati to begin the long trip east back to her beloved New England. She left behind the Cincinnati of fresh memories of grief and loss but also took with her memories of the seventeen years in which she and Calvin had numerous experiences supporting the local Underground Railroad. Both sets of memories would prove valuable resources for the next stage in her literary life.

Relocating to New England because of Calvin's new position at Bowdoin led to an extraordinarily tumultuous time for Harriet. The complexity of moving the household from Ohio to Maine, the lingering grief of losing Charley, the birth of another child (also named Charley in his late brother's memory), and the effort to reestablish a comfortable home for two adults and six children on Calvin's meager salary left her with little free time to rekindle her writing career.

Yet, amid these daunting barriers to resuming Stowe's literary life were two important sources of inspiration that helped reignite it. First, the Compromise of 1850 admitted California as a free state, formed the territories of Utah and New Mexico as popular sovereignties, and ended the slave trade in the District of Columbia. To balance these actions for Southerners, Congress strengthened the laws for apprehending escaped slaves. The Fugitive Slave Law required Northerners to cooperate in the capture and return of fleeing enslaved people. Anyone supporting the Underground Railroad now would be subject to arrest and indictment. For even lukewarm abolitionists in the North, this new law was an affront to individual freedom. The Beecher and Stowe families—among thousands of others—were outraged by this new turn of events. Harriet, in a letter to her sister Catharine, wrote: "Your last letter was a real good one, it did my heart good to find somebody as indignant a state as I am about this miserable wicked fugitive slave business—why I have felt almost choked sometimes with pent up wrath that does no good."[8]

The second source of inspiration—one of a positive nature— was a request from the editor Sarah Josepha Hale for a biographical sketch of Stowe as a key contributor to *Godey's Lady's Book*. Hale was putting together content for *Woman's Record; or, Sketches of all Distinguished Women, from "the Beginning" till A.D. 1850*. Surprised and honored to be included in distinguished company and to have been singled out by a woman with national literary standing, Stowe quickly submitted a brief biography to Hale's editorial office. To accompany Stowe's biographical sketch, Hale chose an excerpt from the writer's *The Tea Rose* to appear with the bio. Accompanying Stowe's entry were warm words that acknowledged her promise as a writer from one of America's leading editors of the day, Sarah Josepha Hale: "None of our female writers excel Mrs. Stowe in the art of entertaining her readers; the only regret is that she does not write more."[9]

With renewed motivation and confidence, Stowe turned to the *National Era*, an antislavery magazine, to publish articles on abolition. Following these pieces, she wrote a story that evolved into a serial in the magazine starting in June 1851. Her writing for this project drew on her personal experience participating in the Underground Railroad in Cincinnati and her contact with the family's black domestic worker, Eliza Buck, and other free blacks in the area. Stowe also consulted Theodore Weld's 1839 book *American Slavery as It Is*. (Weld was a student at the Lane Theological Seminary when Stowe's father was president.) She also sought advice on content from Frederick Douglass in July 1851.[10]

Stowe drew on the narratives published by former slaves as well, such as Josiah Henson's *The Life of Josiah Henson: Formerly a Slave* and Henry Bibb's *The Narrative of the Life and Adventures of Henry Bibb, Written by Himself*. She had a gift for discerning and capturing speech patterns and dialects in her writing. The dialogue in *Uncle Tom's Cabin* accurately captured the conversational nuances found in African American and white rural Kentucky speech patterns. The factual information Stowe gleaned from secondary and firsthand sources became the narrative scaffolding for *Uncle Tom's Cabin*, but it was Stowe's abhorrence of slavery, lingering grief over losing her son, and creativity in structuring situations and dialogue that blended together to make the novel authentic, emotive, and compelling for thousands of readers.

If it were your Harry, mother, or your Willie, that were going to be torn from you by a brutal trader, tomorrow morning . . . and you had only from twelve o'clock till morning to make good your escape—how fast could you walk?

—HARRIET BEECHER STOWE, *Uncle Tom's Cabin*

From June 5, 1851, through April 1, 1852, *Uncle Tom's Cabin* made a weekly appearance in the *National Era* magazine. Much like Charles Dickens's serialized novels in Great Britain, the weekly appearance of *Uncle Tom's Cabin* in the *National Era* gave the author an opportunity to spread out her writing schedule while, at the same time, keeping readers eagerly awaiting the next installment of the story. (This technique continues to be used successfully in current-day episodic cable television dramas.)

The weekly deadline gave Stowe an opportunity to balance her numerous household duties (receiving help from sister Catharine, who joined the family from Cincinnati) with a writing regimen that she undertook in her husband's office at Bowdoin College. Only two times did her rigorous writing schedule derail when writing *Uncle Tom's Cabin*—once in October 1851 and again in December of that year. When Stowe failed to make her deadlines, the *National Era* ran apologies for its readers:

MRS STOWE'S STORY—We regret exceedingly that the nineteenth chapter of Mrs. Stowe's Story did not reach us till the morning of the day on which the Era goes to press and after all its matter, except one column was set up. It shall appear next week.[11]

In 1852 Calvin accepted a chair in sacred literature at Andover Theological Seminary in Andover, Massachusetts. Mindful of her continuous deadline obligations and finding it difficult to balance literary duties and increasing household demands, Stowe decided to accompany her husband to his new position at the seminary. There, Harriet toiled without interruptions in a quiet room at Andover, while Catharine watched over the Stowe's children in Brunswick.

By March 1852 publisher John P. Jewett signed a contract with Harriet Beecher Stowe to publish *Uncle Tom's Cabin* as a book. In the first week of the book's release, it sold 10,000 copies. A year after its release, *Uncle Tom's Cabin* had sold 300,000 copies. Considering "pass along" readership, the book must have reached millions of readers. As Professor Amanda Claybaugh has commented, "The book was published in an era when novels were treated as a kind of communal property, borrowed from circulating libraries, passed from hand to hand, read aloud to entire households at a time; knowing this, one reviewer speculated that *Uncle Tom* had ten readers for every one copy sold."[12]

Two New York religious papers—one antislavery (*The Independent*) and the other proslavery (*New York Observer*)—became cynosures of the contrasting points of view regarding slavery in America. The *Observer* dismissed Stowe's work as "anti-ministerial" and "unlady like." Conversely, *The Independent* invited Stowe to be a frequent contributor as an antislavery voice for the paper. The flashpoint for much of the controversy occurred when Rev. Joel Parker, a Presbyterian minister from Philadelphia, entered a $20,000 libel suit against Stowe for quoting the reverend in chapter 12 of the book and footnoting the source. Parker complained, "After painting a scene of shocking inhumanity, [Stowe] holds me up to the public, in an odious light, by representing me as uttering sentiments that seem to justify, or at least to palliate, the cruelties which you have described."[13]

The crux of the offending quote was that slavery was no worse than any other human frailty. Unfortunately for the miffed minister, Stowe had picked up the quote from a newspaper report, where Parker's words had been cited verbatim. Faced with Stowe's increasing fame and admiration and with the documented evidence of the reverend's words, the Parker suit faded away.

What didn't subside was the anger and challenges from Southern sources, perhaps fueled by the Reverend Parker episode. For Southerners, Stowe's book went far beyond her refutation of the theological justification for slavery that many found in the Old Testament of the Bible. *Uncle Tom's Cabin* plunged a knife in the heart of their economic system with its slaveholder underpinnings. Further, this highly effective case for abolition came from a woman. Harriet Beecher Stowe was an independent-thinking New Englander who did not fit in the early nineteenth century's "cult of true womanhood." Sixteen years before *Uncle Tom's Cabin* had been published, Angelina Grimké and Sarah Grimké had linked two patriarchal institutions—slavery and the subordination of women in the United States. Now a powerful abolitionist novel—written by a woman who relished her sovereignty as a woman, a writer, and a wife—reached millions of sympathetic readers with a clear and convincing picture of human suppression.

The novel took on slavery as it had never been explained before; Harriet Beecher Stowe's detailed, human stories of cruelty and suffering featured well-drawn characters who either earned the sympathy or the revulsion of readers depending on their roles in the narrative. Neither Northern nor Southern proponents of slavery were spared from her vivid writing, which was based on her belief that slavery was "evil and only evil." Protestant clergymen who saw a biblical justification for slavery were treated with equal distain in the *Uncle Tom* saga. Referring to *Uncle Tom's Cabin*, Henry Wadsworth Longfellow (an undergraduate classmate of Calvin Stowe's at Bowdoin) wrote: "Never was there such a literary *coup-de-main* as this."[14]

Proslavery advocates bombarded the press with claims that the book was filled with distortions, exaggerations, and outright lies. The scenes that depicted cruelty to slaves were atypical of normal behavior among slaveholders, critics held.

Rather than counter objections point by point, Stowe employed a different strategy. She produced a publication that explained the credibility of her characters, the veracity of the scenes described, and the body of law that existed to protect the institution of slavery. It appeared under the ponderous title *A Key to Uncle Tom's Cabin—Presenting the Original Facts and Documents upon Which the Story Is Founded Together with Corroborative Statements—the Truth of the Work.* Stowe's approach in the document was to support her case with facts, examples of real people, writings of proslavery journalists and clergy, and numerous newspaper classified ads offering rewards for runaway slaves.

In the court of public opinion, Stowe confounded her critics with facts, data, legal findings, and documented examples of cruelty and human maleficence toward other human beings. The raw reality of enslaved humans was pulled out into the open by a determined forty-one-year-old mother who was outraged at how fellow humans were treated in a nation that was founded on the basis "all men are created equal."

The power of *Uncle Tom's Cabin* to change public opinion about the true nature of slavery and the need to end it is indisputable. Abraham Lincoln was reported to have said when first meeting Harriet Beecher Stowe at the White House in 1862: "So you're the little woman who wrote the book that made this great war."[15]

"And what do you think will be the end of this?" said Miss Ophelia.

"I don't know. One thing is certain,—that there is a mustering among the masses, the world over; and there is a dies irae [day of wrath] coming on, sooner or later . . . My mother used to tell me of a millennium that was coming . . . all men should be free and happy."

—HARRIET BEECHER STOWE, *Uncle Tom's Cabin*

As Harriet Beecher Stowe made her case with pen and ink for freeing the enslaved, abolitionist John Brown made his case with sword and blood. Messianic in appearance and speech, Brown in 1855 brought his form of abolitionism to Kansas, where he had no problem abducting five men with proslavery convictions and splitting their heads open with his sword. His violent approach continued in the Midwest, later reaching a climax in 1859 in Harpers Ferry, Virginia. There, on October 17, Brown sought to spark a slave rebellion by arming the local slaves with weapons from the Harpers Ferry U.S. armory and arsenal. The raid failed miserably; eight of Brown's men were killed—including two of his sons—and Brown was taken prisoner. He was tried on charges of treason, insurrection, and murder. Having been found guilty on all charges, he was hanged on December 2.

As committed an abolitionist as Harriet Beecher Stowe, Brown chose violence over persuasion for freeing the slaves. Despite their very different tactics, both Stowe and Brown were equally successful in shaking Southerners with their demands to end the "peculiar institution." Both Stowe and Brown knew that a day of reckoning was at hand and that the nation would pay a steep price.

> I, John Brown am now quite certain that the crimes of this guilty land will never be purged away, but with blood.

—JOHN BROWN, December 2, 1859[16]

5

The "Seething Hell of War"

As the decade of the 1860s began, the sectional differences that had shaped the previous ten years hardened, became irreconcilable. The residents of the North, in large part, saw slavery as incompatible with the expression of liberty stated by the Founding Fathers: "All men are created equal." In the South the economics of slavery, combined with a presumed biblical justification of bondage, led the white residents to coalesce in a position diametrically opposed to that of their fellow citizens in the North. Deeply held personal opinions further shaped political positions during the antebellum period. Determining how to deal with the westward growth of the nation and the admission of new states to the Union required forcing decisions by these polarized regional factions. Would these states be slave or free?

Historian James McPherson has described this collision of positions: "The slavery issue would probably have caused an eventual showdown between North and South in any circumstances. But it was the country's sprawling growth that made the issue so explosive. Was the manifest destiny of these two million square miles west of the Mississippi River to be free or slave? . . . By 1860 it could no longer be deferred."[1]

The concept of nullification—the idea that states could separate themselves from the Union if they believed that the central government had abridged their sovereign powers—was first raised during the War of 1812 when New England Federalists briefly entertained secession (the Hartford Convention). In 1832 the nullification issue came up again when South Carolina claimed a right to nullify a federal tariff, which it was resisting, and President Andrew Jackson threatened to send troops to that state.

Secession raised its head again in 1860 after Republican Abraham Lincoln (formerly a Whig Party member) was elected president of the thirty-three states then in the Union and with a thirty-fourth, Kansas, about to join. On December 20, 1860, South Carolina formally seceded from the Union, followed closely by Mississippi, Florida, Alabama, Georgia, and Louisiana. Soon afterward Texas and Virginia joined them. New York City attorney George Templeton Strong wrote in his diary: "This treasonable inflammation—secessionitis—keeps on making steady progress, week by week."[2]

Tensions continued to build as the two sides—Union and Confederate—edged toward armed confrontation. On April 12, 1861, at 4:30 a.m. the first guns were sounded in Charleston Harbor as Confederate artillery discharged four thousand rounds at the Union-held garrison of Fort Sumter. Maj. Robert Anderson, Union commander of Sumter, surveyed the partially destroyed fort—its interior on fire—and his outnumbered, exhausted troops, and decided that he had no other course than to surrender. The U.S. flag was struck, the Confederate States' flag raised, and the American Civil War was underway.

The Confederacy began mobilizing an army soon after states seceded. By the fall of Fort Sumter, the South had enrolled sixty thousand men in its army. The Union, meanwhile, was just starting to respond to Lincoln's call for seventy-five thousand, ninety-day militiamen (based on a 1795 law that provided for bringing state militias into federal service). Soon realizing that a three-month enlistment term was remarkably unrealistic, the president called for forty-two thousand three-year volunteers for the army, along with increasing the regular army by twenty-three thousand more men, and the navy by eighteen thousand sailors.

According to historian McPherson, the North ultimately drew on a deeper pool of men than the South had. "Actual Union manpower superiority was about 2.5 to 1. From 1862 onward the Union Army enjoyed approximately this superiority in numbers. But because of its earlier start in creating an army, the Confederacy in June 1861 came closer to matching the Union in mobilized manpower than at any other time in the war."[3]

Both Union and Confederate volunteers were recruited from

and organized by their place of residence. Friends, neighbors, and relatives served together in the ranks. The members of the 155th Pennsylvania Regiment, for example, came from the same neighborhood in Pittsburgh. Friends and schoolmates often showed up together at recruiting offices to enlist with the hope of serving together. (Battlefield casualties in the ranks thus were deeply felt since the men wounded or killed were often longtime friends or, in some cases, related.)[4]

As desirable as the enlistment of large numbers of Union troops was on the surface, the president recognized that able bodies alone were not sufficient to go into battle. In a July 4, 1861, message to Congress, Lincoln stated, "One of the greatest perplexities of the government is to avoid receiving troops faster than it can provide for them."[5]

Northern states and municipalities helped fill the gap in resources caused by the federal recruitment of troops. Arms, uniforms, and related military equipment were funded by the states and some cities that had the financial resources. (Civic pride helped fuel the competition to see that local troops were properly outfitted.) Initially the zeal of state and local governments to provide uniforms resulted in a panoply of outfits that caused confusion among soldiers in the field as they sought to distinguish friendly troops from their foes by their uniforms.

Soon after the armed conflict began, both North and South came to the grim realization that they were ill-prepared to handle the inevitable casualties. The volume of wounded soldiers and the nature of their wounds quickly overwhelmed the medical organizations of both sides. The large-caliber, low-velocity bullets (minié balls) that were used by both sides resulted in devastating damage to human tissue and bone. The default treatment of such wounded bodies was often amputation. The casualties suffering from blood loss, infections from a host of sources, and trauma put military doctors to the test. Combining the medical damage done in the field with the lack of hygienic measures in camps and hospitals and the resulting spread of diseases such as dysentery, army military medical units were rapidly overwhelmed.

Inspired by the British Sanitary Commission founded during

the Crimean War, a group of Northern physicians and women established the U.S. Sanitary Commission in 1861 to support the beleaguered U.S. Army Medical Department. Physician Elizabeth Blackwell led the efforts to address the Union's medical crises by holding an organizing meeting at the Cooper Institute in New York on April 29, 1861, and helped form the Women's Central Association for Relief to coordinate the efforts of small, local organizations and to train nurses. This association, started by and largely comprising female volunteers, became an important part of the U.S. Sanitary Commission. Women were beginning to take a larger role in meeting the medical crises of the Union Army.[6]

The U.S. Sanitary Commission raised funds for medical treatment and provided bandages, clothing, and food for soldiers. But the commission ran into strong headwinds from the U.S. Army Medical Department, which wanted to restrict the newly formed commission to "investigating and advisory only." Commanded by a surgeon general who was the product of forty-three years in the regular army, the sclerotic bureau was not able to make the changes required by the expanding war. The regular army instead pushed back on "the sensation preachers, village doctors, and strong-minded women" of the U.S. Sanitary Commission.[7]

Outraged over the intransigence of the army's medical corps, U.S. Sanitary Commission executive secretary Frederick Law Olmsted complained: "It is criminal weakness to entrust such responsibility as those resting on the Surgeon-General to a self-satisfied, supercilious, bigoted blockhead, merely because he is the oldest of the old mess-room doctors of the frontier-guard of the country." Lincoln responded to the impasse by replacing the curmudgeonly surgeon general with William Hammond, a thirty-three-year-old physician who quickly saw the value of the commission. He also issued an order in July 1862 that required one-third of army nurses in general hospitals to be women. (At the conclusion of the war in 1865, over three thousand women in the North had served as paid army nurses. Several thousand women also were volunteers in the medical arena.)[8]

Hammond appointed Dr. Jonathan K. Letterman as the medical director of the Army of the Potomac. Letterman was a medical innovator who instituted the concept of triage for handling the wounded, a robust ambulance corps, and the noncombatant medic. He also established procedures for improving camps' sanitary conditions in the Army of the Potomac.[9]

With the restrictive grip of the U.S. Army Medical Corps now relaxed, women began to flow into Northern army units to take on critical roles, which they met with success and earned eventual recognition by the army's leadership. Mary Ann ("Mother") Bickerdyke worked tirelessly to improve the soldiers' hygiene and found favor with Ulysses S. Grant's senior officers for her attention to camps' sanitary conditions. She was the only female allowed in advanced base hospitals by Gen. William T. Sherman.[10]

I was often with her on little walks about town, and the girls and boys seemed to vie with each other in forestalling any wish of hers. Their affection and chivalry was received so graciously and naturally that it was a pleasure to witness.

—FANNY CHILDS VASSALL, writing about Clara Barton as a teacher in New Jersey

---

My school boys . . . are reading and crying over Uncle Tom's Cabin and wishing all sorts of good luck to Uncle Tom and the contrary to his opponents.

—CLARA BARTON, Bordentown School, New Jersey

Oxford, Massachusetts, fifty miles west of Boston, attracted Huguenot settlers in the early eighteenth century. Farming and milling occupations sprang up along the nearby French River. There Dr. Stephen Barton—an ardent revolutionary delegate to the Committee of Correspondence and Safety, and later a grandfather of Clara Barton's—became known as a colonial philanthropist and respected anti-monarchist among the town's leadership. His son, Stephen, born in 1774, became an earnest soldier who served with the army of Gen. "Mad" Anthony Wayne in the Northwest Territory. From this resolute stock of New Englanders, Clara Barton was born on Christmas Day in 1821.

Stephen and his wife, Sarah, were the parents of five children, each born approximately two years after the other—until Clarissa Harlowe Barton arrived eleven years after her youngest sibling and seventeen years after her eldest. Capt. Stephen Barton retained his military ways and habits long after his discharge from the army. (According to daughter Clara, "His soldier habits and tastes never left him.") Clara's mother, Sarah, had a fiery temper, was "outspoken on the subject of women's rights," and had a reputation for using earthy language when she was angry.[11] Some have suggested that being raised in this volatile household of two strong-willed parents explains why Clara Barton never married.[12]

Captain Barton loved his youngest daughter, and the feeling was mutual. Clara wrote of him later in life as "a calm, reasonable, high toned, moral man, also of great natural vigor and strength, athletic . . . in all things cheerful –generous & kind but very firm."[13] For young Clara, her father had achieved what she aspired to in her life: providing service to his country, helping others, facing conflict with bravery and resolution, and having a kind, compassionate heart.

As the youngest child in the Barton family, Clara received frequent tutoring from her admiring siblings. Sally taught her to read and spell at an early age. Stephen helped her gain an understanding of mathematics and the rudiments of bookkeeping. David addressed her physical abilities by instructing her in horsemanship, which she eagerly took up. (She retained this skill and interest though her adult years.) David played another role, albeit unintentional, in her education. After falling from a barn roof he was working on, David was treated by local physicians with extensive bloodletting using leeches. He grew progressively weaker, and it was due to Clara's intervention and attentive care that he was nursed back to good health over a two-year recuperation. Not only did her brother benefit but Clara's key role in her brother's convalescence boosted her confidence in her ability to be of help to others as well. The seeds were planted for a nursing capacity that would prove important for treating wounded soldiers in the future.

At the suggestion of a knowledgeable family friend, Clara Barton was encouraged to enter the teaching profession.[14] By age eighteen, she had passed examinations and began teaching in Oxford schools. As Barton's confidence grew in the classroom so did her reputation as a gifted teacher. Within a few years, she established a school for the children of workers in her brother's mill. As much as she enjoyed and was challenged by the teaching profession, she was increasingly aggravated by the low salaries paid to female teachers. She told the Oxford School Board, in response to a contract with an anemic salary offer, "I may sometimes be willing to teach for nothing, but if paid at all, I shall never do a man's work for less than a man's pay." The board withdrew the low salary originally offered and paid her what she requested—equal pay.[15]

Eager to take on a larger challenge and responsibility, Barton went to Bordentown, New Jersey, where she proposed opening a public school to local officials. Overcoming indecisive adults and ambivalent students (especially boys), she persevered. The school she established flourished, attracting scores of students who saw its value and winning over skeptical adults. Funds were soon raised to build a new school and expand the educational program.[16]

Barton's persistence and winning ways with the students soon saw her classroom exceed its expected ceiling of fifty students to reach fifty-four. She taught the basic lessons in mathematics and reading, and even pushed the advanced students to tackle more ambitious topics. For one group of boys, for example, she assigned the reading of recently published *Uncle Tom's Cabin* and led a discussion in class. Her students were deeply moved by the book. Boys in Bordentown who were thought to have been lost to the benefits of public education became, under Barton's tutelage, successful scholars and ardent admirers of their teacher. The young boys appreciated Barton's "kind words and smile of recognition" that had been missing in their prior classroom experience.

The Bordentown School continued to add students and classrooms as its success blossomed. In the community Barton was seen as the chief architect of the school's growing success and reputation. Then in 1854, in an act of incredible obtuseness, the school board brought in J. Kirby Burnham to head the school, and Barton was to continue as a "female assistant" at a salary less than half of Burnham's pay. The new head of the school quickly proved to be a dictatorial and contentious leader who alienated Barton and many of the female teachers in the school. Seething over being rejected for the head position because of her gender and over the unraveling of the school's reputation by an inept administrator, Barton left Bordentown. She was brokenhearted over her own professional ill-treatment and the disintegration of the quality of the school she had worked so hard to found and build. Four months after Barton left the Bordentown School, Burnham was sacked, and the school underwent a restructuring to undo the effects of his incompetence.

Discouraged and stunned at the collapse of her teaching career, Barton was convinced that her education profession was behind her. She needed to apply her organizing abilities and skills of persuasion in another field. Moreover, it necessitated a geographical move to leave the bad memories of New Jersey behind her and to seek a more promising future in a fresh, new location.

Much as her reasons for moving to Bordentown, New Jersey, Clara Barton's motives for relocating to Washington City in mid-1854 are unclear. Washington in the 1850s was more rustic than cosmopolitan, lacking adequate public water and sewage treatment. The narrow social amenities it offered revolved around Congress and the small federal government. Slavery was still lawful in the nation's capital. Barton, as a lifelong New Englander, would have found the city overwhelmingly Southern in manners and style with few exceptions. Amid this strange new environment, Barton quickly contacted the congressman from her home district and soon—through her persistence, personal charm, and impressive résumé—parlayed her connection to obtain a position as a clerk in the U.S. Patent Office.

Barton found the work challenging and interesting in its scope, and the remuneration was far better than she had received as an educator. And much to her satisfaction, her pay was equivalent to that paid to male clerks. She excelled at her work and continued to be a productive, effective office worker despite the hostility of her male coworkers and the decidedly anti-female bias of some senior federal bureaucrats who did not want men and women to mix in the workforce. Barton's self-assurance and her positive relationship with U.S. Patent Office commissioner Charles Mason further disturbed her male colleagues. They resented the favor she curried with Mason and interpreted her confident, professional attitude as haughty.

Barton's patent office work was buffeted by office politics even as she proved to be a conscientious, skilled employee. Then the political tides shifted. Her sponsor, Alexander DeWitt, lost his reelection bid in Barton's home district, and the Buchanan administration was looking to reward its political followers with jobs in the federal government. Clara Barton was not aligned with the new administration's political views, so once again she found herself without a job. She headed back home to Oxford.

After two years of fighting depression, drifting from minor job to minor job, and taking courses, Barton was called back to the patent office after Abraham Lincoln's election in November 1860. She returned to the same office with the same coworkers from her prior time at the patent office. She even was able to go back to her old room at Almira Fales's boardinghouse. Some things had changed, however. The pro-South milieu in Washington City had taken on a more malignant tone. Sensing an undercurrent of instability in the patent office's ranks, Barton decided to shore up her position by aligning herself with a political patron. (Commissioner Mason had left the U.S. Patent Office in July 1855.) Barton targeted Henry Wilson, the senator from her home state, Massachusetts.

When the affable, ambitious Wilson met the personable and poised Barton, it was mutual infatuation at first sight. Little did she know when meeting Wilson for the first time that he would do much more than protect her patent office position. He would be of immeasurable help in supporting her future ambitions, which would eventually launch her into national prominence. Never a passionate abolitionist in the antebellum period, Barton's lukewarm disdain for the seceding Confederate States suddenly came to a boil on April 19, 1861, following the Union surrender at Fort Sumter.

I don't know how long it has been since my ear has been free from the roll of a drum. It is the music I sleep by, and I love it.

—CLARA BARTON

If my countrymen are to suffer my place is with them, my Northern brothers are here in arms danger and death staring them in the face and I cannot leave them.

—CLARA BARTON

When the news of the Confederate forces firing on Fort Sumter reached Clara Barton, she was alarmed and indignant. Writing to a cousin, she said, "From the bottom of my heart, I pray that the thing may be tested, may the business be taken in hand and proved not *if* we have a Government, but *that* we have one." She was especially enraged that two of her coworkers at the patent office were blatant Southern sympathizers. (She urged U.S. Patent Office commissioner D. P. Holloway to dismiss the rebel fellow travelers because of their presumed disloyalty to the federal government. Holloway demurred.)

A week after Fort Sumter, an incident occurred closer to home both in geography and with direct connection to Barton. Troops of the Sixth Massachusetts Regiment, on their way to Washington City, were changing trains in Baltimore when they encountered a large group of secessionist sympathizers that cast paving stones and other debris at them. Trained to handle civil disturbances and street riots, the Sixth Massachusetts used bayonets and rifle butts to subdue the riotous crowd. The conflict escalated, and the troops fired musket volleys into the enraged crowd. At the conclusion of the engagement, sixteen persons had been killed—twelve civilians and four Union soldiers.

Barton saw the Baltimore riot as "a great national calamity" and that "the darkest page of our country's history is now being written in lines of blood."[17] Reboarding their train to Washington City, the Sixth Massachusetts was quartered in the Senate chamber upon arrival. No other barracks were available. Barton lost no time in visiting the Massachusetts regiment at the Capitol and worked diligently to obtain supplies and food for the troops. She was successful in providing provisions from a variety of sources for her home state's soldiers. These actions taken on behalf of the Sixth Massachusetts fueled her desire to do even more and shortened her patience with the feckless male government bureaucrats and military leaders who were proving ineffective and incompetent. Unlike her mentor, Senator Wilson, those men who underestimated this slender, five-foot-tall woman who demonstrated impeccable grace *and* resolution were in for an abrupt education in the artfulness of Clarissa Harlowe Barton.

The 1861 mobilization of the Union Army was without precedent in U.S. military history. Thousands of fresh troops had to be quartered, outfitted in uniforms and weapons, and fed. The Federal Army's Commissary and Quartermaster Corps were unable to meet the needs of this burgeoning armed force. Further complicating the solution, military camps were filthy, fetid breeding grounds for illnesses such as diarrhea and dysentery. Even the newly formed U.S. Sanitary Commission, tasked with improving military hygiene and camp sanitation, struggled with the scope and extent of the need.

In this vacuum, Barton saw her calling to provide medical supplies and related goods to ease the burden on an army where 30 percent of the troops were on sick call in June 1861.[18] She visited the camps near Washington City to provide supplies, taking with her Dr. R. O. Sidney, a friend from the post office. Dr. Sidney could provide some medical guidance while also ameliorating any concerns surrounding Barton's visiting the soldiers in camp as a single woman. (Common wisdom in the mid-nineteenth century was that any single woman in the camps was at worst a prostitute or at best a "woman of easy virtue.") Barton also continued to tap her friends in Massachusetts and New Jersey, her former residences, and sent appeals for items for the troops. The informal network of "dear sisters" responded generously to Barton's frequent and compelling pleas for support. This network included a relationship with the Ladies Relief Committee of Worcester, Massachusetts, that was formed to distribute supplies to Worcester County soldiers. Barton became one of its primary distribution channels.[19]

On Sunday, July 21, 1861, Union troops engaged the Confederates at Manassas Junction, Virginia, a mere twenty-five miles from Washington City. The battle was a disaster for the Union troops under Gen. Irwin McDowell. Union casualties and the subsequent lack of medical treatment were appalling. Some of those fortunate enough to be transported to Washington for medical care were brought to the top floor of the patent office, where Barton saw firsthand the human toll from one of the first significant engagements of the Civil War.

Barton's continuing work in soliciting supplies filled her own boardinghouse room with boxes; she then rented space in a nearby warehouse to store items. Within six months she had filled three warehouses. The goods ran the gamut from raspberry vinegar, honey, soap, and lemons to items that appealed to the soldiers' desire for tobacco and whiskey.[20] As the donated and purchased supplies continued to flow in, Barton realized that her good intentions fell short of addressing the most acute problem, treating the wounded and diseased soldiers on the front line.

Pursuing her desire to take supplies to the war's front and to take an active role in the care of wounded soldiers, Barton approached Col. Daniel H. Rucker, head of the Quartermaster Depot of the District of Columbia, calling on him in his austere office. Rucker initially rebuffed her, but Barton persisted and announced that she had three warehouses of supplies ready to go to the front lines. Barton's passionate plea, backed by the three warehouses of evidence of her ability to deliver, caused the gruff colonel to relent. He gave Barton the use of a wagon and driver, as well as signed permission to take government transportation—including passage by boat—to a Union depot in Virginia. Also, to her delight, he obtained a pass for her signed by Surgeon General Hammond. Along with a small party of assistants, Barton traveled to the Fredericksburg, Virginia, area, and distributed the supplies. Her task complete, she returned to Washington to accumulate more supplies.[21]

Not long after returning to Washington, Barton learned of a campaign unfolding near Culpeper, Virginia. She obtained another pass. Along with a female companion, she transported a load of stores to the port of Alexandria, Virginia, and took the supplies by railroad to Culpeper. There in August 1862, Barton saw the wounded transported from the battlefield at Cedar Mountain. In addition to providing medical supplies, Barton helped address the needs for bandages, the care of amputees, and the cleaning of the blood-covered floors. She later wrote of her experience at the field hospital near Culpeper: "Suffering lay on every side, our ample stores diminished with a rapidity truly appalling when we looked upon so many brave and noble patriots needing everything—possessing nothing. . . . Would you know how our men bear their sufferings? Oh, how I wish I had words to tell you of all the patience, the nobility of soul, the resignation, and bravery of our gallant troops."[22]

Her time at Culpeper convinced Barton that this work required her full-time attention. Commissioner Holloway granted her a leave of absence while she performed fieldwork with the Union Army. A coworker would fulfill her U.S. Patent Office duties and receive half her salary. Holloway generously gave Barton the other half of the salary as a small stipend for her work in supporting the war effort.

Less than three weeks after the Battle of Cedar Mountain, the Union Army—this time led by Gen. John Pope—returned to the Manassas battleground, hoping to block a potential invasion of Washington City by the Confederate Army under the leadership of the much-feared Maj. Gen. Thomas "Stonewall" Jackson. The battle at Manassas and the following action at Chantilly, Virginia, resulted in sixteen thousand Union casualties out of a force of sixty-five thousand men.[23] When Secretary of War Edwin Stanton learned of the devastating loss and the number of wounded soldiers, he quickly called for volunteer nurses to assist with administering medical treatment for the troops. Stanton's army medical director Dr. Thomas A. McParlin supported his plea by placing announcements in Washington City newspapers and on hotel bulletin boards asking for civilian surgeons and nurses to help with the medical aftermath of the fighting at Manassas. Both Stanton and McParlin knew the need was great, but they had no idea of the ghastly scene at the battlefield, where scores of corpses—both men and horses—covered the ground and thousands of wounded soldiers remained uncared for on the abattoir-like battlefield.

Answering the call and with supplies and three assistants, Barton quickly boarded a train bound for Fairfax Station. A number of the wounded from Manassas and Chantilly had been transported to the station and were awaiting treatment at the "evacuation hospital." One of the surgeons who met Barton and her team was Dr.

James Dunn, who had worked with Barton at Culpeper weeks earlier and had a high regard for her professionalism and commitment. (Dr. Dunn and Barton would meet again as they treated the wounded at Antietam Battlefield in September 1862.)

Barton and her assistants immediately began helping by performing rudimentary medical tasks: making and applying compresses, fashioning slings, using tourniquets, and changing bandages. While treating one badly wounded soldier, Barton was grasped by the man, who murmured to her: "Don't you remember me? I am Charley Hamilton who used to carry your satchel home from school." She kindly responded that she remembered him and that he was her "faithful pupil." Barton later wrote about the incident: "That mangled arm will never carry a satchel again."[24] Not only was Barton performing important medical duties in treating wounds but she also provided words of comfort and consolation to dozens of grievously wounded men who were beyond medical help yet were soothed by a sympathetic ear and a kind word.

Following its success at the Second Battle of Manassas, the Army of Northern Virginia, under the leadership of Gen. Robert E. Lee, launched an invasion of Maryland. Barely catching her breath after the devastation resulting from Manassas and Chantilly, Barton was even more convinced that she was needed on the battlefield and that she had to be in place just before and during a battle to be effective. Through an anonymous but reliable source, she learned of the Confederates' move into Maryland on September 13, 1862. She quickly approached her "patron saint" Colonel Rucker to obtain a wagon and a pass so she could venture to Harpers Ferry, where she anticipated the casualties from the certain engagements in Maryland would go. Rucker granted her request. On Sunday, September 14, she and her assistant, Cornelius Welles, loaded the wagon the army provided with bandages, canned foods, lanterns, and other crucial materials, and then departed for Frederick, Maryland.

During the time Barton left Washington City, the Battle of South Mountain was fought several miles west of Frederick. A wagon train of two hundred ambulances provided by Dr. Letterman was used to transport the wounded from the battlefield. Stores, including important medical supplies, intended for battles in Maryland were stopped short of Frederick when the Confederates destroyed the railroad bridge at the Monocacy River. Barton's medical supplies were now even more critical.[25]

Traveling over South Mountain, Barton, Welles, and their teamster passed through the middle of what had been a fierce battle just before their arrival. At one point, Barton asked to stop their wagon so she and Welles could see if any wounded men had survived. They walked the now-still battlefield and assessed those men left behind. None would survive. Letterman's ambulances had cleared the field of all the wounded who had any glimmer of hope of survival.

By September 16 Barton, Welles, the loaned teamster, and their wagon of supplies had reached the Army of the Potomac near Sharpsburg, Maryland. There was, Barton later wrote, an "impending sense of gloom." The air was "soggy" and noxious. "It was all used & made fetid by the press of human beings & animals."[26] For the first time, Barton was where she longed to be, at the very brink of a major battle. Where combat was imminent. Where she could treat the wounded with minimal delay.

The battle that unfolded over the next twenty-four hours would be one of the bloodiest engagements of the Civil War, with horrifying casualties on both sides. It would be the battle where Barton's friend, Dr. James Dunn, would confer on her the nom de guerre "the angel of the battlefield."[27]

6

Noble Watchwords and Inspiring Ideas

By January 1863 the Civil War was twenty-one months old, and there was no end in sight for the two opposing armies. The Union had catastrophic encounters in Virginia during the Peninsula Campaign, at the Battles of First and Second Manassas, and at Fredericksburg. The Battle of Antietam in Maryland had resulted in enormous casualties on both sides with no clear winner. Now, in January, with horrific human losses in its wake, the Union Army faced the humiliation of being literally mired in a "Mud March" with its men, horses, and equipment bogged down in Virginia roads that had turned into a quagmire during torrential rains. The nadir of morale had surely been reached by the officers and men of the Army of the Potomac.

Three changes would ultimately help alter the mood of despair to one of confidence and optimism for the Union's cause. Two of those changes would be made by the president of the United States: he formulated and signed the Emancipation Proclamation, which pushed the cause of ending slavery front and center in the war effort; and as commander in chief, he realized he needed to reassess the generals who were executing the war for the Union. The third factor was the appearance of a rousing anthem—written by a forty-two-year-old poet—that would inspire and motivate Union civilians and soldiers, from privates to generals.

> Our men in the field do not lack food or clothing or money, but they do lack noble watchwords and inspiring ideas such as one worth fighting and dying for.
>
> —SAMUEL GRIDLEY HOWE, February 1862

Born Julia Ward on May 27, 1819, she was one of six surviving children in the family of Samuel Ward and Julia Cutler Ward. Another daughter, also named Julia, had been born in 1816 and died of whooping cough three years later. The second Julia was named in honor of her mother and in memory of her deceased sister. Samuel Ward was a wealthy, self-made man who excelled in the world of banking and finance in New York City. The children of Samuel and Julia Cutler Ward lived privileged lives in the splendor of an opulent house situated on the tip of Manhattan. Their friends and social contacts were the moneyed elite of early nineteenth-century New York.

Julia Cutler Ward was a strict Calvinist whose views of predestination of the elect, sin, and damnation were not shared with the same intensity by her husband. She was also a published poet who had a poem included in Rufus Griswold's anthology *The Female Poets of America.*[1]

On November 11, 1824, Julia Cutler Ward died giving birth to her seventh child, Annie. She was only twenty-seven. For young Julia, the death of her mother would haunt her for the rest of her life. These memories were especially vivid when Julia married and gave birth to her own children. After Julia Cutler Ward's death, Samuel took up his wife's Calvinist beliefs and imposed an austere lifestyle on his six children. He shielded his daughter Julia especially from influences outside their home at Sixteen Bond Street. Education, friends, and life experiences were all carefully controlled within Samuel Ward's splendid but restrictive home. In later years, Julia described her childhood experience under her father's rigorous religious purview: "The early years of my youth were passed in seclusion not only of home life, but of a home life most carefully and jealously guarded from all that might be represented in the orthodox trinity of evil, the world, the flesh, and the devil."[2]

In her secluded existence as a youth, Julia was exposed to gifted teachers and mentors who tutored her in languages (she was fluent in six) and literature. She studied piano with a London-trained teacher and dance with a French dancing master. Shielded from the theater by her father, who considered plays "distinctly of the devil," young Julia wrote her own dramatizations to satisfy her interest in the theater. She also displayed an interest and talent for writing poetry. Modern critics have characterized young Julia as having "poetic talent."[3]

As often is the case with precocious children, some adults saw Julia as a bright, refined young lady with much promise. To others, she was—in intellectual Margaret Fuller's estimation—"as affected as she could be."[4] As the eldest of three sisters known as the "Three Graces" outside their home, Julia was singled out as "Diva," a sobriquet that continued to be used in her adult life.

Protected from the coarseness of the outside world while partaking distilled doses of highbrow culture, Julia found herself a prisoner in a grand but confining castle: "I seemed to myself like a young damsel of older times, shut up within an enchanted castle. . . . And I must say that my dear father, with all his noble generosity and overwhelming affection, sometimes appeared to me as my jailer."[5]

Then, as with the fairy-tale princess, there came galloping into Julia's world a knight—a chevalier of the Order of St. Savior—armed not with a sword but a doctoral degree in medicine and cloaked in the armor of righteousness. Samuel Gridley Howe swept into Julia Ward's life and—the eighteen years difference in their ages notwithstanding—proposed marriage to Julia and rescued her from her gilded cage. Or was it an exchange of one gilded cage for another?

Samuel Gridley Howe was a handsome, heroic humanitarian who held an undergraduate degree from Brown University and a medical degree from Harvard. Finding a conventional medical practice too mundane after he completed medical school, Howe volunteered for medical service with the Greek army during Greece's War of Independence from the Turks. Howe was one of many romantic adventurers steeped in a classical education who wished to join with the spirits of Odysseus, Socrates, Plato, and Homer to help fight Turkish oppression. Another fellow volunteer, the poet Percy Bysshe Shelley, announced: "We are all Greeks."

Enthusiasm among many of the volunteers diminished over time, but Dr. Howe's experience in Greece lasted six years, and those who knew him best said he came back a changed man. Howe returned to the United States as a motivated, committed philanthropist who was intent on applying his medical expertise to good works. Soon after returning home, Howe was approached to head the newly created school for the blind in Boston. A facility was found to house the school, students began arriving, and contributions poured in for funding. The Perkins Institution for the Blind quickly grew in size and reputation under Dr. Howe's leadership.

In the summer of 1841, Julia, her younger sisters Louisa and Annie, and other friends decided to visit the Perkins Institution. While being shown the facility, someone called out, "Oh, here comes Howe on his black horse." Remembering the incident in her later years, Julia reported, "I looked out also, and beheld a noble rider on a noble steed."[6]

Julia was infatuated by the man on horseback, Chevalier Samuel Gridley Howe (or simply "Chev" as he came to be called). He entered Julia's life and caused profound changes, some of which she would cherish and others she would despise as she struggled to achieve her own independent dreams.

There were some early clues just before their marriage that Julia was trading one dominating, controlling Samuel (her father) for another. Samuel Howe had written to his soon-to-be-bride: "I give you fair warning; I shall not help you out of the cocoon state at all; you are a sweet, pretty little mortal, & shall not be immortal if I can help it, this many a long year. . . . I advise you not to show even a . . . feather, for I shall unmercifully cut them off, to keep you prisoner in my arms."[7]

Biographer and historian Valarie Ziegler has summarized Julia's transition from Julia Ward to Julia Ward Howe:

> The duties of marriage and motherhood thus intruded on the study opportunities of a woman who still defined herself in terms of her intellectual accomplishments. Household cares also isolated her from the company of men—with whom she identified—and from the intimacy of other women who might have helped her understand that she was not alone in enduring

frustration and the loss of self. . . . In short, Julia would discover that life with Samuel Howe was much like life with Samuel Ward: in both instances she was isolated, dominated by men, and in search of intellectual achievements that could lift her above the lot that true womanhood had assigned her.[8]

Despite the prospect of a constrained future with Samuel Howe, the bride was launched into marriage with an enchanting honeymoon trip to England and the Continent. The newly married couple sipped tea with Florence Nightingale and author Thomas Carlyle, was given a guided tour of London by Charles Dickens, met Pope Gregory XVI, and generally were in the company of Europe's elite.

On March 12, 1844, after just over a year of traveling in Europe, Julia Ward Howe gave birth to the couple's first child in Rome. Named Julia Romana—her mother's and grandmother's name coupled with that of her birthplace—the new baby and the prospect of motherhood in a foreign city caused Howe to sink into a prolonged period of depression. (As a wife and mother, she chose to be called Julia Ward Howe rather than Mrs. Samuel Gridley Howe, a preference she kept for the remainder of her life.) The glow of the sensational honeymoon experience in Europe slowly faded with the birth of Julia Romana and the couple's return to the United States and their hometown of Boston.

Spartan in his tastes and desire for creature comforts, Dr. Howe was delighted to be offered quarters in the Doctor's Wing of the Perkins Institution for the Blind. On the one hand, he saw these rooms as a convenient and appropriate home for his new wife and child. (There were economic advantages also, as the Howes did not have to spend money on rent.) Julia Ward Howe, on the other hand, saw their quarters in the institution as cold, bleak, and further incentive for her husband—already deemed a chronic workaholic—to blur the line between work and family.

Writing to her sister several years after her marriage, Howe confessed: "I have come to him, have left my poetry, my music, my religion, have walked with him in his cold world of actualities. There I have learned much, but there, I can do nothing—he must come to me, must have ears for my music, must have a soul for my faith—if my nature is to sing, to pray, to feel—his is to fight, to teach, to reason. . . . We sleep apart and baby lies in my arms."[9]

During this time of marital strain, Howe continued to write. Some of her poems were published in *Female Poets of America* in 1848. Also during this time, she wrote an unpublished novel about a hermaphrodite named Laurence. Inspired by *Sleeping Hermaphroditos* sculpture she saw in the Villa Borghese in Rome, the unfinished novel chronicles the life and trials of a hermaphrodite raised as a boy who attracts both male and female admirers with tragic consequences. In 2004, nearly 160 years after it was written, a scholar organized Howe's material and published the manuscript.[10] The rationale for writing what became known as *The Hermaphrodite* can be assigned a litany of Freudian motives, but the fact remains that Howe did not bring her work to fruition as a published piece. She may have feared the reaction it would cause, she may have been unhappy with what she had written, or she simply may have been writing for her own creative outlet during a period of personal frustration and anger.

In August 1845 Howe gave birth to a second daughter, Florence "Flossy" Marion Howe, named after Florence Nightingale whom the parents had met in England during their honeymoon. Now with a second child added to the family and continuing pleas from his wife, Samuel Howe purchased a farmhouse and six acres a short distance from the institution as their new home. Samuel's generosity in agreeing to move to their own home was facilitated by funds he obtained from an antenuptial agreement negotiated with the Ward family.

The Howe family soon called their new home—infinitely cozier than the cold hallways of the institution—Green Peace because of the tonic effect of its bucolic surroundings. While Julia decorated the family's first personally owned home, Chev enjoyed gardening, growing flowers, fruits, and vegetables in their "Garden of Eden." The bliss of Green Peace was short lived, however. Julia Ward Howe grew more and more despondent over the remote location of their home, far from the amenities and cultural advantages of Boston and the people whose company she enjoyed. Samuel, who constantly badgered his in-laws about controlling Julia's money, was able to wrest some funds from the trust to invest in real estate. The doctor's speculative endeavors were generally unsuccessful. Chev's financial acumen fell far short of his medical skills; consequently, the family was consistently short of funds for the growing household. In 1848 a third child, a son named Henry "Harry" Marion, was born, putting an additional strain on the household budget.

While her daughter Julia Romana Howe, reflecting later in life, saw the tension between Julia and Samuel as an indication of the "full life of each [that] enriched and sustained the other," Julia Ward Howe viewed her world as buffeted by two diametrically opposed forces. Biographer Ziegler explains Howe's dilemma: "Accustomed to the ethereal world of art, music, and literature, she found the drudgery of household duties required of her as a wife and mother extremely trying."[11] Howe's ability to negotiate with her spouse was influenced not only by her husband's obdurateness but also by the hand she held in their card game of marriage: she had the card of marital intimacy with which to bargain (with its concomitant risk of pregnancy). But as yet she had limited tangible accomplishments in the area where she most wanted to achieve success—by having her work published and the resulting financial independence that they would bring. This untenable situation would soon bring the Howes to the brink of a marital rupture.

In February 1850 a fourth child was born to Julia and Samuel. Laura Elizabeth Howe was named in honor of Laura Bridgman, a deaf and blind patient of Dr. Howe's at the institution. Howe had taught the young Bridgman girl to read and communicate with extraordinary success. The young girl repaid her appreciation with unqualified devotion and obedience to her doctor-teacher. A woodcut from the time depicts young Bridgman—who had achieved international recognition for her abilities—sitting in Dr. Howe's lap, with the unfortunate visual suggesting her as a ventriloquist's dummy. Laura Bridgman was the physician's beau ideal of a woman—unquestioningly obedient and dependent.

Just four months after Laura Elizabeth was born, the Howes traveled to Rome on vacation with their two youngest children, Harry and the baby. They left seven-year-old Julia Romana and five-year-old Florence behind (a situation the two oldest children would resent years later as adults). By October Doctor Howe, refreshed and rejuvenated by his European sojourn, returned home to Boston, leaving Julia and the children in Rome. Julia reveled in her freedom from Samuel and wrote: "I found myself free and untrammeled. . . . I was absolutely intoxicated with the joy of freedom and used to dance . . . singing 'Liberty, Liberty!'"[12]

To the shock of her relatives, Julia Ward Howe decided to rent an apartment, not in the American expatriate quarter, but in the Via Capo le Case near the Trevi Fountain in Rome. She further confounded her friends and relatives by taking Hebrew lessons from a Roman rabbi. Julia found the rabbi an excellent language instructor and an informed source for theological discussions.

During her time in Rome, Howe was also introduced to a thirty-three-year-old Princeton graduate and lawyer Horace Binney Wallace. The pair shared an interest in literary subjects, in art, and in visiting Rome's tourist sites. She may have been infatuated by this literate, humorous, and charming aesthete, but Wallace's interest was dependably platonic. In January 1851 Wallace left Rome for Naples and Greece, returning to Rome briefly before visiting Paris, and then going home to Philadelphia. Howe's sisters and friends feared a hint of scandal in the Howe-Wallace relationship, and they urged Julia and Chev to reconcile and join each other in Boston. She took the advice of others and left Rome in August, returning home to Green Peace in September after a fifteen-month absence.

According to Howe biographer Elaine Showalter, Howe spent the time on the return trip to America "reading, brooding about Wallace, and writing poems."[13] Howe and Wallace may have met in New Jersey while she was calling on a relative in the spring of 1852, but this visit has not been verified. Wallace, overcome by whatever demons haunted him, committed suicide by cutting his throat in Paris that December. Howe deeply grieved the loss of her kindred spirit, Horace Binney Wallace.

The winter, like a college boy's vacation,

Seemed endless to anticipate, and lay

Stretched in a boundless glittering before me,

Unfathomable in its free delight.

Or if horizon-bounded like the sea,

I saw new seas beyond—the sweeping line

Limits the known, but not the possible.

—JULIA WARD HOWE, "Rome"

By 1863 a confluence of circumstances in Julia Ward Howe's life—her separation in Rome from her demanding husband, her romantic interlude with Horace Binney Wallace, and her unfettered creativity and literary productivity while away from her domestic responsibilities in the States—encouraged her to submit a group of poems to a publisher. She elected not to share her foray into the publishing world with Chev; instead, she sought advice from the couple's friend Henry Wadsworth Longfellow. She submitted her manuscript to James Fields at the publishing house of Ticknor and Fields. Only five months earlier, Fields had rejected a draft manuscript written by Chev as "too wordy and not welded together strong enough to hold the ... public attention."[14]

After reading the galley proofs and receiving advice on revisions from Longfellow, Julia Ward Howe was exhilarated when her book was published on December 23, 1853. This volume of poems, *Passion-Flowers*, was an achievement that demonstrated to her that she could succeed in pursuing her literary dreams and be recognized as a writer of considerable talent. Chev, however, was furious when he found out about *Passion-Flowers*. First, his wife had kept him in the dark about her efforts; added to that, his good friend Longfellow was an accomplice in this secret. Chev also found the content to be inappropriate, if not salacious; and, further wounding his ego, Julia had been accepted for publication by the same group that had rejected his work.

Passion-Flowers was well received by the public and favorably reviewed by the literary establishment. Theodore Parker, a Boston Unitarian minister, quoted excerpts in his Christmas sermon. John Greenleaf Whittier wrote: "It is a great book—it has placed [Julia Ward Howe] at the head of us all. . . . God bless thee for it." Nathaniel Hawthorne reported: "I, for one, am much obliged to the lady, and esteem her beyond all comparison the first of American poetesses." But Hawthorne pondered, "What does her husband think of it?"[15]

Dr. Samuel Gridley Howe detested the book. He was offended that his wife had achieved success without his knowledge or permission. He found the verses exposed the brittle state of their marriage and were a public embarrassment. His ego, damaged by his wife's achievement, the snide comments of friends and acquaintances, and the gossip following the book's release, caused Chev to lash out physically at Julia. He demanded that sections be rewritten in the second edition.

Petulant and controlling, Chev insisted on resuming their sexual relationship (after a hiatus of eighteen months) and took steps to returning to the institution as their living quarters, leaving Green Peace to be used to house pupils. Julia was devastated to relinquish their home at Green Peace. By mid-February 1854 she was pregnant with their fifth child.

Howe's second book of poems, *Words for the Home*, was published in February 1857 by Ticknor and Fields. Among the poems were references to her friendship with the late Horace Binney Wallace, verses referring to the beating of her friend senator Charles Sumner by Rep. Preston Brooks of South Carolina in the Senate chamber, and another poem that suggested that Elizabeth Barrett Browning's poetic achievements depended on her use of opium. This book of poems received lukewarm reviews by critics and earned the lifelong wrath of the Brownings. *Words for the Home* was not the follow-on success to *Passion-Flowers* that Howe was expecting.

She continued to pursue her literary interests with a different form of expression. Her play *Leonora, or the World's Own* was performed in New York at the Lyceum Theatre to mixed reviews. Another of her plays, *Hippolytus*, was written by Howe for actor Edwin Booth, brother of John Wilkes. Production of the play faltered for a variety of reasons—not the least of which was the taint of the Booth name—and was not brought to the stage until March 1911, six months after Julia Ward Howe's death.

With her literary career faltering, Julia and Chev did find a common bond in their growing involvement in abolitionism. Their interest found an outlet in serving as joint editors of the newspaper *The Commonwealth*, an antislavery publication that promoted the Free Soil Party and the immediate end of slavery. Husband and wife became increasingly more radical in their position on slavery, and both began to cultivate friends who held similar positions. For Chev this included a relationship with what came to be known as the "Secret Six."

Samuel Gridley Howe, Unitarian minister Theodore Parker, ardent abolitionist Franklin Sanborn, minister and literary critic Thomas Wentworth Higginson, wealthy businessman Luther Stearns, and philanthropist Gerrit Smit joined to take action—not just talk—and write about abolition. Finding their perfect embodiment of aggressive abolitionism in John Brown, the group funded his plan to raid the U.S. armory and arsenal at Harpers Ferry and incite a slave rebellion. John Brown visited the Howes' home in Boston, where Julia Ward Howe met him at the front door: "At the expected time, I heard the bell ring, and, on answering it, beheld a middle-aged, middle-sized man, with hair and beard of amber color, streaked with gray. He looked a Puritan of the Puritans, forceful, concentrated, and self-contained."[16]

The Secret Six gave Brown both moral and financial support. The men approved of his motivations and the violent practices he employed, and they provided the funds required to launch the Harpers Ferry raid. However, the Secret Six had no interest in participating directly in the raid. The group left that to Brown and his recruits. Frederick Douglass also abjured taking part in the raid, considering it "doomed to failure."

After Col. Robert E. Lee of the U.S. Army captured Brown in October 1859, letters from the Secret Six to Brown were discovered in his rented farmhouse near Harpers Ferry and were quickly published in the *New York Times*. Horrified by this revelation, four of the six disavowed their involvement in the raid. Only Parker and Higginson stood by their support of and involvement with Brown. (John Brown never identified his supporters.) Chev fled to Canada and, from his safe position in Montreal, wrote a letter to the *New York Tribune* denying his knowledge of or support for John Brown's raid. Chev returned to Boston in December once the furor over Brown's raid had died down and was present for the birth of his sixth child, Samuel, on Christmas Day. By early January, Chev returned to Canada ostensibly to conduct studies on "methods for the education of the blind." Or perhaps to let the John Brown incident cool down further.

Chev was not alone in sullying the Howe family name during this period. In the winter of 1859, Julia Ward Howe traveled to Cuba and wrote travel letters to be published in the *Atlantic Monthly* and later published as a book. While composing an often witty and highly descriptive travelogue of her adventures, Howe also wrote accounts of slavery and race that were demeaning and deeply offensive. She wrote that the slave "must go to school to the white race, and his discipline must be long and laborious. . . . [T]he ideal Negro is the Negro refined by white culture, elevated by white blood, instructed even by white inequity."[17] Abolitionist William Lloyd Garrison was appalled by Howe's Cuba book. It represented the nadir of her literary achievements that she worked so hard to perfect. Upon reading her Cuba letters, Chev announced to friend Theodore Parker that the content "made me sad."

The attack on Fort Sumter and the resulting announcement of war deeply troubled the Howes. Samuel soon found an appropriate (and safe) way to further the cause by serving as a member of the U.S. Sanitary Commission. Julia, however, found her ability to contribute constrained by her family duties, especially the care of her infant son. Further, she claimed that she had no affinity for helping prepare bandages or packing medical supplies, yet she felt strongly about the need to preserve and defend the Union and was frustrated by her inability to play an appropriate role.

When Chev announced that as part of his U.S. Sanitary Commission duties he wanted to visit Washington City and the Massachusetts troop encampments in and near the capital city, Julia asked to accompany her husband so that she could experience firsthand the realities of the war. The Howes left Boston accompanied by their pastor James Freeman Clarke, Massachusetts governor John Andrew and his wife, and Edwin P. Whipple and his wife, Charlotte. As they approached Washington City, Julia noted troops gathered near fires who were standing picket duty, guarding the railroad lines. Perhaps this sight was the inspiration for her verse written later: "I have seen Him in the watch-fires of a hundred circling camps."

During her visit, Julia Ward Howe was asked to speak to the First Massachusetts Heavy Artillery by the unit's colonel, William P. Greene. Reluctantly, she finally consented, and, in her words, "I stood and told as well as I could how glad I was to meet the brave defenders of our cause and how constantly they were in my thoughts."[18] Chev was present neither for his wife's brief, impromptu address to the soldiers (he would not have approved of a woman taking that role) nor when she and the other members of the Boston contingent met with President Lincoln in a White House drawing room. The conversation was primarily between Lincoln and Governor Andrew. Howe recorded her lasting memory of the meeting years later in her book *Reminiscences, 1819–1899*: "I remember well the sad expression of Mr. Lincoln's deep blue eyes, the only feature of his face which could be called other than plain." For his part, Abraham Lincoln had no idea that the petite, forty-two-year-old Bostonian who sat with him that day would write the stirring anthem that would bring tears to his eyes years later when he heard it sung before cheering crowds.

While in Washington City, Julia and Chev's schedules ran on separate paths, and they occupied separate rooms in Willard's City Hotel. After she visited the troops at Munson's Hill in Northern Virginia and returned to Willard's later that day, Chev was not present when she awoke and wrote the verses that became "The Battle Hymn of the Republic." Nor, contrary to her later account, was her baby son with her when she wrote in the dark to not "wake the baby." The baby, Sammy, was home in Boston.

Howe wrote her first draft of the poem quickly and went back to bed. In the morning she made some changes to her draft and shared it with her friend and traveling companion, Charlotte Whipple. Julia Ward Howe felt this work was sound, an opinion Charlotte shared. After Howe returned to Boston from Washington City, she made some minor revisions and sent a copy to her friend and editor of the *Atlantic Monthly*, James Fields. Her forwarding note to Fields said, "Do you want this, and do you like it, and have you any room for it in the January number [issue]?"

Fields did want the poem, and in February 1862 it appeared prominently in the *Atlantic Monthly*. Howe family tradition is that Fields came up with the title "The Battle Hymn of the Republic." The poem became a hymn, sung to the tune of "John Brown's Body," and slowly spread "into the newspapers, thence to army hymn-books and broadsides."[19] By December 1863 Julia Ward Howe delivered a reading of the hymn at the dedication of John Brown's statue in Boston. In February the following year, the "Battle Hymn" was performed for President Lincoln. The hymn caught the public's attention in the North because it combined the spiritual qualities and nobility of a nineteenth-century hymn while having the syncopated tempo of a military march. It could be sung in church pews and while marching in ranks to battle. It had the power to uplift spirits and be a call to action.

Why did Julia Ward Howe succeed in writing this iconic anthem while efforts by others came up short? Biographer Elaine Showalter describes the way Howe's talents came together to produce a piece of historical significance: "Her lifelong knowledge of biblical imagery, her decades of training as a poet, and her own longing to be part of the war effort, fueled and fused her creative imagination. She drew upon images from her reading, from sermons, from her dreams, from her unconscious, from her anger at her husband, and from her view of the Civil War as a holy war."[20]

Motivation in a time of war requires a combination of circumstances. The Civil War was no exception. Victories on the battlefield, an inspired sense of purpose, and visionary, effective leadership must combine to inspire both the soldiers who fight and the citizens who support them. The early stage of the war—1861 to early 1863, with few exceptions—was a time when Union victories were rare, and Union morale was at its nadir. For the Union, a sense of purpose was rekindled by the Emancipation Proclamation and Julia Ward Howe's moving anthem. Northern victories in 1863, later coupled with Lincoln's bold moves to change the leadership of the Union Army in the spring of 1864, would coalesce to turn the corner for a Union victory. This destiny was anticipated in the haunting words of Howe's anthem:

> He has sounded forth the trumpet that shall never call retreat;
> He is sifting out the hearts of men before his judgment seat:
> Oh! Be swift, my soul, to answer Him! Be jubilant my feet!

7

Tending to the Wounded and Missing

Following her service at Antietam in September 1862, Clara Barton was close to a physical collapse. She had lost fifteen to twenty pounds on her already slim physique and was suffering from a self-diagnosed bout of typhoid fever. Placed on a coverlet at the bottom of a Union Army wagon, she was taken back to her room in Washington City to recover from her mental and physical exhaustion. She shocked herself when she looked in a mirror after returning to Washington and saw that her face was "the color of gun powder, a deep blue."[1]

Even in her depleted condition, Barton wrote to her friend Mary Norton: "When I think what I have been through I wonder that I have as much strength as I have, but I shall never fail while this war lasts—my strength will be as my day, and I will be able to serve faithfully to the end. . . . I should be ungrateful to complain if my strength failed a little sometimes, but it is only for a little; in two weeks I shall be strong and well as ever."[2]

And she was. On October 9, 1862, she was distributing medical supplies in Alexandria, Virginia, aided by her quartermaster colleague Col. Daniel Rucker, who assisted her with transportation and documents granting passage to the army at Camp Misery. The convalescent unit was described as a place where "10,000 luckless souls were confined in their reeking purgatory. They lived in dirty, floorless tents, mostly without blankets, and were poorly clad and racked by malnutrition and disease."[3]

The camp, located near Alexandria, offered the worst medical care in the Union Army. In addition to the squalor and lack of adequate clothing and blankets, the camp was a breeding ground for infections, dysentery, and other illnesses that were rampant.

Camp Misery lived up to its name. Undeterred by the magnitude of the camp's problems, Barton worked long days to see that medical supplies provided by the U.S. Sanitary Commission and U.S. Christian Commission were properly distributed. Progress at the camp was slow and incremental in the face of all this human suffering, but always the optimist, Barton lauded the support of the federal government: "I don't know how I should succeed in my work without the full cooperation and kind care of the Government— they not only never deny me a request but try to anticipate my wants and necessities."[4]

Sleep my weary men. Rest for tomorrow's battle. Enjoy your dreams tonight, of your sister, or wife, or mother. They may yet live to dream of you cold, lifeless and bloody, but this dream, soldier, is the last, paint it bright, dream it well. . . . Already the roll of the moving artillery is sounding in my ears, the battle draws near, and I must catch one hour's sleep for tomorrow's labor.

—CLARA BARTON, letter to Elvira Stone, December 12, 1862

By mid-October Colonel Rucker contacted Barton and implored her to go back to the Army of the Potomac: "They will fight again. Can you go—and what transportation do you want?"[5] Rucker exceeded Barton's request by supplying four army wagons and an ambulance. Additionally, he provided four experienced teamsters for the wagons and a driver for the ambulance. To assist her, Barton recruited her nephew Sam Barton and her loyal assistant, Cornelius Welles. Together they loaded the wagons with more supplies than Barton had ever been responsible for up to that date. She had clearly earned the confidence of the quartermaster unit in Washington City.

On their way to the Antietam area—the army under George McClellan had not yet left its encampment near Sharpsburg, Maryland, a month after the battle (McClellan was proving accurate Lincoln's complaint that the general "had the slows")—Barton was challenged by her teamsters. Unlike Welles, Sam, and the ambulance driver, the rough-hewn teamsters resented that they were being managed by a woman. As she had done in the past and would do many times again in the future, Barton won over the teamsters by showing them respect, by demonstrating she was a tireless worker, and by ensuring they were properly fed, nursed if sick, and treated as skilled coworkers. The teamsters soon were convinced. They apologized to Barton for their insubordination and, going forward, became committed, loyal workers. Even though she was a woman, they claimed, they would "get accustomed to that."[6]

On October 26 Barton's wagon train caught up with the Army of the Potomac, which was now, finally, underway and pursuing Lee's army across the Potomac River into Virginia. She arranged to join Gen. Ambrose Burnside's IX Corps, the advance unit, as it moved down the Blue Ridge Mountain range. Barton later wrote of her experiences during this travel with the Army of the Potomac as a sublime period in her life. She was delighted to be among the soldiers, hearing the sounds of men marching, eating hardtack (sometimes accompanied by her marmalade), and singing "John Brown's Body" around the campfires at night. (The song would soon be replaced by Julia Ward Howe's "Battle Hymn of the Republic," which used the same melody.)

Barton considered herself one of the troops. "I am a U.S. soldier." She often said of the Army of the Potomac, "[It] is my own army."[7] The feeling between Barton and the soldiers was mutual. She had the respect of the men of IX Corps with whom she traveled, and the Twenty-First Massachusetts Regiment considered her a "daughter" of the regiment. In the regimental history written following the war, Barton was complimented as "a 21st [Regiment] woman to the backbone."[8] Soldiers up and down the ranks appreciated Barton's dignity, her work ethic, and her fierce commitment to the fighting men. It was this combination of traits that won Barton her well-deserved reputation in the Army of the Potomac.

And Clara Barton found her work with the Army of the Potomac immensely satisfying. She took responsibility willingly and was recognized as a team member who could be counted on to perform her assignments with skill, devotion, and bravery. Time and time again she was able to transcend the mid-nineteenth-century perception of what women were capable of doing in a "man's world." By the close of 1862 Barton, perhaps for the first time in her life, had a clear sense of purpose and the confidence that comes with success and with recognition from the people who mattered most to her—her family and the U.S. Army.

Barton's accomplishments did not come without a price. The wagon train ride through Virginia during the late autumn of 1862 and exposure to numbing cold weather caused inflammation in her hands. Despite a dose of narcotics and minor surgery, the problem continued. This infection, along with an allergic reaction to smoke from a dogwood-fueled fire that caused her face to swell, sent Barton back to Washington City to recover. During Barton's health challenges, McClellan had been relieved as commanding general of the Army of the Potomac and was replaced by Burnside. McClellan, a general who exercised such caution he was considered virtually inert by his military and civilian leaders, was replaced by a general who had an astonishing lack of confidence in his own ability to lead.

Barton's recovery time was brief. By early December, her conscientious assistant, Welles, sent her a message urging her to return to the Army of the Potomac and reminded her: "Your place is here."[9] She needed little prodding. On December 7, along with supplies, she was en route by government boat to Aquia Creek, an important Union logistics base in Virginia. Barton discovered that an old friend from the Twenty-First Massachusetts was stationed there as a quartermaster officer. Always conscious of how her network of friends could be recruited to support the cause, she suggested to the quartermaster how he could help. The next morning Barton, along with the large quantity of supplies she had obtained, was on an army train headed to Falmouth Station near Fredericksburg, Virginia.

The Army of the Potomac, in anticipation of attacking Fredericksburg on the Rappahannock River, was bivouacked at Falmouth. More than 100,000 men were encamped and waiting for the arrival of pontoons that could be assembled into a bridge to cross the river. They were going to attack Fredericksburg—midway between Richmond and Washington City—as a preliminary step in the Union Army's drive toward the Confederate capital. "On to Richmond!" was the Union rallying cry.

Barton was taken from Falmouth Station to the Lacy House (also known as Chatham Manor) overlooking the Rappahannock and Fredericksburg on the opposite side of the river. She was given a room in the mansion that she shared with a "Miss G." Officers from the Twenty-First Massachusetts found out that "Miss Barton" had arrived and began calling on "the angel of the battlefield." As comfortable as the Lacy House was for her lodging, Barton expressed that she would have preferred "a good tent, floor and stove"—the type of quarters given to soldiers. (And certainly *not* a residence that was the property of generations of slave owners.) Despite the accommodations, Barton was pleased that she was situated near where a major battle would be fought. Once again it seemed that Barton's satisfaction was directly proportional to her proximity to a battlefield.

The long-awaited pontoons began to arrive, and on the evening of December 12, Barton wrote her sentiments about the expected battle that would follow the next day as she looked at the landscape surrounding the Lacy House:

> The campfires blaze with unwanted brightness, the sentry's tread is still but quick—the acres of little shelter tents are dark and still as death, no wonder for as I gazed sorrowfully upon them, I thought I could almost hear the slow flap of the grim messenger's wings as, one by one, he sought and selected his victims for the morning sacrifice—sleep weary ones, sleep and rest for tomorrow's toil. . . . Already the roll of the moving artillery is sounding in my ears, the battle draws near, and I must catch one hour's sleep for tomorrow's labor.[10]

Clara Barton's observations in this letter to Elvira Stone the night before the Battle of Fredericksburg were prescient regarding what followed the next day. The long-awaited pontoons were configured as a bridge spanning the Rappahannock by Union engineers, who came under intense fire from Confederate snipers located in houses and warehouses in Fredericksburg.

On December 13, just before first light, Burnside ordered the attack to begin. A dense fog shrouded the army's initial movements as the men crossed the pontoon bridge, but as the fog lifted, the clearly visible Union troops were raked by heavy, unrelenting Confederate artillery fire. Confederate artillery commander Edward Porter Alexander reported to his superior, Lt. Gen. James Longstreet: "General, we cover that ground now so well that we will comb it as with a fine-tooth comb. A chicken could not live on that field when we open on it."[11]

While Union infantry flowed across the completed pontoon bridge and federal artillery began bombarding the Confederate position from Stafford Heights, Barton insisted that she be allowed to cross the river to support the medical teams deployed in Fredericksburg. She joined Dr. J. Calvin Cutter, surgeon for the Twenty-First Massachusetts. Barton and Welles were constantly engaged, setting up a soup kitchen, assisting doctors with the wounded, and offering words of comfort and encouragement to the men waiting to be treated for their wounds.

During the afternoon, the fighting progressed to Marye's Heights, a slope adjacent to the city. Unit after unit of Union troops stormed the ground toward a narrow sunken road bordered by a stone wall; behind it lines of Confederate soldiers fired down on their approaching enemy without surcease. The result was a devastating loss of life among the Union ranks. By the end of the day, 900 Union soldiers had been killed and 7,000 wounded as they struggled to take the heights.[12] By dusk Union leadership realized the futility of the assault on Marye's Heights, pulled back the troops, and reformed their units in Fredericksburg. After dark the survivors, accompanied by ambulances filled with the wounded, crossed the pontoon bridge back to the other side of the Rappahannock. A pitiless, cold rain shrouded their retreat.

Barton returned to the Lacy House in the evening. She encountered the wounded of II Corps who were being treated at the house, which was now serving as the corps's hospital. About 280 wounded soldiers had been taken to the Lacy House from the battlefield. Here Barton saw dozens of men and their amputated limbs. Described by Walt Whitman, who was also present at Fredericksburg, there was "at the foot of a tree, immediately in front, a heap of feet, legs, arms, and human fragments cut, bloody, black and blue, swelled and sickening—in the garden near, a row of graves."[13]

Barton was everywhere: outside the house serving soup and inside feeding the wounded, providing pillows for amputees, and making her rounds while trying to avoid slipping on the floors that were slick with blood. She later reported that she had to wring the blood from the bottom of her dress because it was weighing her down. This work was not for the faint of heart.

Clara Barton was consistently in the midst of battlefield action during the Battle of Fredericksburg. An artillery round was reported to have struck the pontoon bridge when Barton was crossing the Rappahannock. A fragment of the round tore away a part of her skirt. Another documented close call for Barton came when Confederate artillerymen were considering targets on the Union side of the Rappahannock. Artillerymen asked J. Horace Lacy, the owner of the Lacy House and an embittered Confederate former resident, for permission to fire on the two women standing on the house's veranda. These "unbidden guests," as Lacy called them, were Clara Barton and Miss G (the only two women who were at the Lacy House.) Lacy's desire to have the house fired upon to "reduce Chatham to the dust" was denied by Robert E. Lee, who saw no need for the "unnecessary effusion of blood."[14] Clara Barton had General Lee to thank for sparing her life in December 1862.

After the battle, Barton continued to help the wounded soldiers by aiding with evacuations and trying to make the wounded as comfortable as conditions allowed as they began their transportation to hospitals in Washington City. One day during this time she was surprised when her tent flap opened, and Senator Wilson, her friend and advocate, appeared to check on her welfare. Wilson was there following the battle in his capacity as chairman of the U.S. Senate Committee on Military Affairs. His initial reaction to the events surrounding Fredericksburg was that the Union Army needed more men, including the thousands of former slaves whom he believed should now bear arms for the Union following their emancipation.

While at Lacy House, Barton had begun keeping a campaign diary that noted where men were taken for treatment and which men died, along with when and where they were buried. She started with the Massachusetts regiments, but she soon would expand the scope of this record keeping, chronicling the wounded, missing, and dead over time. It was yet another example of her ongoing commitment to the soldiers who gave so much to their country. Someday the war would be over, but for Clara Barton the anguish and grief of those families whose loved ones were among the unidentified dead or missing would inspire her to continue her work in honoring those who had given "the last full measure of devotion." Barton summed up her commitment in a letter to friend Mary Norton: "I am so happy in doing any little things I am able to, and glory so in any trifling sacrifice I am called upon to make that I frequently think I ought to be the happiest person in the world— and indeed Mary I think I become happier every year of my life, notwithstanding this terrible war which would crush me to my grave if I could not labor in it."[15]

Clara Barton's efforts did not go unnoticed by civilian and military leadership. To aid Barton's passage to encampments and battlefields to conduct her work in early 1863, Maj. Edward Preston, a provost marshal in the Federal Army, wrote a letter of introduction that glows with praise:

> The bearer Miss Clara Barton visits the 10th Army Corps for the purpose of attending personally to the wants of wounded soldiers. She has rendered great service for all the great battles that have been fought in Virginia for the last six months. She acts under the direction of the Surgeon General, and with the authority of the Secretary of War. The smoke of battle, the roar of artillery and the shrieks of shot and shell do not deter her from administering to those who fell. . . . Here she is highly respected and all bestow upon her much praise.[16]

By January 1863 the advances in medical treatment within the Union Army had made significant progress. Dr. Jonathan Letterman, working in the U.S. Army Medical Department, and with support from the U.S. Sanitary Commission, had shaken up the army's old, moribund medical bureaucracy and made major strides in caring for the huge number of casualties. According to historian Stephen B. Oates: "The [Medical] Department now had 2,000 commissioned surgeons in command of almost 10,000 personnel, plus access to thousands of horse-drawn wagons and ambulances."[17]

The U.S. Sanitary Commission, staffed with skilled civilian medical personnel—including the illustrious Dr. Samuel Gridley Howe, spouse of Julia Ward Howe—made important advances in improving conditions in Union encampments. Deaths from disease versus enemy fire were high—two Union soldiers died from disease for each one killed in combat—but this death rate was better than what was experienced in contemporary wars. For British soldiers in the Crimean War, the rate of disease to combat deaths was four to one; for Americans in the Mexican War, the rate was seven to one.[18] Diseases such as dysentery, typhoid, and pneumonia—due, in large part, to unsanitary camp conditions—were the principal causes of death.

Dr. Letterman and the U.S. Sanitary Commission were able to make many improvements in the men's care and the camps' conditions despite the conclusion of some historians that "medical services represent one of the Civil War's most dismal failures."[19] The sheer volume of casualties, the thousands of men living in crowded, unsanitary conditions, and the elementary state of the medical arts in the 1860s presented staggering obstacles for the U.S. Army Medical Department and its civilian partners.

Some important advances were blocked by the army's bureaucracy and petty infighting. For example, Surgeon General Hammond had recommended that the medical department create its own ambulance corps with men specially recruited and trained to staff the ambulances. Hammond, with the support of the U.S. Sanitary Commission and backed by Sen. Henry Wilson, recommended that twelve thousand volunteers and five hundred commissioned officers be recruited for this purpose. (Clara Barton wrote to Senator Wilson in support of a bill to establish this service.)

Despite the strong arguments for an independent ambulance corps from practitioners in the field who could vouch for the need for such a unit, the desk-bound bureaucrats prevailed. Secretary of War Edwin Stanton and General in Chief Henry Halleck criticized the independent ambulance corps as "impractical." The bill died.

Even with these bureaucratic obstacles along the way, Dr. Letterman was ultimately successful in creating an ambulance corps for the Army of the Potomac, and it eventually spread to other Union units and became law in 1864. Historian James McPherson credits Letterman's ambulance corps with becoming a model for future military medical units: "Wearing special uniforms and imbued with high morale, these noncombatant medics risked their lives to reach the wounded in the midst of battle and evacuate them as quickly as possible to surgeons' stations and field hospitals. The ambulance corps became a model for European armies down to World War I; both the Germans and French adopted the system in the Franco-Prussian War."[20]

8

The Prolonged War

As the war dragged on from the devastating Union losses at Fredericksburg, a growing movement to enlist black soldiers began to gain momentum. Once the hope of black leaders, abolitionists, and Northern Radical Republicans, an increasing group of Union proponents saw the value in expanding the pool of able-bodied men to serve in the armed forces for the Union cause. Once considered a war that would be brief and require limited manpower, by early 1863 the reality of a prolonged war was apparent to the citizens, the military, and the political leadership. Initially, on the one hand, many Union leaders saw the enlistment of free and formerly enslaved black men as a way to shift noncombat roles from white soldiers to black troops. In the thinking of the time, white soldiers could turn their shovels over to black men, exchanging the tools of manual labor for the tools of war. That would permit whites to engage in "real" fighting, leaving the routine, noncombat duties to black troops.

Frederick Douglass, on the other hand, saw the role of black soldiers as an integral part of the combat effort and a path to citizenship for the black man. "Once the black man get upon his person the brass letter, U.S., let him get an eagle on his button, and a musket on his shoulder and bullets in his pocket, and there is no power on earth which can deny that he has earned his right to citizenship."[1] For Douglass the black soldier clearly had all the qualities necessary to serve on the front line and should not be relegated to the menial tasks of the army. The path to citizenship involved a role in combat.

Slowly and inexorably in the Federal Army, regiments of free black soldiers began to spring up organically, despite the senior leadership's foot-dragging. Louisiana and South Carolina (in Union-controlled areas), Kansas, and Massachusetts began actively sending black units into the field. The Union Navy, meanwhile, had enlisted men of color to build a cadre of skilled seamen to man the fleet. Black sailors held roles integral to the successful operation of ships in positions such as deckhands, firemen in the engine rooms, and coal handlers. Black sailors also held more menial roles such as cooks and stewards in the officers' wardrooms. (In battle, however, those men serving in these roles were called on to perform combat duties.) Regardless of the roles they played in the Union Navy, the fact was that life aboard U.S. Navy vessels was a truly integrated workforce where one's skill and experience as a mariner trumped skin color.

As a result of the growing numbers of free and formerly enslaved blacks in the U.S. military, an important change occurred in the raison d'état of the war among the Union leadership. According to historian James McPherson, "The organization of black regiments marked the transformation of a war to preserve the Union into a revolution to overthrow the old order. Lincoln's conversion from reluctance to enthusiasm about black soldiers signified the progress of this revolution. By March 1863, the president was writing to Andrew Johnson, military governor of Tennessee. "The bare sight of fifty thousand armed, and drilled black soldiers on the banks of the Mississippi, would end the rebellion at once."[2]

Confederate reaction to the increasing number of blacks in the Union Army was immediate, predictable, and harsh. Captured black soldiers were executed on the spot or shot "while trying to escape." White officers who led black troops and were captured were subject to trial as "criminals engaged in inciting servitude insurrection," and the punishment was death.[3] In no cases were black soldiers or their white officers to be treated as conventional prisoners of war. This extreme position taken by the Confederate military was the chief reason for the breakdown in prisoner of war exchanges between both sides that had been observed earlier in the war.

In a situation filled with irony, South Carolina—the state that led the secessionist, proslavery position under the guidance of the late senator John C. Calhoun—became the epicenter of the recruitment and deployment of black Union forces as the war progressed. The War Department ordered Brig. Gen. Rufus Saxton, the military governor of the Sea Islands in South Carolina, to raise five regiments of black soldiers. Recruits were to be drawn from free blacks who populated the islands and contrabands freed from enslavement in the area. For the first black regiment officially authorized in the war, Saxton established the First South Carolina Volunteer Infantry under the leadership of Thomas Wentworth Higginson from Massachusetts.

Colonel Higginson was a graduate of Harvard, a Unitarian minister, and an abolitionist with strong bona fides. Starting in the 1850s, he had organized free blacks in Boston to protect fugitive slave Anthony Burns, storming the city courthouse in an attempt to free him from captivity. Next Higginson aided John Brown's activities in Kansas and later became a member of the Secret Six, which supported Brown's raid on Harpers Ferry. Following Brown's execution after the raid, Higginson raised funds for Brown's widow. He studied military theory and tactics, recruited troops for the Union Army, and in the summer of 1862 joined the army. Minimizing his own personal safety by serving as a leader of black troops in the Deep South and adamantly rejecting claims that the black soldier lacked bravery, Higginson eagerly took to his role as the regimental commander of the First South Carolina Volunteers, considering that it "fulfilled the dream of a lifetime."[4]

The Second South Carolina Volunteer Infantry was organized shortly following its fellow regiment. Col. James Montgomery was appointed to the position of regimental commander. Unlike Higginson, Montgomery was not a New Englander but came from Ohio. Like Higginson, however, Montgomery was a minister and had served with the militia and John Brown in Kansas. Higginson and Montgomery shared a strong abolitionist fervor and a commitment to the cause of black liberation, but they differed on one key tenant: Higginson was a stickler for military protocol and behavior, including an aversion to troops under his command plundering civilian goods and wantonly destroying property, while Montgomery had no compunction about sacking the territory through which he and his men were passing. One of his most notable raids in South Carolina was famous for the extent of his plundering and the person who accompanied him and supported the raid.

After Harriet Tubman's impressive work operating a successful Underground Railroad from Maryland to upstate New York—and eventually to Canada when the Fugitive Slave Act made U.S.-based sanctuaries ineffective—at the start of the Civil War she saw a role for her skills and experience in support of the Union cause. Soon after the war started, Tubman accompanied Maj. Gen. Benjamin Butler's Massachusetts regiment to Fort Monroe in Hampton, Virginia, where she helped black refugees obtain food, clothing, and shelter.

During one of Tubman's trips to Massachusetts, where she spoke about the critical needs of black refugees and sought funds to help them, Governor John Andrew saw the value that she could bring to the Massachusetts forces serving in South Carolina. Andrew asked her to travel to Beaufort, South Carolina, and take an active role as a nurse and scout for the army. The governor recognized that beyond her abilities as a nurse, Tubman had experience that could be readily applied in South Carolina: "She would be a valuable person to operate within the enemies lines in procuring information and scouts."[5] Once in South Carolina and under the direction of Maj. Gen. David Hunter, the commander of the Department of the South, Tubman immediately began working with the hundreds of displaced black persons and applying her nursing skills to help hospitalized soldiers.

At this stage in the war in South Carolina, soldiers in hospitals were suffering primarily from the diseases that were rampant in that climate and topography, not battle wounds. The swamps, marshes, creeks, and ditches that surrounded the area were fertile breeding grounds for diseases spread by mosquitoes. Tubman applied her skills as an experienced herbalist and nurse. But in line with Governor Andrew's thinking, Tubman possessed another skill that would be valuable to the Union Army in South Carolina.

Tubman's connection with Colonel Higginson began in Boston, where she had worked with him on abolition activities, including speaking in his church on the moral imperative of freeing enslaved people. Now, in his military position, Higginson tapped Tubman for duties beyond the hospital. He knew she could move among the local population in rural South Carolina to ferret out military intelligence, so Tubman began scouting the region outside the military-held area of Port Royal. During these incursions, Tubman was able to conduct "much and very valuable service acting as a spy within the enemy lines."[6] While the precise details of her scouting activities during her early time in South Carolina are not well documented, it is certain that Tubman was eager to prove herself as one who could perform military service (scouting, spying, and recruiting contraband men for the Union Army), as well as nursing duties in the field hospitals.[7]

Tubman's reputation as the "Moses of Her People" and as "General Tubman" was well known among the leadership of the black troops in South Carolina. General Hunter and Colonel Higginson, along with Colonel Montgomery, who commanded black troops in South Carolina, were longtime abolitionists and familiar with Tubman's work dating to her experiences with the Underground Railroad and her connection with John Brown. They knew her talent for working in dangerous and clandestine activities and her absolute commitment to the abolitionist cause. They also knew that she had the will, the wherewithal, and the perseverance they could count on. As the mobilization of black troops in the Union Army in South Carolina began to roll out, Tubman was tapped for an assignment with Colonel Montgomery that would draw on all her skills as an evolving military figure.

Montgomery was eager to test his newly recruited and trained Second South Carolina Volunteers by leading them on a raid into the Confederate-occupied territory near Port Royal. The objective was to traverse up the Combahee River and disrupt rebel supply lines and seize stores. Thanks to advance work by Tubman and her scouts, Montgomery knew that the area held stores vital to the Confederate Army and their exact location.

Tubman and the colonel planned the route of the raid, and she helped enlist the aid of local black watermen who knew the river and its connecting waterways and who could help identify the Confederate "torpedoes" (mines) that were placed along their intended route up the river. Under the cover of darkness, the raid was launched from Port Royal with three vessels—the *John Adams*, the *Harriet A. Weed*, and the *Sentinel*—transporting approximately three hundred infantry and a small group of artillerymen to man the boats' guns. Tubman and Montgomery were both aboard the *John Adams* in the lead.

By dawn on June 2, the small flotilla was at its objective, twenty-five miles upriver from the coast and in the heart of the location of the Confederate supplies they wanted to seize or destroy. The troops confiscated rice, corn, some cotton, and horses along with other farm animals. What they could not transport, they destroyed to deny their use by the Confederates. Barns, homes, and mills were torched, and a pontoon bridge at Combahee Ferry was demolished. Troops smashed irrigation system sluice gates to flood the fields, making them unusable for growing crops.

Montgomery also wanted Tubman along on the raid to assist with another objective—to encourage enslaved people to leave the area's farms and plantations, and seek their freedom by being relocated to the federally controlled area. Montgomery's rationale that Tubman could "speak a word of consolation" to her "people" was icily received by Tubman: "They wasn't my people any more than they was his [Montgomery]—only we was all Negroes."[8] She was able to calm a potentially hazardous situation as fleeing slaves almost swamped the boats sent to carry them away to freedom. Tubman sang and began clapping her hands to the beat. The people waiting to be transported were calmed and joined her, singing, clapping their hands, and shouting "Glory" as her melody broke the tension and panic. According to accounts that followed, 730 contrabands were taken away by the vessels.

An eyewitness reporter from the *Wisconsin State Journal* wrote that "the black woman who led the raid, and under whose supervision it was originated and conducted," addressed the group, and the words she spoke "would do honor to any man, and it created quite a sensation." The article concluded by reporting: "Col. Montgomery and his gallant band of 300 black soldiers, under the guidance of a black woman, dashed into the enemies' country, struck a bold and effective blow, destroying millions of dollars' worth of commissary stores, cotton, and lordly dwellings and struck terror to the heart of a rebellion, brought off near 800 slaves and thousands of dollars' worth of property without losing a man or receiving a scratch! It was a glorious consummation."[9]

The surgical strike up the Combahee River by Montgomery's "fleet" in South Carolina infuriated the Confederate leadership, which characterized it as a wanton act of destruction and pillaging. The men's reaction may have been further inflamed had they known the raid was the work of three hundred contraband men and a formerly enslaved black woman.

Tubman's Combahee River exploits received significant coverage in the North, where *The Commonwealth* newspaper of Boston identified her by name as a principle player in the event. Minimizing her own role and focusing on "we colored people," Harriet Tubman was especially pleased that the raid demonstrated that they could conduct themselves with bravery and honor in the face of the enemy.[10]

She was also proud that the raid had liberated 730 enslaved people and that not one Union soldier lost his life in the engagement. Colonel Montgomery joined Tubman in appreciating that virtually all the able-bodied males in the group of the newly freed persons enlisted in the Union Army (100 to 180 by some counts).[11]

The raid was not without its critics in the Union's leadership of the South Carolina Volunteers. Colonel Higginson, despite his impeccable abolitionist credentials, found Montgomery's tactics of "burning and pillaging" during the conduct of his operations unacceptable. Further, Montgomery's reliance on unchecked violence in situations was unnecessary and repugnant behavior for a military unit. Higginson rebuked Montgomery—and Tubman through her association with and endorsement of Montgomery's actions—in reports to his superiors.

Soon after the Combahee raid, Montgomery led his regiment down the coast to seize a port town, but Tubman did not accompany him. She felt her role in helping the men, women, and children freed during the June 1–2 raid took priority, and she was uniquely qualified to perform this unfinished business. In a letter she dictated to Franklin Sanborn in Massachusetts, she stated:

"I am trying to find places for those able to work, and provide for them as best I can, so as to lighten the burden on the Government as much as possible, while at the same time they learn to respect themselves by earning their own living."[12]

In July plans were underway for the Union troops stationed at Port Royal to conduct an assault on Charleston. The initial offensive was to take Fort Wagner, the heavily fortified earthwork defending the approach to Charleston Harbor. The Fifty-Fourth Massachusetts Volunteer Infantry Regiment, a black unit led by white abolitionist and prominent Bostonian colonel Robert Gould Shaw, was to take the lead role in the assault. As Tubman continued her humanitarian duties, she also served as a cook. She helped support the troops as they readied for the assault on Fort Wagner and later told sources that she had served Colonel Shaw his last meal the night before the battle.[13] Tubman also knew that two of Frederick Douglass's sons, Lewis and Charles, served with the regiment.

Tubman's lyrical account of the battle at Fort Wagner was recorded by historian Albert Bushnell Hart forty years afterward in his book *Slavery and Abolition*. (Hart met Tubman in Boston.) According to Hart, Tubman told him: "And then we saw the lightning, and that was the guns; and then we heard the thunder, and that was the big guns; and then we heard the rain falling, and that was the drops of blood falling; and when we came to get in the crops, it was the dead that we reaped."[14]

The blood indeed fell at Fort Wagner. The Union suffered 1,515 dead, wounded, and missing. Of those total casualties, 256 came from the Fifty-Fourth Massachusetts, including its regimental commander; Robert Gould Shaw was killed leading his troops.

The wounded were taken to hospitals in Beaufort, South Carolina. There Tubman worked most of her waking hours treating the steady stream of wounded that came to the hospitals as the fighting continued until early September. In the late fall of 1863, exhausted by her nursing duties and wanting to return to her family in upstate New York that she felt needed her attention, Tubman left South Carolina. After briefly visiting relatives in upstate New York and Canada, in February 1864 Tubman returned to South Carolina, where she was welcomed by Maj. Gen. Quincy Gillmore, who understood her immeasurable value in military skills such as scouting and intelligence gathering, in serving as a nurse, and in performing the prosaic duties of cook and laundress. Tubman's considerable talents, work ethic, and commitment to the Union cause made her a welcome addition to the Union Army's Department of the South. She was the indispensable woman.

During a lull in fighting and a pocket of inactivity in her own life following the Battle of Fredericksburg, Clara Barton yearned to be back amid the "fiery trial" of combat to demonstrate her courage, to prove her usefulness, and to satisfy her appetite for adventure among valiant men. As the war wore on, medical treatment improved in the U.S. Army's Medical Department, and the U.S. Sanitary Commission began to gain traction as the primary civilian organization treating the wounded. Barton's freelance style of operating was meeting resistance from a number of official quarters, not the least of which was the nursing organization operating under the direction of Dorothea Dix. In an attempt to secure her own undisputed control of nursing activities, Dix did not welcome any invasion by Barton on her turf.

Senator Wilson, without Clara Barton's knowledge or permission, named her brother David a quartermaster in the Union Army. Clara Barton was taken by surprise, her sister-in-law (David's wife) was furious, and David was perplexed but complied with the senator's offer. Wilson's intent was to provide a channel for Clara Barton to continue her work and still operate within the growing wartime military bureaucracy. David was given orders to report to South Carolina in March 1863 with XVIII Army Corps and prepare for attacks on Charleston. With the War Department's permission (no doubt orchestrated by Senator Wilson), Clara Barton sailed from New York on April 2, 1863, to serve with her brother in the Department of the South.

Once in South Carolina, Barton found little to occupy her other than social activities. A captain Lamb and Col. John J. Elwell competed for her attention like two smitten schoolboys. Barton was a willing player, flirting with both men in the social milieu in which she found herself. Meanwhile, her brother's role as quartermaster was turning into disaster—a catastrophe for David and an embarrassment for his sister.

Her relationship with Colonel Elwell blossomed into an infatuation bordering on a love affair. The couple spent time together riding horseback, exchanging letters, and addressing each other with affectionate nicknames. Then the war muscled its way into their affair. Barton and Elwell turned from their romantic activities to gather essential supplies before the expected second assault on Fort Wagner. Aboard the steamship *Fulton*, the pair watched the bombardment of the fort in anticipation of the Union assault.

After the bombardment, Clara Barton followed the troops ashore on Morris Island. There she treated wounded soldiers, including her friend Colonel Elwell who had fallen from his horse after being struck by a Confederate round during the assault. She and her assistant Mary Gage helped establish a field hospital and treated the numerous wounded from the Fort Wagner engagement. Fort Wagner was eventually taken after heavy Union losses. The ultimate prize, Charleston, would not fall to Union forces during this campaign. The "pestilent nest of heresy, Charleston," as Charles Francis Adams referred to the city in his diary, would remain in Confederate hands until the end of the war.[15]

Barton's world began to close in on her after Fort Wagner. Officials and medical personnel resented her demands and imperious nature. Without the cover of an official sponsor, Barton was dismissed from Morris Island. She managed to return for a brief period but soon received word from General Gillmore, the general in charge, that her services were no longer required. Further closing the door to her options in the medical area, Dorothea Dix, who lead the U.S. Sanitary Commission's nursing staff, would brook no challenge to her absolute control in the Department of the South. On the last day of December 1863, Clara Barton boarded a boat that would take her home to Washington City.

According to biographer Elizabeth Brown Pryor, Barton's conflicts in South Carolina, where she "gave little speeches on her achievements, delivered in a self-congratulatory tone that was indicative less of pride than justification," led to a lasting behavior. "She would never again drop this dark cloak of self-righteousness apology. For the remaining fifty years of her career, Barton would feel the need to anticipate dissatisfaction, even to falsify information, to avoid unfavorable comment."[16]

The one affirming aspect of Barton's time in South Carolina was her friendship with Frances D. "Aunt Fanny" Gage, who managed one of the contraband plantations in Port Royal. (It was an experiment to introduce formerly enslaved people to a work experience that paid wages.) Gage encouraged Barton's evolving feminist positions, including on the subject of women's suffrage. In a letter to friend Mary Norton, Barton wrote: "I most devoutly wish that intellect, education and moral worth decided a voter's privileges and not sex, or money or land, or any other unintelligent principle."[17] Gage's humanitarian impulses, her advocacy for justice, and her persistence in the face of obstacles were a model for Barton, thirteen years Gage's junior, for the remainder of Barton's long and productive life.

When Clara Barton left South Carolina with all its memories, both positive and negative, she also left behind Colonel Elwell, her friend, her kindred spirit, perhaps her lover. They separated with heavy hearts, knowing that their relationship could not continue. After the war, Elwell returned to Cleveland and his wife, resumed his career in medicine and law, and over the years that followed wrote Barton "passionate and tender letters recalling their love affair in 1863."[18]

Clara Barton and Harriet Tubman were in South Carolina during the same time in the summer of 1863. They both witnessed the Battle of Fort Wagner and were both on Morris Island following the fighting to treat wounded soldiers. They also owed their presence in South Carolina to their military and political friends in Massachusetts who believed in their potential to contribute to the war effort. They had a common friend in Colonel Higginson of the First South Carolina Regiment. Both women shared a commitment to helping others affected by the war and were drawn by a similar strong desire to be in the middle of the action. Yet there is no historical record of their meeting in South Carolina. They were two shooting stars crossing the night sky of the Civil War, burning brightly and moving in the same direction but remaining on separate paths.

Back in Washington City, Barton tapped all those officials who in the past had helped her achieve permission to journey to the front lines. Now brigadier general Rucker, Senator Wilson, and even Secretary of War Stanton were targets of her lobbying efforts for authorization to return to the battle front. Bureaucratic red tape, an order by newly appointed general in chief Ulysses S. Grant to bar all women and civilians from the Army of the Potomac, and the long, controlling grasp of Dorothea Dix at medical units nearly ended Barton's relentless initiative to provide her services to the wounded. But the reality of Grant's aggressive fighting tactics in the Overland Campaign being conducted in Virginia changed the picture. Thousands of casualties swamped the abilities of the army's medical units and the U.S. Sanitary and Christian Commissions to cope with the volume of wounded men. Practicality prevailed. Barton was issued a pass from General Rucker's office that was signed by the acting surgeon general, Joseph K. Barnes, to travel to Virginia. Barton soon found herself in Belle Plain, the center for casualities rolling in from the Overland battlefields.

After a brief period, Barton departed Belle Plain for Fredericksburg with her traveling companions Mrs. Brainard from the Michigan Soldiers' Relief Organization and a young clergyman (whose name is unknown) from the U.S. Christian Commission. Clara and her two coworkers went to work in Fredericksburg and provided care for the scores of wounded. The task was overwhelming. A U.S. Sanitary Commission volunteer estimated that there were fourteen thousand wounded in the city compared to the prewar population of Fredericksburg of five thousand.[19]

As accustomed as she was to battlefield casualties, Barton was appalled by the numbers of wounded coming to Fredericksburg from the Overland battles of the Wilderness and Spotsylvania Court House. Soldiers lay in wagons waiting their turn to be treated by army surgeons. Barton observed, "The dark spot in the mud under many a wagon . . . [telling] only too plainly where some poor fellow's life had dripped out in those hours of dreadful darkness."[20]

Once again in Fredericksburg, Barton had met her objective of being in the midst of the suffering where she could contribute and feel she was helping the war effort. And yet the casualties were even more staggering than her first experience in the town during December 1862. "I cannot but think that we shall win at last," she wrote to an associate, "but Oh the cost . . ."[21]

Distraught over the lag in treating casualties, Barton pleaded with Senator Wilson to push for an improvement in the transportation of the wounded. When Wilson urged a speedy resolution, Secretary of War Stanton balked; he doubted the severity of the situation. Wilson pushed back, threatening a Senate investigation if the War Department could not or would not comply. The War Department quickly dispatched Quartermaster General Montgomery Meigs and his staff to Fredericksburg. Disturbed by what he found at Belle Plain, Meigs directed army engineers to restore the railroad tracks between Falmouth Station and Aquia Creek that had been destroyed by the Confederates.

Thanks to the combined efforts of Barton, Wilson, and Meigs, train service was quickly restored, and the wounded were transported to hospitals in Washington City for treatment. A senator, a general, and a female civilian worked together and made a difference.

Fig. 1. Acknowledging Harriet Tubman's contribution to freeing enslaved people, Frederick Douglass wrote: "The midnight sky and the silent stars have been the witness of your devotion to freedom and your heroism." This is the earliest known photograph of Harriet Tubman, thought to have been taken in 1868 or '69 when Tubman was in her mid-forties. Photo courtesy of the Library of Congress and the Smithsonian National Museum of African American History and Culture, Benjamin F. Powelson, photographer.

Fig. 2. Following the Battle of Fort Wagner in South Carolina, Tubman was quoted as saying: "And then we saw lightning, and that was the guns; and then we heard the thunder, and that was the big guns; and then we heard the rain falling, and that was the drops of blood falling; and when we came to get in the crops, it was the dead that we reaped." Photo courtesy of the Library of Congress, Harvey B. Lindsley, photographer, ca. 1873.

Fig. 3. Speaking to her biographer, Sarah H. Bradford, Tubman reported: "Now I've been free. I know what a dreadful condition slavery is. . . . I have seen hundreds of escaped slaves, but I never saw one who was willing to go back and be a slave." Woodcut from Sarah H. Bradford's *Scenes in the Life of Harriet Tubman*, 1869.

Fig. 4. Harriet Tubman in her home in Auburn, New York, 1911. She told Sarah Bradford, "Why, didn't I tell you Misses, it wasn't me, it was the Lord! . . . The Lord could take care of me till my time came and then I was ready to go." Photo courtesy of the Library of Congress.

Eng.ᵈ by A.H.Ritchie.

Fig. 5. The daughter, sister, and spouse of Protestant ministers, Harriet
Beecher Stowe radiated piety and compassion. Yet it was undergirded by a
fierce commitment to freedom and justice. Engraving courtesy of the Library
of Congress, Alexander Hat Ritchie, artist, ca. 1870.

Fig. 6. Harriet Beecher Stowe, ca. 1850. On writing *Uncle Tom's Cabin* she said, "I wrote what I did as a woman, as a mother. I was oppressed and broken-hearted with the sorrows and injustices I saw." Photo courtesy of the Library of Congress.

Fig. 7. Harriet Beecher Stowe, ca. 1880. "Deeds of heroism are wrought here more than those of romance, when defying torture, and braving death itself, the fugitive voluntarily threads his way back to the terrors and perils of that dark land, that he may bring out his sister, or mother, or wife." From *Uncle Tom's Cabin*. Photo courtesy of the Library of Congress.

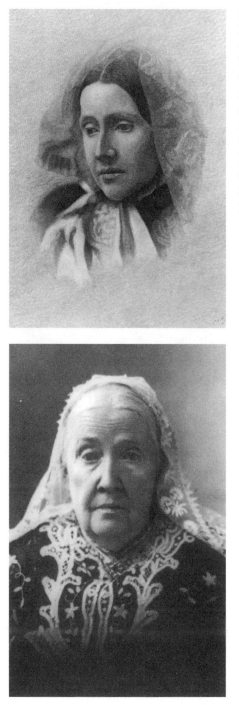

Fig. 8. Engraving of Julia Ward Howe, ca. 1887. In 1843 Howe wrote in her diary: "My pen has been unusually busy during the last year—it has brought me some happy inspiration, and though the golden tide is now at its ebb, I live in the hope that it may rise again in time." Photo courtesy of the Library of Congress, Caroline Amelia Powell, engraver; Josiah Johnson Hawes, photographer.

Fig. 9. Julia Ward Howe, ca. 1902. "He is coming like the glory of the morning on the wave. / He is wisdom to the mighty, he is succor to the brave. / So the world shall be his footstool, and the soul of Time his slave. / Our God is marching on." Julia Ward Howe omitted this sixth and final verse of "The Battle Hymn of the Republic" perhaps because of its strong apocalyptic overtones. Photo courtesy of the Library of Congress.

Fig. 10. Julia Ward Howe, 1904. Following the Civil War, Howe became a pacifist, proclaiming: "From the bosom of the devastated earth, a voice goes up with our own. It says: 'Disarm, disarm!' The sword of murder is not the balance of Justice. Blood does not wipe out dishonor, nor violence vindicate possession." Photo courtesy the Library of Congress.

Fig. 11. Julia Ward Howe, 1908. Well into her elder years, Julia Ward Howe's public lectures usually concluded with her audience requesting that she sing "Battle Hymn." Journalists who reported on these occasions wrote that there was "not a dry eye in the house" during these performances. Photo courtesy of the Library of Congress.

Fig. 12. Engraving of Clara Barton taken from a ca. 1863 Civil War photograph. As a young teacher Barton made the following statement to the Oxford, Massachusetts, School Board: "I may sometimes be willing to teach for nothing, but if paid at all, I shall never do a man's work for less than a man's pay." Photo courtesy of the Library of Congress.

Fig. 13. Clara Barton, ca. 1863. Reflecting on her time spent with the Union Army, Barton said, "I don't know how long it has been since my ear has been free from the roll of a drum. It is the music I sleep by, and I love it!" Photo courtesy of the Library of Congress.

Fig. 14. Clara Barton, ca. 1904. Addressing a veterans group following the Civil War, Barton admonished the crowd, "You glorify the women who made their way to the front to reach you in your misery, and nurse you back to life. You called us angels. Who opened the way for women to go and make it possible? Who but the detested 'clique' who through the years of opposition, obloquy, toil, and pain had openly claimed that women had rights, should have the privilege to exercise them." Photo courtesy of the Library of Congress.

Fig. 15. Sarah Josepha Hale, ca. 1831. As a thirty-nine-year-old widow and mother of five, Hale wrote the best-selling novel *Northwood* in 1827. The book's popularity soon helped her land the position of editor at the *Ladies' Magazine*. She remained editor of that publication and later the affiliated magazine *Godey's Lady's Book* for nearly fifty years. Portrait by James Reid Lambdin courtesy of Richards Free Library, Newport, New Hampshire.

Fig. 16. Sarah Josepha Hale, ca. 1850. In *Northwood* Hale wrote, "We have
far too few holidays. Thanksgiving Day, like the Fourth of July, should be
considered a national festival and observed by all our people . . . it will be a
grand spectacle of moral power and human happiness, such as the world has
never witnessed." Engraving courtesy of the Library of Congress.

Fig. 17. Sarah Josepha Hale, 1880. Less than a week after Hale sent a letter to Abraham Lincoln recommending a national day of thanksgiving, the president issued a proclamation that urged all Americans to observe the last Thursday in November 1863 as a day of thanksgiving. Engraving courtesy of the Library of Congress.

9

"With Malice toward None, with Charity for All"

The Overland Campaign, led by the Union Army's new general in chief, Ulysses S. Grant, demonstrated that federal troops were now directed by a relentless warrior who would not shy away from aggressive encounters with the Confederates as many of his predecessors in the Army of the Potomac had in past campaigns. And the cost was high. Maj. Gen. Gouverneur K. Warren, who commanded the Army of the Potomac's V Corps, reported: "For thirty days it has been one funeral procession past me and it has been too much!"[1] Warren's comment was hardly hyperbole. During the spring campaign starting in early May to mid-June 1864, the Army of the Potomac had sixty-five thousand casualties, or "three-fifths of the total number of combat casualties suffered by the Army of the Potomac during the *previous three years*."[2]

Abraham Lincoln, reflecting on the human loss and sensing the political repercussions for the upcoming presidential election, said in a speech to the U.S. Sanitary Commission in June 1864 that the "terrible war" had "carried mourning to almost every home, until it can almost be said that 'the heavens are hung in black.'"[3] Astute observers also knew that Robert E. Lee had thirty-five thousand casualties during the same period and that the heretofore evanescent Army of Northern Virginia had been pinned down in a defensive position around Petersburg and Richmond, Virginia. During the summer and fall, Grant had severed most of the key supply lines from the South to Lee's army.

As Union morale sank in the summer of 1864 and editorials flooded Northern Democratic newspapers alleging that a peace could be forged if emancipation would be set aside, Lincoln chose to stay the course. "It [the war] is and will be carried on so long as I am President for the sole purpose of restoring the Union. But no human power can subdue this rebellion without using the Emancipation lever as I have done." Lincoln reasoned that the 130,000 black soldiers and sailors fighting for the Union desired nothing less than the achievement of emancipation. "If they stake their lives for us they must be prompted by the strongest motive—even the promise of freedom. And the promise made, must be kept."[4]

Then, on September 1, 1864, came news that would breathe new life into the Union cause and shatter the South, as well as change the dynamics of the presidential election of 1864: General Sherman took Atlanta. He sent a telegram to the president that reported: "Atlanta is ours, and fairly won." George Templeton Strong, a New York lawyer, seemed to sum up the feelings of the North in his September 3, 1864, diary entry: "Glorious news this morning—Atlanta taken at last!!! It is (coming at this political crises) the greatest event of the war."[5]

Much hard fighting and loss of life still lay ahead before peace would begin to be forged at Appomattox Court House in April 1865. The siege of Petersburg, the Shenandoah Valley Campaign led by Maj. Gen. Philip Sheridan, the Battle of Five Forks, and numerous other engagements would be fought, men grievously wounded, others lost, and lives changed forever.

As the war began to reach a denouement, Abraham Lincoln had already begun to think about the conclusion of the hostilities and what came next. Reunion was foremost on his mind as he addressed the crowd at his second inaugural ceremony. The conclusion of his brief address carried with it a note of reconciliation and hopes for the reunion of the Northern and Southern states. "With malice toward none, with charity for all, with firmness in the right as God gives us to see the right, let us strive on to finish the work we are in, to bind up the nation's wounds, to care for him who shall have borne the battle and for his widow and orphan, to do all which may achieve and cherish a just and lasting peace among ourselves and with all nations."[6]

Another American had been thinking about reconciliation and

unity at the national level for a number of years. Sarah Josepha Hale, a nationally known magazine editor and ardent patriot, had been advocating for a national day of thanksgiving for over thirty years. Now, with the shadow of Civil War hanging over her beloved country, Hale thought it the opportune time for the nation to recognize its nearly ninety-year history of independence with a celebration of thanksgiving.

Now the purpose is to entreat President Lincoln to put forth his Proclamation, appointing the last Thursday in November as the National Thanksgiving for all those classes of people who are under the National Government particularly, and commending this Union Thanksgiving to each State Executive: thus by the noble example and action of the President of the United States, the permanency and unity of our Great American Festival of Thanksgiving would be forever secured.

—SARAH JOSEPHA HALE, September 28, 1863

Her similar appeals to the four presidents who had preceded Lincoln went unanswered. But now, Hale reasoned, the time was right. The faint but favorable winds of national reconciliation were beginning to stir, and the American president had a vision of a reunited country. The seventy-five-year-old "editress" of the *Lady's Book* was once again going to appeal to the nation's chief executive to help fulfill a dream she had been pursuing since she was a young woman. Hale, whose birth coincided with the birth of America's constitutional government, saw a national day of thanksgiving as a unifying event, providentially inspired, and a connecting experience for the country and for the families of proud, grateful citizens of the republic. Differences in geography, station in life, and political preferences would be put aside to enjoy those aspects of American life that united all: liberty, freedom, and an unrestrained opportunity to prosper based on hard work.

Courage and skill are not to be taught by lectures . . . they must be acquired by practice, and improved by braving danger; and the younger we begin our lessons the better.

—SARAH JOSEPHA HALE, *Northwood*, 1827

On October 24, 1788—six months before George Washington took the oath of office as the first president of the United States—Sarah Josepha Buell was born to former Revolutionary War officer Capt. Gordon Buell and Martha Whittlesay Buell in Newport, New Hampshire. Their one-and-a-half story farm house sat on four hundred acres of land overlooking the valley where the Sugar River flowed. Sarah was the third child and first daughter born to the couple; their fourth child, Martha, was born four years later. Public education was in its infancy in the new nation and not available to children from families of modest means in rural New Hampshire. Therefore, Mrs. Buell schooled her children at home, where she relied on the Bible and *Pilgrim's Progress* to teach reading and to impart a religious education. She was also said to have been a gifted storyteller and had a love of learning she transferred to her four children.[7]

Sarah shared her mother's passion for reading, and while in her early years, she read *The Mysteries of Udolpho* by Ann Radcliffe and David Ramsay's *The History of the American Revolution*. Both books had a profound impact on young Sarah and to some degree would influence her most of her adult life. *The Mysteries of Udolpho* was a romance novel filled with supernatural occurrences, a foreboding castle, and adventures involving the dashing Valancourt and his love interest, the beautiful Emily St. Aubert. And, most important to Sarah, this book was written by a female author.

Equally enthralling to Sarah, Ramsay's *History of the American Revolution* provided the stirring details of the seminal American event that occurred shortly before Sarah was born and in which her father was a participant. Reading this book and hearing her father's tales of his firsthand experiences would create an indelible sense of patriotism that guided her throughout her life. About these early literary influences Sarah wrote later: "The wish to promote the reputation of my own sex, and to do something for my own country, was among the earliest mental emotions I can recollect. This love of country was deeply engraved on my heart, by reading when I was not more than ten-years-old, Ramsey's [sic] *History of the American Revolution*. It made me a patriot for life."[8]

In a later time, Sarah's intellectual gifts as a young girl would have made her a natural candidate for attending a college or university; however, in the early nineteenth century, this was not possible because of her gender. Sarah had to confine her further education to what she could learn at home by reading with her mother and relying on another important family asset, her brother Horatio, who applied to and was accepted by Dartmouth College in nearby Hanover, New Hampshire. Horatio respected his sister's academic potential and willingly shared his textbooks and tutored Sarah during school breaks. Horatio graduated with top honors from Dartmouth, and his sister received the equivalent of a college education by absorbing this transfer of knowledge from brother to sister.

Sarah Buell began teaching in a small, private school in the Newport area following the mentoring she received from her brother. She was paid by the families of the students; the curriculum included reading, some Latin, mathematics, and the classics. Records show that Sarah operated and taught in the school for four years.

With his two sons away from the family farm to launch their own careers—Charles on a sailing ship at sea and Horatio attending Dartmouth—Gordon Buell decided to sell his farm and enter a business where he would not be dependent on their labor. The Buells built a small inn in Newport and named it the Rising Sun Tavern. (Inexplicably, the front of the structure faced west, so the back of the building received the beams of morning light from the rising sun.) Sarah and her sister, Martha, helped run the inn.

Shortly after starting the inn, the Buell family suffered a trio of tragedies: Charles was lost at sea, his body never recovered; young Martha died of tuberculosis; and her mother died the following month. Heartbroken, Gordon sold the tavern but retained rooms in the inn where he and Sarah could live. By this time, Horatio was on his own, studying to practice law in Glens Falls, New York. In operation only a year, the Rising Sun had many unhappy memories for both father and daughter. Yet a positive event occurred at the Rising Sun Tavern.

David Hale, one of the inn's boarders, was a young attorney just starting out in the practice of law. Sarah and David were quickly attracted to each other and began a courtship that would last two years.[9] The duration of their engagement was not due to any uncertainty about the relationship but conformed to the custom of the day of not marrying during a period of mourning. The deaths of the mother, sister, and eldest son were still very much a part of the Buell family's lives; David Hale respected this time of grieving and waited patiently for Sarah's hand in marriage. During their courtship, Sarah continued to teach, and David established a successful, growing law practice in Newport.

On October 23, 1813, the couple was married in a small ceremony among close friends. Sarah Josepha Hale turned twenty-five the day after the wedding. The bride, a brunette with pale skin, delicate features, and large hazel eyes and of average height, was seen as an attractive match with her tall, "good-looking groom."[10]

Not only physically compatible, the Hales were also compatible in their intellectual interests. The newly married couple settled into a daily routine that included a two-hour period where both read and wrote together. Sarah later reported on these hours they set aside: "Two hours out of twenty-four. How I enjoyed those hours."[11] Sarah's writing time with David allowed her the opportunity to write poems and short stories, some of which were published in local periodicals and newspapers. Sarah also started a writer's group with some of her women friends who had literary aspirations. The Newport coterie was committed to writing for publication; however, the women used noms de plume when published, not wanting attention that would detract from their roles as wives and mothers. Hale used the name Cornelia when her works were published.[12] (The use of noms de plume had a long history in both Europe and America as women writers sought to hide their gender, perhaps with the hope of attracting both male and female readers. Amatine Lucile Aurore Dupin, the French novelist, for example, wrote under the name George Sand. Male authors wishing to conceal their identities also used pseudonyms during the period. Alexander Hamilton, James Madison, and John Jay wrote the Federalist Papers using pen names.)

Two years after their marriage, Sarah gave birth to a son, David, named for his father. In 1817 their second son was born. Horatio was named for his uncle, Sarah's educational mentor when she was a young girl. In the autumn of 1818, Sarah was expecting their third child when she was diagnosed as having tuberculosis, the same disease that had caused her sister's death less than a decade earlier. David Hale was reluctant for his wife to follow the doctor's recommended treatments of bloodletting, emetics, and confinement indoors. Leaving his two small sons in the care of family members, David took Sarah to the New Hampshire mountains for a regimen of fresh air, a fruit diet, and rest. It worked. Sarah recovered and praised her husband's health recovery plan, calling it the "grape cure" because of her consumption of grapes whenever they were available. The following spring, Sarah gave birth to the couple's first girl, Frances Ann. Whether it was David's unconventional path to improved health or a misdiagnosis by the family's physicians, Sarah regained her strength and never suffered any serious illnesses for the remainder of her long life.

The Hales continued to live lives of good health and growing prosperity and never abandoned their times set aside for reading and writing, even amid their busy days. In 1820 a second daughter, named Sarah Josepha after her mother but called Josepha, was added to the family. In September 1822 the happy and comfortable life of the Hales underwent a devastating change. While participating in a trial in a nearby town, David was caught in a storm in his carriage that chilled him in his soaking wet clothes. His exposure resulted in pneumonia. He died on September 25, leaving behind his wife, Sarah, pregnant with their fifth child. The baby, William, was born weeks after his father's untimely death.

As a thirty-four-year-old widow with five children younger than the age of eight and virtually no savings, Sarah had few options open to her in early nineteenth-century America. The usual paths included finding an eligible man—perhaps a young widower—to marry or relying on welfare from a local church or a government widow and orphan fund or, worst of all, giving up her children to relatives or placing them in orphanages. None of these options was acceptable to the recent widow. Her former profession as a teacher, before she was married David, was closed to her because public schools did not hire married women in the early nineteenth century. She had experience helping her father run the Rising Sun as a successful business, so with the financial help of David's Masonic lodge, Sarah and her sister-in-law, Hannah Hale, started a millinery shop in Newport. The sisters-in-law sold hats and other women's clothing. The business helped Sarah bring in much-needed funds, and Hannah was able to provide babysitting when Sarah worked in the shop.

Sarah Josepha Hale, meanwhile, continued writing both poetry and prose, submitting her work to newspapers, magazines, and other publications in New Hampshire and Boston. The Masons of New Hampshire also helped her publish a volume of her poems, *The Genius of Oblivion*, which was released in 1823. The small volume received praise from readers and was soon followed by a prize awarded by the *Boston Spectator* and the *Ladies' Album* for her poem on charity. During this time, her work was also published in the *Atlantic Monthly* and the *Literary Gazette*. A selection of her poems was also published in *The Memorial*, a small gift book—a type of volume popular in the early nineteenth century.

Encouraged by her literary successes, Hale reduced her involvement in the millinery shop and began writing a novel that she submitted to Boston publishers Bowles and Dearborn in 1827. The book *Northwood* was accepted and published the same year. Hale now felt she had a reliable income stream coming from doing what she loved—writing. *Northwood* launched her into the view of readers in the public and leaders in the publishing profession.

Sarah's two-volume work was one of the first fictional accounts featuring slavery in the United States, preceding *Uncle Tom's Cabin* by twenty-five years. *Northwood, or Life North and South* was unequivocal about the necessity of eliminating slavery, but it also attempted to depict the similarity between North and South—both borne out of the Revolutionary War experience—and advocated unity between the regions. The main character in the novel, Sydney Romilly, shuttles between North and South while fulfilling his family's duties. Sydney sees benefits and positive qualities in both regions yet finds himself torn between his New England father's abolitionist beliefs and his South Carolina uncle's proslavery position. He seeks some common ground.

Author Hale's themes in the novel reflect her own admiration for conciliation, benevolence, charity, personal freedom, and piety. Her strong, practical, and independent New England persona shines through most of her characters in the book. One of her leading players in the book says: "Happiness can never be compelled to be our companion, nor is she oftenest won by those who most eagerly seek her. She most frequently meets us in situations where we never expected her visits; in employments or under privations to which we have become reconciled only by a sense of duty."[13]

The novel quickly became a best seller in the United States. It was reprinted in Great Britain under the title *A New England Tale*. The book was reprinted several times following its initial publication, but in 1852, following the release of *Uncle Tom's Cabin*, a revised version was printed and published. While Hale was an early advocate for abolition, she thought Stowe's book too provocative and that it would generate a sudden, violent change that would divide the nation. In the new preface of the reprint, Hale wrote:

> *Northwood* was written when what is now known as "Abolitionism" first began to disturb seriously the harmony between South and North. . . . That it is easier to burn the temple than to build one, and that two wrongs never make one right, are points conceded by all; yet all seem not to have considered what is quite as sure, that fraud and falsehood never promote the cause of goodness, nor can physical force make or keep men free. . . . Hoping that *Northwood* might in some degree aid in diffusing the true spirit, I have consented to its republication at this time.[14]

In the final chapter, which she revised, Hale wrote: "Let us trust that the pen not the sword will decide the controversy now going on in our land, and that any part women may take on the former made will be promotive of peace, and not suggestive of discord."[15]

Hale's moderate, peaceful approach to abolition proposed in 1852 was doomed to fail amid the growing tensions leading up to 1861. Lincoln's view alas prevailed: "Every drop of blood drawn by the lash shall be paid by another drawn by the sword."[16]

One reader of the original version of *Northwood* was so impressed by the author's skills that he offered her the position of editor for a women's magazine he was about to launch. Rev. John L. Blake wanted to start a magazine written for women such as those published in England. The *American Ladies' Magazine* would feature articles for women not only to help them be better parents and housewives but also to broaden their horizons in the world of literature and art. Sarah Josepha Hale seemed the ideal candidate to lead such an ambitious endeavor.

The offer from Reverend Blake was a dream come true for a widow who was constantly concerned about her family finances. The position offered a steady income stream in work that Hale considered her life's calling. Two factors about the job concerned her. A new publication—especially one directed at women—might be a huge financial risk. Women, after all, would have to ask their husbands to pay for the subscription. Was that, Hale worried, sustainable? And the job would be located in the magazine's office in Boston, requiring Hale to move her family to a city a hundred miles from Newport.

Hale was able to convince Blake that she could serve as the editor for several months of the start-up while still living in Newport. Blake agreed. She overcame her concern that the new magazine might founder and saw the potential rather than the downside of a publication that appealed primarily to American women. For the children, Hale worked through a reasonable solution that met the needs of all. Son David was entering the U.S. Military Academy at West Point, where he would board. The youngest son, William, would live in Boston with his mother. Her second-eldest son, Horatio, would live with her brother Horatio and his wife in Glens Falls, New York. Daughters Frances and Josepha, who attended Miss Fiske's Seminary for Young Ladies in Keene, New Hampshire, would live with her late husband's brother and wife there. All members of the family who would be caring for Hale's children were supportive of her new position and delighted that this talented and independent woman had overcome the death of her husband and the potential financial crises it might have entailed. She had provided for all of her children both financially and emotionally during a challenging time for the family.

Despite her success as a writer and editor with a strong financial foundation of her own making, Sarah Joseph Hale never forgot the precarious times she faced as a young widow. She wore black clothing, the traditional attire of a widow, for the rest of her life as if to remind herself not only of the loss of her beloved David but also of the tenuous financial state of being a widow in the nineteenth century.[17]

Hale took on her new editorial responsibilities with creativity and enthusiasm. Knowing that husbands controlled household finances, in her introduction of the first issue of the *Ladies' Magazine*, she appealed to men to buy their wives a subscription to the publication. It would result for each wife, Hale promised, in a female reader who would improve her mind, enhance her homemaker skills, and never "cause her to be the less assiduous in preparing for his reception or less sincere in welcoming his return."[18] Husbands willingly subscribed, and advertisers generously supported the new publication. In addition to her keen sense for marketing the new publication, Hale also adhered to a consistent editorial approach that focused on the promotion of educational opportunities for women; the encouragement of original literary material from American authors, including women; and the backing of worthwhile, nonpolitical causes.[19]

The *Ladies' Magazine* flourished under Hale's editorial leadership. However, in the early years of the 1830s the publication experienced a falloff in subscriptions and increasing account delinquencies from subscribers due to national economic turbulence. During the winter of 1833–34, the "Biddle panic" occurred; interest rates jumped, businesses failed, and thousands of workers lost their jobs. Initially Hale was resistant to join forces with publisher Louis Godey's new magazine for women—*The Lady's Book*—when the publisher suggested a joint venture, but Hale came to see the economic wisdom of combining the two publications. The deal was sealed when Godey, as part of his purchase agreement, insisted that Hale should be the editor of the new combined publication.

We have too few holidays. Thanksgiving Day, like the Fourth of July, should be considered a national festival and observed by all our people . . . it will be a grand spectacle of moral power and human happiness, such as the world has never witnessed.

—Squire Romilly in *Northwood*

Hale's vision of a nationally observed day of thanksgiving first surfaced in her novel *Northwood* published in 1827 and then republished in 1852. The appropriateness and power of a national observance of thanksgiving was expressed by the highly respected father of the novel's main character. A detailed, lush description of the thanksgiving feast in the fictional Romilly household in rural New Hampshire was drawn from Hale's own experience celebrating thanksgiving in the Buell family with feasting and prayer. The concept of a national observance of thanksgiving was not original to Hale. The first proclamation of Thanksgiving came from President George Washington in 1789, a year after Sarah Josepha Buell Hale was born. Some states continued to observe Thanksgiving on the fourth Thursday of November, but a national observance faded after Washington's term as president ended.

For a person born during the formation of the constitutional government in the United States and having participated, as a child, in the warm and inspiring celebration of a communal feast, Hale had a strong motivation to see the national observance continue. Perhaps more than those who followed in later years, Hale honored the Founding Fathers as those "great men who knew no North or South." Unity, loyalty to the American family, and providential inspiration for the national government were Hale's guiding principles for her campaign to help establish a national day of thanksgiving.

From her role as the editor of the *Lady's Book*, Hale would lead the way for establishing a national day of thanksgiving. With a barrage of editorials and letters, she launched a campaign in 1847 following a trip to her childhood home in Newport, New Hampshire, that convinced her that Thanksgiving, as with the Fourth of July, warranted its own day on the calendar for a time of national recognition and celebration.

Writing in the *Lady's Book*, Hale announced: "From this year, 1847, henceforth and forever, as long as the Union endures, the last Thursday in November be the Day set apart by every State for its annual Thanksgiving. Will not the whole press of the county advocate this suggestion?"[20] Following this appeal, Hale wrote letters to governors, congressmen, and anyone else in positions of authority she thought could further her cause. She followed up by placing two editorials per year in the *Lady's Book*: the first early in the year, asking that states and territories join the cause of setting aside a day of thanksgiving, and a second editorial in November to report on the progress of national participation.

By 1862 twenty-nine states and territories were participating. Only Vermont and Virginia were holdouts, and Hale was working on them. Earlier she had turned to the president for an endorsement. Zachery Taylor was the first chief executive to receive a Thanksgiving Day appeal from Hale, but there was no response from Taylor. Nor did she hear from Millard Fillmore, Franklin Pierce, or James Buchanan. This lack of response led Hale to step up her appeals to the White House.

On September 28, 1863, Hale sat down again to write to an American president. Her persistence and zeal for the cause was reflected in her letter and undimmed by the fact that her youngest daughter, Josepha, had died suddenly the previous May. Her letter is businesslike, cites the support of two key governors, and invokes the support of her friend secretary of state William Seward.[21] Her letter also clearly sets out the importance of the role the president has to play.

The lawyer president must have been impressed with Mrs. Hale's presentation of her case. Less than a week following her letter, the president issued a proclamation that urged Americans to observe the last Thursday in November as a day of thanksgiving.

I do, therefore, invite my fellow-citizens in every part of the United States, and also those who are at sea and those who are sojourning in foreign lands, to set apart and observe the last Thursday of November next (November 26) as a day of thanksgiving and praise to our beneficent Father who dwelleth in the heavens. And I recommend to them that, while offering up the ascriptions justly due to Him for singular deliverances and blessings, they do also, with humble penitence for our national perverseness and disobedience, commend to His tender care all those who have become widows, orphans, mourners, or sufferers in the lamentable civil strife in which we are unavoidably engaged, and fervently implore the interposition of the almighty hand to heal the wounds of the nation and to restore it, as soon as may be consistent with the Divine purposes, to the full enjoyment of peace, harmony, tranquility, and union.

—ABRAHAM LINCOLN, October 3, 1863

Hale was delighted that her work to secure top-level endorsement for a national day of thanksgiving was complete with Lincoln's signature on an unambiguous proclamation. It was another tangible step on the path toward bringing the nation together initiated by Lincoln. The reality, however, was that the war would not end for another year and a half, and North-South enmity would not abate. Still there was a spirit of reconciliation when Lee and Grant met at Appomattox Court House in April 1865 during the surrender ceremonies. Grant's terms for surrender were remarkably generous, and the Union Army's senior officers took pains not to humiliate their former foes as the Confederates laid down their arms at Appomattox.

Despite the lack of pervasive goodwill between North and South, Hale remained optimistic about the prospects for reconciliation and a continuance of the Thanksgiving proclamation even after Lincoln's assassination. Writing in 1867, Hale's book *Manners* reflected her optimism for the future:

> Our late beloved and lamented President Lincoln recognized the truth of these ideas [regarding Thanksgiving] as soon as they were presented to him. His reply to our appeal was a proclamation appointing Thursday, November 26, 1863 as the day of National Thanksgiving. But at that time, and also in November 1864, he was not able to influence the States in rebellion so that the festival was necessarily incomplete. Since the close of the war, these obstacles have been removed, and President Johnson's Proclamation for the National Thanksgiving on the last Thursday of November, 1866, was observed over all the country. This family union of States and Territories in our Great Republic was fixed and hallowed by the people in the ninetieth year of American Independence.[22]

Hale's optimism about the longevity of Thanksgiving as a national holiday was not unwarranted. It did take until 1941—ninety-four years after the start of Sarah Josepha Hale's quest and sixty-two years after her death—for a joint resolution of Congress to settle the holiday's date as the fourth Thursday in November.

10

"Joy My Freedom!"

Joy my freedom!

—A freed slave, Greensboro, Georgia, 1865

I am lost in amazement when I think of what has been done these last four years. . . . If my faith in God's presence and real living power of the affairs of man ever grows dim, the end of slavery makes it impossible to doubt.

—HARRIET BEECHER STOWE, 1866

The American Civil War was the radical surgery that removed the cancer of slavery from the nation but left in its wake devastating consequences that required years of healing to restore wholeness and health to the country. Farmlands and many cities were destroyed south of the Mason-Dixon line. In total, both sides lost more than 620,000 fighting men in the four years of warfare; 360,000 Yankees and at least 260,000 Confederates lost their lives in combat or to war-related illnesses.[1]

In addition to the physical destruction of lands and buildings along with the many casualties on the battlefield, the South lost the underpinning of its labor market following the liberation of four million slaves. Historian Eric Foner wrote: "Transformation of slaves into free laborers and equal citizens was the most dramatic example of the social and political changes unleashed by the Civil War and emancipation."[2]

Lincoln's generous peace terms and presumed measured approach to reconciliation and Reconstruction came to an abrupt end on April 14, 1865, at Ford's Theater. Reconstruction was now in the hands of Andrew Johnson, the new president, who was a

Southerner and former slave owner. Wishing to avoid a vacuum in presidential leadership that would hold the South accountable for the rebellion and its consequences, Radical Republicans, who held power in Congress and had public approval in the North, found Johnson's policies toward the South too lenient. The Republicans were seeing evidence that the South was instituting its own draconian postwar restrictions on blacks. The enactment of black codes in the South sought to regulate African Americans' labor activities and put them in a subordinate position legally and socially. Some rights—property ownership, contractual rights, marriage—were granted to black persons under the codes, but other fundamental rights, such as the right to testify against a white person, to serve on a jury, or to bear arms, were restricted.

Radical Republicans passed the Civil Rights Act of 1866 to help prevent discrimination in the South against black citizens. Johnson vetoed the bill; Congress immediately overrode the veto. Further, the Radical Republicans put in motion a proposed amendment to the Constitution (what would become the Fourteenth Amendment) that set up a national definition of citizenship forbidding any state to deprive any citizen of life, liberty, or property without due process.

The elections of 1866 further strengthened the number of Radical Republicans in Congress. This meant their bills were now veto-proof as they had the necessary numbers to override any presidential veto. The Radical Republicans continued their aggressive Reconstruction plans, rolling over President Johnson and challenging the judiciary to approve their policies. This zealous approach by Congress eventually led to charges of impeachment against the president. The House of Representative presented eleven charges against President Johnson to the Senate to initiate the impeachment process. Eventually, as the appetite to impeach the president waned, the Senate voted for acquittal, and the Radicals backed off their pressure on the chief executive.

Recognizing that the liberation of formerly enslaved people was a matter of enormous economic consequence in the South, the federal government established the Freedmen's Bureau in March 1865 to facilitate the transition from slavery to freedom. Julia Ward

Howe's husband, Samuel Gridley Howe, was one of three members of the American Freedmen's Commission that helped establish the Bureau of Emancipation. The precise duration of the bureau's mandate was a source of disagreement, but the organization was able to issue supplies and establish educational facilities to assist former slaves and, in some cases, to help black people settle on abandoned or confiscated Southern lands. (Rations distributed by the bureau were dispersed to whites as well as blacks in the South who were facing starvation immediately following the war.)

The federal government's role in redistributing land to former slaves after the war had been discussed as part of the role of the Freedmen's Bureau, but the immediate need to restore agricultural output in the South took precedence. Cotton production by 1879 surpassed that achieved in 1860 in the South due in part to the focus on crop restoration and agricultural productivity. Additionally, tobacco, sugar, and rice crops flourished. Scholars T. Harry Williams, Richard N. Current, and Frank Freidel wrote: "As the great staples, which had been the South's source of wealth before the war, again flowed into the world's markets, the region again had a cash revenue and all classes experienced a measure of wellbeing."[3]

Economic restoration was underway in the South, and political reconciliation was in process. By 1868 Tennessee, Arkansas, North Carolina, South Carolina, Louisiana, Alabama, and Florida were readmitted to the Union after meeting the restoration process spelled out in the Reconstruction acts (Proclamation of Amnesty and Reconstruction, December 8, 1863). By 1870 Mississippi, Virginia, Georgia, and Texas had joined the former Confederate states in the Union.[4] Members of the Republican Party controlled the governments in all ten states with blacks providing the majority support for Republicans. Charges and countercharges of "carpetbaggers" (Northerners who came to the South for political purposes) and "scalawags" (Southern whites who believed they could steer black voters to support their policies) tainted the political discourse in the Reconstruction South.

While economic and political factors were being addressed South of the Mason-Dixon line—albeit with setbacks and challenges along the way—the issue of achieving suffrage for formally enslaved people and granting them their full civil rights ran into daunting resistance from Southern whites. As Frederick Douglass had observed about emancipation: "Verily, the work does not end with the abolition of slavery, but only begins."[5]

The post–Civil War period was a transformative time for both the North and the South. In the South, challenges resulted from the abrupt loss of slave labor as these states struggled to maintain their economies using wage labor. In the North, the economic momentum, fueled by industrial growth required by the war, continued in the postwar economy at an undiminished pace. Historian Foner has characterized this period: "If economic devastation stalked the South, for the North the Civil War was a time of unprecedented prosperity."[6] Clara Barton's advocate and mentor, Sen. Henry Wilson of Massachusetts, summed up the condition of the North in 1867: "The loyal States have accumulated more capital, have added more to their wealth, than during any previous seven years in the history of the country."[7] Those industries associated with the conduct of the war for the North benefited most, with railroads, the meat-packing industry, banking, manufacturing, and textile factories—especially New England woolen mills— realizing robust growth and lucrative profits.

Reformers in the North were energized and confident over their success in the abolition of slavery. Emboldened by their impact in taking on slavery, reformers—many of them women—adopted new causes in social welfare and temperance (addressing a social ill rising from young men drinking to excess in the military, according to some.) Actions to support liberated blacks through the Freedmen's Bureau also drew women into its ranks, especially teachers who were enlisted to help with education. More than a thousand teachers, the majority of whom were women, were sent to teach over 200,000 Southern black students.

The Northern women who participated in activities associated with the war became familiar with public action. As they increased their interest in these activities, their work gave them confidence that they could succeed in like endeavors. Furthermore, this work helped them develop organizational experience that involved management, administrative, and planning skills. As women took on larger roles and began exercising leadership of programs, they became acutely aware that their roles were hampered by social and political restrictions that kept them in subordinate positions. Women were discovering that perceptions needed to change regarding women's roles in American society and that women's political power—that is, women's right to vote—needed to be addressed. As Historian Foner has commented, "The war enlarged the ranks of women who resented their legal and political subordination to men and believed themselves entitled to the vote in recognition of their contribution to Union victory and to the end of slavery."[8]

Harriet Beecher Stowe

It's a matter of taking the side of the weak against the strong, something the best people have always done.

—HARRIET BEECHER STOWE

After her success with *Uncle Tom's Cabin*, Stowe wrote two more novels in the decade that followed the release of her world-renowned antislavery work. *Dred* and *The Minister's Wooing* were published to critical acclaim and commercial success. (Stowe proudly wrote to her husband, Calvin, that *Dred* sold "one hundred thousand copies . . . in four weeks.")[9] The three novels assured her place in the literary pantheon of nineteenth-century America, but *Uncle Tom's Cabin* was the novel that would secure her reputation for the ages. During this time, Stowe established a strong professional relationship with James Fields, a partner in Ticknor & Fields, one of the most successful publishing houses in the nineteenth century. Fields was also the editor of the *Atlantic Monthly* and in this position sought to feature talented female authors. Stowe's recognized skills as a writer and her association with Fields helped ensure her continued access to the leading literary outlets of the time.

In the midst of her successes as an author, tragedy continued to haunt the Stowes' male offspring. Their sixth child, Charley, died of cholera in 1849. Henry, a nineteen-year-old student at Dartmouth College, drowned while swimming with classmates in the Connecticut River in July 1857. Frederick, the oldest son, enlisted in the Union Army. During the Battle of Gettysburg in July 1863, he was struck by a shell fragment that because of its location, lodged in his ear, could not be removed by military surgeons. Ringing, throbbing sensations, and severe headaches resulted in the young man turning to alcohol for relief. For the following several years, he struggled with alcoholic binges, a business failure in Florida, and despair over the discredit he brought to his mother and father, who, despite his problems, continued to love and support him. In 1871 Frederick signed on with the crew of a merchant ship sailing to the horn of South America. He was last seen in the port of San Francisco. Then he vanished forever.

At the conclusion of the war, Stowe applauded William Lloyd Garrison's dissolution of his Anti-Slavery Society. In Stowe's opinion, "The great deed [was] done." Abolitionist Wendell Phillips disagreed. He saw a longer-term need to establish civil rights for African Americans before declaring the deed was done and victory celebrated. Reconstruction with its black codes and nascent Ku Klux Klan organization soon had Stowe rethinking the certainty of black people's freedom during the postwar period. But for the most part, her writing was silent on the subject of rights for formerly enslaved people.

Stowe's writing after the war focused on the home and the values of domestic life while she and Calvin undertook a major home-building project in Hartford, Connecticut. Located in an area of Hartford known as Nook Farm, the Stowe's new home—called Oakholm—made them neighbors of Mark Twain's. Book royalties flowed in, and these additional financial resources, along with a desire to exchange the harsh winters of New England for the warmer climate of Florida, led Harriet and Calvin to establish a second home on the east side of the St. Johns River in Mandarin, Florida. In the sunny climate of Florida, Stowe hoped to stimulate her creative juices to complete the romance novel she was working on. Published as *Oldtown Folks*, the book received unfavorable, even searing reviews, from critics: "warmed over from previous use," "liked it less than anything she ever wrote," "tedious."[10] Bret Harte's review of his fellow writer's work in *Oldtown Folks* was merciless. He wrote in his conclusion that it was "time for Stowe and all she stood for to exit the scene."[11]

As she had with *Uncle Tom's Cabin*, Stowe fought to counter the critics and promote her book. It worked. In three months, *Oldtown Folks* had sold twenty-five thousand copies despite the scathing reviews by the literary establishment. Sensing a bias against women writers in *The Nation* newspaper, from which some of the most virulent criticism emanated, Stowe wrote the editor E. L. Godkin to protest about *The Nation's* male book reviewers. They were, Stowe complained, filled with "rudeness & heedless discourtesy" that were "as much out of place in literary criticism as in a private parlor."[12] (Henry Clapp, editor of the *Saturday Press*, waggishly labeled *The Nation* as *Stag-Nation*.)

Editor Godkin quickly apologized to Stowe for the harsh review of her *Oldtown* stories. But the damage was done. Women writers, including Stowe, saw rampant prejudice from the male reviewers in *The Nation*. These critics characterized women authors as writing "earnest, sentimental" works that dwelled on the "morbid and painful in life." When female characters stepped outside their prescribed gender roles in works written by women authors, male critics described them as "indelicate" or "unfeminine women."[13]

Women with demonstrated literary credentials, such as Lydia Maria Child, Anna Dickenson, and Harriet Beecher Stowe, banded together in a women's network of writers who demanded fair, unbiased reviews of their works that went beyond conventional depictions of women. Elizabeth Cady Stanton suggested, "Cultivated, carping men of letters, who are all the time criticizing the women of this country who do write and speak should rather work to open the doors of Harvard to both sexes."[14] Stowe, in a letter to Sara Willis Parton in October 1868, complained that Henry James was "an insolent man who is unable to comprehend [a female author's] goodness or greatness."[15]

Sensing in Stowe a kindred spirit regarding women's rights, Stanton and Susan B. Anthony wanted Stowe to serve as an editor of their publication, *Revolution*. Stowe was not pleased with the publication's name, but for Stanton and Anthony, who had spent several years building the journal's reputation, a name change was not negotiable. At the same time, Stowe was immersed in publishing "The True Story of Lady Byron's Life," so she offered a polite "no, thank you" to Stanton and Anthony.

"Lady Byron's Life" represented a departure for Stowe into the genre of nonfiction. The article chronicled the humiliation and betrayal of Lady Byron by her spouse, the poet Lord Byron. Told from a woman's viewpoint, the story crackled with reports of sexual tension and allegations of adultery and incest against the acclaimed poet. Critical reaction to this piece published by the *Atlantic Monthly* was swift and filled with outrage: "a disgusting story," "revolting and obscene." Male critics came to the defense of Lord Byron. Women, however, such as Elizabeth Cady Stanton, saw the story as one exploring a fundamental issue in male-female relations: "Mrs. Stowe's fearful picture of the abominations of our social life . . . will do much to rouse wise men to new thought on the social wrongs of the race, for whatever enslaves woman debases man; together we must rise or fall."[16]

Much as she had done with *A Key to Uncle Tom's Cabin* in response to negative reviews of *Uncle Tom's Cabin*, Stowe sought to counter criticisms of her eighteen-page Lady Byron article with a book, *Lady Byron Vindicated*. Unlike *A Key*, documents and similar tangible, written evidence were not readily available to build a substantial case in the Byron matter. Additionally, the lag in bringing the book to press and to the court of public opinion impeded her momentum in responding to her critics. Her success with *Uncle Tom's Cabin* and *A Key* to counter criticism was not repeated. A lack of substantial, compelling evidence and delays in responding to criticism resulted in Stowe's losing her case with the literary world and the general public.

Stowe suffered physically and emotionally from the adverse reaction to the Lady Byron story. In the opinion of biographer Joan D. Hedrick, "*Lady Byron Vindicated* vindicated neither Lady Byron, the case of women's rights, nor Stowe's reputation."[17]

The continuing anti-woman bias among male literary critics and the toll taken by the Lord and Lady Byron article on public opinion caused Stowe's reputation to suffer. While her reputation was redeemable over time, her ability to be a major contributor in women's rights and the suffrage movement was handicapped. The acclaim she enjoyed after publishing *Uncle Tom's Cabin* and her other successful novels was significantly diminished.

Harriet Tubman

Sir, you are a Copperhead scoundrel. I thank you or nobody to call me a colored person. I will be called black or Negro, for I am as proud of being a black woman as you are of being white.

—HARRIET TUBMAN, 1865

Tubman remained at Fort Monroe in Virginia after the war ended to provide nursing care for wounded black soldiers. Concerned about the "dreadful abuses" she saw in the hospital at the fort, she returned to Washington DC to make these problems known to federal officials. Using a contact provided to her by her friend (and landlord) secretary of state William Seward, Tubman took her case to Dr. Joseph K. Barnes, the surgeon general. She pointed out that fatalities for black soldiers were twice that of white soldiers being treated for their wounds. Dr. Barnes appointed Tubman "Nurse or Matron of the colored hospital."

Before leaving Washington to assume her duties at Fort Monroe, Tubman approached Seward about receiving pay for her wartime service. Seward, who was recovering from grievous wounds suffered as part of the Lincoln assassination plot, requested that Maj. Gen. David Hunter, with whom Tubman had served during the South Carolina campaigns of 1863, look into the matter. Despite her appeals, neither Tubman's position at the Fort Monroe hospital nor her payment for wartime services was addressed. Discouraged and needing money to pay her debts, Tubman headed to Auburn, New York, to raise funds and take care of her elderly parents. On the way to her home, Tubman stopped at Lucretia Mott's home near Philadelphia. The two talked about "Freedmen and their right to vote," a subject of great interest to both Tubman and Mott.[18]

If she thought the war had settled the issue of blacks' civil rights, Tubman soon saw the discouraging reality of the situation even in the North. She boarded the Philadelphia to New York train with a valid half-price ticket to travel to Auburn. Once on board, the conductor ordered her to sit in the smoking car while using abusive language and racial epithets. Tubman refused to be relegated to the smoke-filled car. Enraged, the conductor, with the assistance of two male passengers, forcibly removed Tubman from her seat. During the scuffle her arm was broken, her shoulder wrenched, and her ribs bruised, if not broken, as she was thrown from the train car. After recuperating in New York City, she continued on to Auburn, where she was nursed back to health by friends and family. A family friend looked into bringing a lawsuit against the railroad, but witnesses either would not agree to testify or could not be found. The lawsuit was abandoned.[19]

Following her return to Auburn, Tubman suffered from physical ailments connected with the attack on the train. Her condition prevented her from working to support her relatives and the impoverished boarders lodging at Tubman's house. The group only escaped starvation during the winter through the gifts and donations of friends and neighbors who saw the dire condition of Tubman's household. Meanwhile, she continued to pursue her claims for back pay due for services with the Union Army as a scout and nurse. Her appeals for just compensation never wavered.

One well-meaning person who sought to bring Tubman's accomplishments to the public's attention was Sarah Bradford, a writer whose works included romantic novels and short stories.[20] Bradford solicited testimonials and remembrances about Tubman from prominent people who knew her. Author Bradford spent time interviewing Tubman and recording her recollections. The result proved to be a tepid biography, written in haste and eliminating many of Tubman's personal stories and reflections. Less than half of the 132-page book was material written by Bradford. The remaining pages were letters written by those who knew Tubman personally and articles about her reprinted from newspapers. While the resulting book, *Scenes in the Life of Harriet Tubman*, fails in many ways as a serious biography, it does provide an important glimpse into her life and goes to considerable lengths to present an authentic account substantiated by testimonials. That it was published soon after her accomplishments described in the book (1869) gives the work the benefit of being a proximate account.

Biographer Kate Clifford Larson has concluded: "Tubman's narrative in *Scenes* challenged conventional stereotypes of black womanhood. To be sure, in its twin themes of resistance and liberation, it followed conventions that a predominately white audience had come to expect and understand from black memoirs. Yet more than this, *Scenes* recounts an experience that is simultaneously very personal and collective. . . . Tubman offered her life as representative of the horrors of slavery, and also staked a claim, based on an African American intellectual and spiritual tradition, to full participation in the public discourse about the still-uncertain fate of millions of ex-slaves."[21]

Julia Ward Howe

Literary affairs confused, I have no market, Chev takes away my voice, and I do not see how or where to print.

—JULIA WARD HOWE, 1865

As the war drew to a close, Julia Ward Howe found her stature in the literary world after writing "The Battle Hymn of the Republic" was withering. Interest in her work was waning, and her husband, Chev, was becoming more obstructive about her literary endeavors. He also discouraged her from accepting public speaking invitations, which were becoming a growing outlet for her creativity. Generally she would combine a reading of "Battle Hymn" with some of her poems. She traveled to Washington to give readings and later traveled to read *Passion-Flowers* to the inmates of a mental institution. Chev, meanwhile, saw his own professional opportunities diminishing, which may have contributed to his lack of support for his wife's speaking invitations. Spousal jealousy led to marital discord.

In 1867 Julia Ward Howe accompanied her husband and children to Europe on a mission to provide relief funds for Crete. She rubbed shoulders with the literary elite in London, performed readings to the American colony in Rome, and then joined her husband in Crete, where she gave readings while her husband sulked and resented sharing the stage with his popular wife. Based on this trip, she wrote the travel book *From the Oak to the Olive: A Plain Record of a Pleasant Journey.* After returning to the United States, Howe started a number of clubs for women to counter the all-male clubs (e.g., Five of Clubs, a Boston men's club) that excluded them.[22] She became the president of the New England Woman's Club and served in that role for almost forty years.

After the Civil War, Julia Ward Howe became more public about her thinking on the evolving role of women. Writing in 1869 she reflected: "The new domain now made clear to me was that of true womanhood—women no longer in her ancillary relation to her opposite, man, but in her direct relation to the divine plan and purpose, as a free agent, fully sharing with man every human right and every human responsibility. This discovery was like the addition of a new continent to the map of the world, or a new testament to the old ordinances."[23]

Now that slavery had been addressed and African Americans had become citizens (the ongoing struggle for their civil rights notwithstanding), Howe thought it time to demand "the full dignity of citizenship" for women. From a personal standpoint, this meant freeing herself from the restrictions placed on her by her husband, Chev. She longed to be free from the controlling grip that he continually sought to exercise over her. Initially Howe was reluctant to align herself with female suffragists, supposing them to be strident, unattractive bullies whose purpose was more to make trouble for men rather than promoting opportunities for women. On reflection later, she realized these perceived characteristics came from newspaper reports (written by men), Chev, and his coterie of male friends.

To determine for herself the nature of the women engaged in suffrage activities, Howe attended a women's rights forum at Boston's Horticultural Hall. Much to her surprise, the speaker, suffragist and reformer Lucy Stone, changed her opinion instantly. Howe reported that Stone was "sweet-faced and silver-voiced, the very embodiment of Goethe's 'eternal feminine' and Stone's views on women harmonized with my own aspirations."[24]

Reflecting on this watershed moment in Boston, Howe later

wrote in *Reminiscences, 1819–1899*: "These champions who had fought so long and so valiantly for the slave now turned a search light of their intelligence upon the condition of women, and demanded for the mothers of the community the civil rights that had recently been accorded the Negro. When they requested me to speak, which they did presently, I could only say 'I am with you.'"[25]

Solidifying her conversion and commitment to this new cause, Howe was elected president of the New England Woman Suffrage Association. A year later Howe became the foreign corresponding secretary of the American Woman Suffrage Association and served as an editor of the organization's publication, *Woman's Journal*. The energy, enthusiasm, and literary skills that Howe had brought to the antislavery movement were now redirected to the cause of women's suffrage.

Clara Barton

To the friends of missing persons: Miss Clara Barton has kindly offered to search for the missing prisoners of war. Please address her at Annapolis, Maryland giving name, regiment, and company of any missing prisoner.

—ABRAHAM LINCOLN, 1865

As she performed nursing duties at the close of the war in Annapolis, Maryland, Barton came in contact with men returning from Confederate prisoner of war camps in the South. Prisoners from Andersonville Prison in Georgia were among those in the worst condition physically and mentally. Seeing those men triggered Barton's next great cause, accounting for missing soldiers at the conclusion of the war.

Facing army officers who deemed it improper that a woman should undertake such a task, bureaucratic roadblocks, and an administration that was focused on concluding the war, not on dealing with the consequences of the fighting, Barton was thwarted as she attempted to gain support to begin a search for missing soldiers. Eventually a perseverant Barton found help from the president to initiate a missing soldier program. (While Barton was meeting bureaucratic dead ends and obstinate federal officials, she also was caring for her dying brother Stephen.)

Soon after Barton received the letter of approval from the president, the country was shocked and grieving over his assassination. A distraught Barton captured the nation's mourning and loss in a poem:

From the northern ocean to the southern seas was only this
A silence born of grief too mighty for words, too deep for moans.
And thus they bore him on
And laid him in the quiet grave among his own.[26]

After a period of mourning, Barton set about tackling the problem of the missing, the unidentified, and the unknown dead. Facing this monumental task, Barton used her own funds to employ several assistants, purchase stationery, and establish the Friends of the Missing Men of the United States Army. As the medical need to keep the hospital at Camp Parole in Annapolis open diminished, Barton looked for ways to accelerate her search for missing soldiers and obtain funding to support these efforts. Using a cost-benefit rationale, Barton wrote: "If it costs the United States four thousand dollars to kill an enemy in battle, is it worth five dollars or ten dollars to discover the fate of a citizen who has been reported missing?"[27]

Barton appealed directly to President Johnson for support and was successful in getting the Government Printing Office to publish the rolls of the missing. At her urging, Sen. Henry Wilson offered to pay the postage for the program's mailings. Barton and her employees developed an initial roll containing fifteen hundred names with a request for information about each. Twenty thousand copies were printed, and copies were sent to every post office in the North. The responses soon flooded in. Barton received up to 150 letters a day after the initial mailing.[28] A second roll of fifteen hundred names was developed and distributed. Barton kept a master list noting all pertinent data for each missing man along with the corresponding names and addresses of those who had provided the information.

Once again, Clara Barton's reputation as the "soldier's friend" proved accurate. For the wounded, the missing, and the dead, Barton felt an obligation to help not only while the war was raging but also long after the guns fell silent.

Sarah Josepha Hale

Our late beloved and lamented President Lincoln recognized the truth of these ideas [regarding a national Thanksgiving celebration] as soon as they were presented to him. . . . But at that time, and also in November, 1864, he was not able to influence the States in rebellion, so that the festival was necessarily incomplete. Since the close of the war, these obstacles have been removed, and President Johnson's Proclamation for the National Thanksgiving on the last Thursday of November, 1866, was observed over all the country. Thus the family union of States and Territories in Our Great Republic was fixed and hallowed by the people in the ninetieth year of American Independence.

—SARAH JOSEPHA HALE, 1868

While President Johnson's proclamation made the Thanksgiving celebration in the United States a matter of executive order, celebrations in the South were not pervasive. It would take years before Hale's optimistic notion of a national day of thanksgiving celebration across all the states and territories would be realized. Hale had helped set in motion the necessary executive proclamation for an observance, but it would take time for the enmity between North and South to dissolve so that Thanksgiving Day became a true national celebration.

As important as Thanksgiving was to Hale, she also continued to focus on her editorial duties as she had since 1828 when she became editor in chief of the *Ladies' Magazine* and then editor of *Godey's Lady's Book* in 1836. Hale found her self-described title of "editress" to be entirely appropriate. It indicated a woman of considerable skill and experience had achieved a leadership position in a profession dominated by men. Far from being a demeaning form of "editor," the editress title acknowledged that she held a chief editorial role fully equivalent to that held by a man.

While serving as an editor who had a working relationship with Nathaniel Hawthorne, Harriet Beecher Stowe, and Edgar Allan Poe in her magazine work, Hale also wrote seven volumes of poetry, six books of fiction, several volumes on cooking and housekeeping, and a nine-hundred-page reference work devoted to women in history.[29]

She also edited over two dozen books of poetry and collections of letters. This work continued throughout the Civil War without pause.
At age seventy-five she decided to conduct her editing work at home
rather than travel to the *Godey's Lady's Book* offices in Philadelphia,
a minor concession by the publication's owner to Hale's advancing
years and a daunting workload. In July 1863 Hale's beloved daughter Josepha died unexpectedly at age forty-two. Josepha had successfully launched and operated Miss S. J. Hale's Boarding and Day
School in Philadelphia for seven years prior to her passing. Josepha's death left her mother despondent; she never fully rebounded.

On a happier note in Hale's life, her five-year-long promotion in
Godey's Lady's Book of a women's college, to be started by Matthew
Vassar, reached a successful conclusion. In September 1865 Vassar
Female College began classes in Poughkeepsie, New York. Hale was
delighted that her advocacy for starting the school was effective, but
she was outraged that the trustees had included the word "female"
in the institution's name. In a letter to founder Vassar, Hale bristled:
"I write this earnestly because I wish to have Vassar College take the
lead in this great improvement in our language. . . . I plead for the
good of Vassar College, for the honor of womanhood, and the glory
of God."[30] Faced with jeopardizing "the good of Vassar," "the honor
of womanhood," and "the glory of God," Matthew Vassar promised a
correction. Several months later he wrote to Hale to tell her that her
"long cherished wishes were realized," and the "vulgarism" associated with the name would be expunged. Henceforth, the school
would be known as Vassar College and that the word "Female"
would be removed from the marble slab on the front of the college.[31]

Hale's commitment to women in the workplace and in higher
education was uncompromising. Her written words and actions
were proof of her position on the changing roles of women. Yet
unlike many of her fellow female activists, she was a woman born
in the eighteenth century, and her upbringing in postrevolutionary
New England not only shaped her views as an independent woman
but also carried with it the weight of tradition. Sarah Josepha Hale
could not accept that women had a right to vote as a growing number of female activists were advocating in post–Civil War America.
It was at the voting booth that Hale drew the line on women's rights.

11

Women in Post–Civil War America

Freedom doesn't come from the clouds, like a meteor.

—ERNESTINE ROSE, women's rights leader

Men, their rights and nothing more; women, their rights and nothing less.

—Masthead of *Revolution* newsletter of the National Woman Suffrage Association

The toxic aspects of the Civil War were all too obvious to the nation as it emerged from the four-year-long conflict. In both the North and the South, widows, grieving mothers, and wives whose husbands had suffered grievous wounds were found in virtually every city, town, and rural crossroad in the country. The nation wept over its losses. Yet beneath this sad toxic stratum of suffering, there was a tonic of opportunity for women, especially those women living in the North and the West. Women who had performed voluntary services, headed organizations that supported the war effort, and took over jobs left vacant by soldiers serving in the armies now found they had the skills, the experience, and the self-confidence to assume responsibilities unimagined in antebellum America.

The teaching profession expanded in numbers and drew women into its ranks as teaching opportunities flourished in the western states and in the South among the formerly enslaved children. The Freedmen's Bureau actively recruited teachers for schools educating black children. To meet this growing need for teachers, women's colleges and coeducational colleges and universities began admitting female students. Between 1870 and 1900, the number of women college students in the nation jumped nearly eightfold from eleven thousand students in 1870 to eighty-five thousand in 1900. Five years after the end of the Civil War, women were 21 percent of students attending college. By the turn of the twentieth century, they represented 35 percent of the student bodies of colleges and universities.[1]

State universities in Kansas, Indiana, Minnesota, Missouri, Michigan, and California began opening their classrooms to female students. In the Northeast, in addition to women's colleges such as Smith, Wellesley, and Vassar being founded, some of the elite universities for men such as Harvard and Columbia took small steps by starting associated "annex" colleges—Radcliffe and Barnard, respectively—for women students. Upper-middle-class young women now found the doors to colleges slowly opening for them, but women from families with modest incomes found the barrier to higher education was financial. Scholarships, grants, or college loans were not available for qualified prospective students. It would be decades after the Civil War before intellectually gifted women who were not from wealthy families had access to other sources of funds to pay for their college educations.

The new systems of mass production that proved so important to wartime production also expanded rapidly after the war. Between 1860 and 1870, the number of manufacturers in the North increased by 80 percent.[2] Patterson, New Jersey was typical. Four silk mills employed 690 workers before the war. Following the war, ten more mills were established, adding jobs that brought the total employment at Patterson silk mills to 8,000 workers. Further fueling the growth of manufacturing, a network of rail lines helped bring products to market at a low price. Despite this explosive growth in the manufacturing sector, women did not enjoy a fair share of the employment opportunities, as women becoming wage earners in industries typically employing men met widespread resistance. Therefore, women found employment in occupations that mirrored their home skills—for example, nursing, teaching, sewing, and domestic service. One occupation that saw rapid growth in female employees was office work. In 1870 there were nineteen thousand female office workers in the United States.

By 1900 that number had grown to seventy-five thousand. In 1870 4.5 percent of office stenographers and typists were women; by 1880 that number had grown to 40 percent.[3]

The expansion west after the Civil War also saw women finding new opportunities that sprang from frontier life. According to historian Harriet Sigerman:

> The frontier provided many ways for women to earn a livelihood while they also worked for the common good. Women started schools in their cabins or were dispatched by school boards to teach. . . . Women also cooked, sewed, and did laundry for others, especially for single men. Some took in boarders or became innkeepers, others peddled produce from their gardens . . . while other women became trail guides, newspaper editors, or professional writers. Some succeeded as ranchers or mine owners, either after their husbands died or because they simply had better business skills than their spouses. Women doctors and lawyers also went west.[4]

Women reformers following the Civil War had little interest in working women—with the notable exception of Susan B. Anthony, who had a keen interest in women's economic status, including employment. Whether the women leading reform efforts considered other issues (prohibition, pacifism, women's suffrage) more pressing or they were satisfied with the progress being made by women on the employment front, other than Anthony, reformers largely ignored expanding occupational opportunities for women.

To meet women's diverse interests and commitments, women's clubs sprang up throughout the nation after the Civil War, with especially strong growth in the Northeast and Midwest. Some of these organizations had a cultural focus such as reading literature and poetry, others involved causes such as temperance (e.g., the Women's Christian Temperance Union), and others had a professional focus. For example, journalist Jane Cunningham Croly started the Sorosis Club in New York City when she was blocked from attending the all-male New York Press Club. The Boston Young Women's Christian Association was started in 1867 to aid single young women coming to cities for employment. The Working Women's Protective Union was started in 1868 to advocate for higher wages and shorter workdays, while the Daughters of St. Crispin was started in 1869 as a trade union for female shoemakers.

In 1869 Elizabeth Cady Stanton and Susan B. Anthony started the National Woman Suffrage Association (NWSA) to work for women's right to vote. Stanton and Anthony refused to support the Fifteenth Amendment that granted black men's suffrage unless women's suffrage was also part of the amendment language. That same year, the American Woman Suffrage Association (AWSA) was established by Lucy Stone and her husband, Henry Blackwell. The AWSA supported the Fifteenth Amendment and worked to establish women's voting rights at the state levels. The two organizations were rivals until 1890 when, after three years of negotiations, they merged into one group, the National American Woman Suffrage Association.

While Northern women's clubs ran the gamut of cultural and political interests, women's clubs in the postwar South reflected more traditional, nonpolitical interests with clubs that sought to involve members in literature and poetry as part of their cultural focus or to work in the temperance movement, the creation of settlement houses, and other missionary endeavors. Suffrage was not on the agenda for most Southern women's clubs. The emphasis on "good works" rather than political causes was due to the strong influence of religious denominations on Southern women's clubs.[5]

Those women who thought that the end of slavery and the institution of black civil rights after the war finally meant an opportunity to grant voting rights for women were astounded at what took place. The Fourteenth Amendment to the Constitution, enacted on July 9, 1868, guaranteed citizens "equal protection under the law" that covered rights for black and white men but not for women of any race. Equally disconcerting, the Fifteenth Amendment to the Constitution, ratified in February 1870, prohibited states from denying citizens the right to vote "on account of race, color, or previous condition of servitude." No mention was made of gender. These two amendments were crucial victories for African American men, but they left women out of one of the fundamental rights of citizenship—the right to vote. Frederick Douglass's statement that when women were "dragged from their houses and hung upon lampposts" like black men, then they too would need the ballot's protection did nothing to encourage support for the voting rights for half of the nation's population.[6]

Harriet Beecher Stowe

Domestic and family duties are not degrading and unworthy of [woman's] powers. . . . We hold that . . . there is nothing as sacred as . . . the time honored institutions of the HEARTH AND HOME.

—HARRIET BECHER STOWE, *Hearth and Home*

When it came to women's rights and the issue of suffrage, Stowe's guiding beacons were the Declaration of Independence and the U.S. Constitution. Voicing her opinion in the decidedly nonfeminist *Hearth and Home* periodical, coeditor Stowe posited: "Now the question arises, which is in fault, the Declaration of Independence, or the customs and laws of America as to woman? Is taxation without representation tyranny or not?" In the same vein, Stowe applauded John Stuart Mill's *The Subjection of Women* (1869) because of its forthright stand on woman having the same natural rights as man. Coeditor Stowe also attempted to enlist Ralph Waldo Emerson to submit a two-column article on women's suffrage for *Hearth and Home,* but her editorial priorities changed and follow-up with Emerson was put aside. Emerson never contributed the piece despite the fifty-dollar payment he was to receive as an honorarium.[7]

All during her time as coeditor of *Hearth and Home,* Stowe demonstrated a nuanced approach to feminism. While she strongly supported women's right to vote, she also saw the positive side of the domestic duties of women. Rather than "free women from the home," she wanted domestic work to be more prized. When women did enter the workforce outside the home, she wanted them to be paid what a man would be paid for an equivalent job. Man was not the enemy, in Stowe's thinking, but a coequal.

At his wife's urging, Calvin Stowe, wearing his biblical scholar mantle, found numerous scriptural references for the justification of women's rights. For Harriet Beecher Stowe, feminists such as Elizabeth Cady Stanton and Susan B. Anthony were too radical in their stands on women's rights, favoring, in Stowe's way of thinking, "free divorce and free love." The very name of the Stanton-Anthony publication for NWSA members, *Revolution*, was anathema to Stowe. Historian Nancy Koester has summarized Stowe's perspective as a feminist leader: "She disliked both frilly femininity *and* strident feminism," for in Stowe's view, "the right kind of woman [was] neither a tyrant nor a martyr."[8]

Stowe's rejection of the "radical" approach to women's rights came to a head when she ridiculed feminist Victoria Woodhall in a thinly disguised character named Miss Audacia Dangyereyes in her novel *My Wife and I*, which was serialized in the *Christian Union* publication from November 1870 to November 1871. Following this serialization and Stowe's public characterization of Woodhall as "a witch" and as having "demonic possession" over her sister Isabella, Woodhall retaliated by accusing Stowe's brother Rev. Henry Ward Beecher of adultery with a member of his congregation. Beecher was eventually exonerated, but the bad blood between Stowe and the progressive wing of the women's rights activists continued.[9]

In addition to *My Wife and I*, which exacerbated the Woodhall-Stowe/Beecher feud, Stowe also continued to write popular society novels that confirmed her ability to capture domestic scenes with veracity and create vibrant dialogue that attracted a loyal following of readers. *Pink and White Tyranny* and *We & Our Neighbors* were works that continued to keep author Stowe in the public eye with homespun narratives featuring women who were bright and independent but did not venture far from the confines of hearth and home. Following these novels, she wrote *Palmetto Leaves* about her experiences in a new seasonal home that she and Calvin enjoyed in Florida. (Some have suggested that these sketches convinced a number of her readers in the cold climates to consider spending their winters in Florida, turning Stowe into the state's first real estate public relations agent.) Next, Stowe wrote a series of sketches she called *Woman in Sacred History*. For this series, Stowe drew on research provided by Calvin.

Beyond her interest in supporting women's causes in her writing (in her own moderate way), Stowe also had a strong interest in animal welfare. She wrote "The Rights of Dumb Animals," an article that was based on sources gathered by the Society for the Prevention of Cruelty to Animals. Supporting a proposed Florida law to protect birds from overhunting, Stowe wrote *The Semi-Tropical* in 1877. Despite her strong advocacy and appeal to the public, the Florida legislature chose not to issue a protective law for birds.

As she grew older, Stowe backed away from her father's rigorous, New England Calvinism, preferring a theology that included more forgiveness and less emphasis on original sin. After the Civil War, both Harriet Stowe and her husband began dabbling in spiritualism, seeking contact with the departed through séances and similar experiences. Publicly, both Harriet and Calvin demurred when asked about their adherence to spiritualism as practiced by notables such as Horace Greeley and William Lloyd Garrison. She insisted, when writing for Christian periodicals, that readers needed to rely on Christianity, but privately she read spiritualist literature and attended séances. When her head guided her emotions, she rallied behind Christianity. When her heart guided her, she practiced some blend of Christianity and spiritualism. Those times when her heart guided her, her thoughts turned to her lost sons, Henry and Fred. Several times she and Calvin sought to communicate with Fred in the spiritual world. In 1883, in a letter to her sister Isabella, Stowe wrote of receiving a message from her son Fred through a medium. Isabella also reported receiving a message from Fred during a spiritualist encounter.[10]

Harriet Tubman

Harriet Tubman, the woman who had been hailed as "the greatest heroine of her age," drifted into obscurity after the Civil War ended and the old abolitionist vanguard began to pass from the scene.

—MILTON C. SERNETT, *Harriet Tubman: Myth, Memory, and History*

It is almost inconceivable in modern times that a person with the visibility and reputation of Harriet Tubman would simply drop from public view, as biographer Milton Sernett has claimed. In fact, in 1893 Dr. M. A. Majors published a piece *Noted Negro Women: Their Triumphs and Activities* as a tribute to African American women. Of the nearly three hundred women whose sketches appear in the work, Harriet Tubman is not mentioned.

Numerous reasons have been given for Tubman's virtual eclipse in the public eye during the last third of the nineteenth century, but three interconnected factors are the most compelling: Tubman's illiteracy, her financial situation, and her commitment to community charities. While books were written about Tubman (e.g., Sarah Bradford's *Scenes in the Life of Harriet Tubman*), because of her illiteracy, Tubman could not write her own book or articles based on her experiences using her own voice. Unlike other prominent women in the latter part of the nineteenth century, Tubman was unable to write her memoir and then take that narrative before audiences in personal appearances.

Coupled with her inability to write her own experiences for an audience receptive to wartime exploits, Tubman's financial state was dire after the war. She had to work to provide for her immediate family and the numerous needy people who came to her seeking food, clothing, and shelter. She had no time for engaging in activities such as public speaking that did not have an immediate cash benefit. (Tubman's numerous appeals to receive back pay or a pension for her military duties during the war were ignored by the federal government.) It was only through financial gifts from friends and neighbors in Auburn, New York, that Tubman and her many dependents were able to survive.

Biographer Emma Telford has written that Tubman's "doors have been open to the needy, the most utterly friendless and helpless of her race. The aged . . . the babe deserted, the demented, the epileptic, the blind, the paralyzed, the consumptive."[11] Tubman's own frail, elderly parents were her responsibility, and her husband Nelson Davis, a Union veteran who married Tubman following his release from the military, was diagnosed with tuberculosis. His care also fell to Tubman as she struggled to provide for the growing number of persons who depended on her support. Tubman's own health was precarious. Recurring bouts of headaches, seizures, and trance-like spells plagued her throughout the post-war years. (As noted in chapter 3, these health issues were likely due to temporal lobe epilepsy that resulted from being struck in the head with an iron weight when she was a young girl.)

Along with her personal and family responsibilities that limited her contact with the national movements springing up after the war, Tubman's own interests focused on those in her community who had urgent needs—usually involving food, shelter, and clothing. While she never expressed it in this manner, Tubman was an advocate of the aphorism "Charity begins at home." In addition to using her own home as a shelter for those she took in, she wanted to establish a residence to provide for the indigent. In 1896 she purchased twenty-five acres adjacent to her property to establish the Harriet Tubman Home.[12] According to her neighbor Helen Tatlock, Tubman accommodated "a great number of young and old, black and white, all poorer than she."[13] Tubman had a sincere interest in women's rights and the civil liberties of African Americans, but in the decades that followed the Civil War, her priority was helping those Auburn neighbors who had immediate, basic needs. Tubman's dreams of caring for others in her community were always greater than her meager financial resources. However, her credo remained constant throughout the difficult times: "Missus, it wasn't me, it was the Lord! I always told him, I trust you. I don't know where to go or what to do, but I expect you to lead me. And he always did."[14]

During the 1870s and 1880s when conventions and gatherings for women's suffrage and black men's rights were being conducted on a regular basis in New England and New York State, Tubman was not involved. Her financial constraints and her focus on local community involvement kept her close to Auburn. Later, perhaps influenced by her longtime friend Lucretia Mott, Tubman did align herself with Susan B. Anthony's National Woman Suffrage Association. Historical details on the exact nature of Tubman's involvement in suffrage conventions are sketchy, but it is known that in November 1896, Susan B. Anthony escorted Tubman to the podium to speak to a women's suffrage convention in Rochester, New York. A *Rochester Democrat and Chronicle* reporter wrote: "With her hand held in Miss Anthony's, she impressed one with the venerable dignity of her appearance . . . through it all there shows an honesty and true benevolence of purpose which commanded respect."[15] Tubman described to the audience her experiences with the Underground Railroad and related events. While her talk did not address the suffrage movement per se, Tubman was the embodiment of the strong, independent woman who had achieved heroic feats on her own against overwhelming odds. She was a model feminist with exceptional bona fides.

Earlier that same year, Tubman attended the inaugural meeting of the National Association of Colored Women in Washington DC. She received a standing ovation upon entering the convention hall, was admiringly addressed as "Mother Tubman," and was revered as a "great black liberator." At the convention she discussed her role in the Underground Railroad and her experiences with the Union Army. Tubman was at the meeting to endorse suffrage for black women without addressing the subject in detail. She also used the opportunity to solicit funds for her home and hospital for the indigent.

After years of hand-to-mouth existence in Auburn, Tubman's financial picture improved slightly in the late 1890s. A new edition of Bradford's *Harriet: The Moses of Her People* was published in 1886 and brought with it increased recognition and a flow of royalties and gifts. In October 1895 Tubman began receiving an eight-dollar monthly widow's pension resulting from her marriage to Nelson Davis. She was also given a lump sum of five hundred dollars to cover the sixty-month delay in the approval process. A few years later, she was given a twenty-dollar monthly pension— eight dollars for being Davis's widow and twelve dollars for her service as a nurse with the Union Army. The funds helped Tubman avoid total privation, but these minimal payments did not reflect her significant contributions during the war.

Queen Victoria—impressed by Tubman's achievements—sent her a silver medal commemorating Victoria's diamond jubilee. The queen also invited Tubman to attend her royal birthday party in England. Tubman, with regret, had to decline the invitation because of her responsibilities and limited funds.

Julia Ward Howe

In my own youth, women were isolated from each other by the very intensity of their personal consciousness. I thought of myself and of other women in this way. We thought that superior women ought to have been born men. A blessed change is that which we have witnessed.

—JULIA WARD HOWE, 1899

Howe's fame associated with writing the "Battle Hymn of the Republic" was the proverbial mixed blessing. Her daughters, writing in their mother's biography *Julia Ward Howe, 1819–1910*, reported: "It was a joy to her to be associated with the *Battle Hymn*, yet she sometimes grieved a little because this so greatly overshadowed all her other literary productions."[16] Howe's fame with "Battle Hymn," however, did open doors for her as she pursued other causes in the latter decades of the nineteenth century—women's suffrage and pacifism.

Howe's prewar position on suffrage changed significantly to her postwar advocacy of women's rights and suffrage. Her "Women's Rights Questions" speech, believed to have been written in the 1840s or 1850s, was in stark contrast to her later position. Historian Valarie Ziegler has referred to the speech as "a parody of Julia's later suffrage writings." In "Questions," Howe separates the outer world of "War, Commerce, in a degree, Government and Public Instruction" as the sole province of men. Women were confined to the "functions of the inner world of home—bearing and raising children, domestic economy, and elementary instruction."[17]

By the 1870s, Howe's position on women's rights had completely changed in both her words and deeds. In an 1885 speech, Howe confided, "No one could be more opposed to woman suffrage than I was twenty years ago. . . . Let me say to fashionable women . . . that the time is coming when suffrage will be fashionable."[18]

In addition to promoting woman's suffrage in her writing and talks, Howe joined the organizations actively advocating women's rights. Aligning herself with the moderate women's rights organization in 1869, the AWSA, she also became the editor of the organization's publication, *Woman's Journal*. Howe was the founder and an active member of the Association of American Women (1876–97), the president of the New England Woman's Club, the cofounder of the Massachusetts Woman Suffrage Association and the New England Woman Suffrage Association, and the founder of the General Federation of Women's Clubs in 1893 and its director for five years.

With memories of the death and destruction of the American Civil War still fresh in her mind, Howe was moved to become an advocate of world peace as the Franco-Prussian War broke out in 1870. The author of the "Battle Hymn" now held: "From the bosom of the devastated earth, a voice goes up with our own. It says: 'Disarm, disarm!' The sword of murder is not the balance of Justice. Blood does not wipe out dishonor, nor violence vindicate possession."[19] For Howe the "terrible swift sword" was sheathed, and the "Hero, born of woman" of her anthem would be admonished not to "crush the serpent with his heel."

Howe called on mothers around the world to embrace a crusade on behalf of peace. She participated in two meetings in New York City to promote peace that attracted capacity crowds. Several years later, Howe visited England to organize the first women's peace conference with global reach. The following year she worked to establish the observance of a Mother's Day for Peace in early June. Through Howe's inspiration, a group in Philadelphia formed a Julia Ward Howe Peace Band and observed a Mother's Day for Peace for over fifty years.[20] Her efforts also led the Federation of Women's Clubs, the Council of Mothers, and the National Council of Women to support world peace. Howe's efforts to promote Mother's Day and world peace together eventually fell victim to commercial interests. In 1912 Anna Jarvis trademarked "Mother's Day" as a commercial holiday, and President Woodrow Wilson made the second Sunday in May a national holiday for Mother's Day in 1914. Howe's Mother's Day for Peace was soon eclipsed.[21]

Meanwhile, Chev Howe's grip on his wife's literary output and speaking opportunities began to wane as his health deteriorated in the early 1870s. On January 9, 1876, he died after suffering a "convulsive attack" at home. After almost thirty-three years of marriage, Julia Ward Howe grieved Chev's passing and the memories they had shared, but she recognized that a door had now opened wide for her. Five days after his death, Howe wrote in her diary: "Began my new life today."[22]

Now unfettered by Chev's restraints, Howe plunged into her suffrage and pacifist activities. Her writing output surged. She authored five books, including a biography of Margaret Fuller, her own autobiography, a volume of poems, and two other books, all published between 1881 and 1899. No longer constrained as a public speaker, Howe was active on the lecture circuit, covering towns and cities from Buffalo to Minneapolis. She read "Battle Hymn" at Longfellow's memorial service and continued her lecture tour in the West: Chicago, St. Paul, Spokane, Walla Walla, Tacoma, Seattle, and Portland. At the Grand Opera House in San Francisco, the audience rose to their feet to sing "Battle Hymn" before its appreciative lyricist.

Howe basked in the glow of her "public rituals of veneration," as historian Valarie Ziegler has described Julia Ward Howe's triumphant return to the public eye. In 1889 while visiting Kansas, one exuberant legislator suggested that she run for the U.S. Senate. She declined, perhaps musing on the irony of being encouraged to run for an office for which she could not vote. Now released from the smothering presence of Samuel Gridley Howe, Julia Ward Howe could join the women she spoke of in her own women's rights exhortations who were liberated and "who found a new scope for their activities."[23]

Clara Barton

Only an opportunity was waiting for woman to prove to man that she could be in earnest—that she had character and firmness of purpose— that she was good for something in an emergency. . . . The war offered her this opportunity.

—CLARA BARTON, 1868

Following the war, Barton immersed herself in the task of determining the fate of missing Union soldiers. Her enthusiasm for the work was fueled by her own efforts at the Andersonville Prison site in the summer of 1865, locating and marking nearly thirteen thousand Union graves. Accompanied by a former prisoner of the camp, Dorence Atwater, and Capt. James M. Moore, the Union officer charged with battlefield cemeteries, Barton was appalled by what she saw: "My heart sickened and stood still, my brain whirled, and the light of my eyes went out, and I said 'surely this was not the gate of hell, but hell itself.'"[24]

What on the surface appeared to be an unsullied attempt to identify the dead Union soldiers and establish a cemetery for them at Andersonville was roiled by discontent beneath the surface. Atwater was accused of both larceny involving the roll of names he had prepared of the Andersonville dead and "conduct to prejudice of good order and military discipline." He was dishonorably discharged from the Union Army, fined three hundred dollars, and sentenced to eighteen months in prison.[25] Barton was outraged that a former prisoner of war who had survived the South's most notorious prisoner camp would be treated as a common criminal over the nebulous ownership of the deceased prisoner list that Atwater had created. (Atwater was released after two months in prison upon an order from President Andrew Johnson.) Additionally, Barton's relationship with Captain Moore was tumultuous. Barton, on the one hand, found he was rude, a backstabber, and marginally competent. Moore, on the other hand, found Barton imperious, vindictive, and all too eager to appeal to her high-level contacts (e.g., Sen. Henry Wilson) when things did not go her way. It was clearly a case of an intense civilian with a fragile ego trying to accomplish much while dealing with a by-the-numbers, regular army functionary.

Barton's financial and emotional resources were being rapidly depleted when her old friend and mentor Francis D. Gage ("Aunt Fanny") came to her rescue. Gage, with help from Barton, petitioned Congress to appropriate fifteen thousand dollars to support Barton's work with missing soldiers. Barton appeared before the Joint Committee on Reconstruction—the only woman to give testimony during the committee's hearings—to review her work. Less than a month later, Congress approved the entire amount requested to reimburse Barton for her efforts on the behalf of missing soldiers and their families. (Barton may have been the first woman to testify before Congress.)[26]

Gage also encouraged Barton to take her war experiences on the lecture circuit and wrote letters to those who might consider Barton as a lecturer. Titling her lecture "Work and Incidents of Army Life," Barton lunged into the speaking engagement world with her usual zeal and energetic pace. She began by delivering lectures in New York State and New England, speaking in schools, churches, town meeting rooms, lyceum halls, and other welcoming venues where large audiences could be addressed. The crowds she attracted were sizable and appreciative. As one newspaper reported: "It was as if this gifted woman found our heartstrings and was skillfully playing a sad minor hymn upon them."[27] Her fame spread. Soon Barton's lecture schedule included towns and cities throughout the Midwest and the West.

Initially having to overcome severe stage fright, this diminutive figure with the mellifluous voice, dressed in black silk, began to take command of the stage. Her experience as a classroom teacher and as a persuasive advocate who had addressed numerous government and military leaders during the war resulted in polished, compelling talks peppered with war stories and other harrowing experiences delivered with a growing theatrical flair. Lecturing before capacity crowds and earning seventy-five to one hundred dollars per talk, Barton was now reaping the financial rewards for her work. (For lectures to benefit soldiers, Barton usually waived her speaking fee.) Thanks to her lecture activities, Barton's bank account was healthy, and her ego was equally well compensated by the accolades surrounding each talk.

While on the speaking circuit in November 1867, Barton met Elizabeth Cady Stanton and Susan B. Anthony as she changed trains in Cleveland, Ohio. Barton found herself a kindred spirit with these two leaders of women's suffrage; she did not need to be convinced to turn her focus to the expansion of women's rights on political and social fronts. Barton continued to lecture on her wartime experiences, but she would emphasize what women were capable of accomplishing, using her own life as an example. Here was a woman who was not merely a proponent of women's rights but also a practitioner with an impressive history of accomplishing what she and others were preaching.

Barton's lectures were advertised in *Revolution*, the publication of Stanton and Anthony's association. At one of her lectures, the introduction of Barton included a negative reference to "the style of Susan B. Anthony and her clique." Barton held back until the conclusion of her talk and then responded to the introduction with fervor: "You glorify the women who made their way to the front to reach you in your misery, and nurse you back to life. You called us angels. Who opened the way for women to go and make it possible? Who but that detested 'clique' who through the years of opposition, obloquy, toil and pain had openly claimed that women had rights, should have the privilege to exercise them. The right to her own property, her own children, her own home, her just individual claim before the law, to her freedom of action, to her personal liberty." Barton concluded her talk with: "Boys, three cheers for Susan B. Anthony!" Barton reported later that "the very windows shook in their casements" in response.[28]

Despite her agreement with the basic principles of the women's rights movement, Barton did differ with the position of suffrage as a core theme. For this reason, she had her name removed as vice president of the National Woman Suffrage Association. She also disagreed with the NWSA position, advocated by Susan B. Anthony, that disapproved of the passage of the Fifteenth Amendment because it gave race precedence over gender. Barton believed that black civil rights were rightly given priority in the constitutional amendment. Women's rights could be addressed later, according to Barton.

On the advice of her physician, as Barton again began suffering exhaustion from her rigorous lecture activities, she went to Europe to restore her health. While in Europe, Barton met people and experienced relief work that would shape her future. In Geneva, Switzerland, Barton met Dr. Louis Appia who was a representative of the International Red Cross. She was fascinated by the concept of a relief organization and immediately saw the application for a Red Cross in America. She also met Grand Duchess Louise of Baden, daughter of Kaiser Wilhelm, who invited her to work in the Red Cross Hospital in Baden. The duchess was also instrumental in getting Barton involved in treating the casualties of the Franco-Prussian War in Strasbourg. The need for an American Red Cross to support relief efforts in the United States became increasingly apparent to Barton as she saw the impact of the Red Cross in Europe. Her European sojourn gave her the contacts, the experience, and the motivation to pursue a Red Cross organization in the United States. Referring to Barton's time in Europe and specifically her relief efforts in Strasbourg, historian Elizabeth Brown Pryor wrote: "This was Clara Barton as she liked best to picture herself: the Lady Bountiful, sowing dignity and hope to the afflicted, reaping loyalty and love in return."[29] Clara Barton now had a cause, a mission that fit her skills, her experience, and her passion for helping those in need.

Returning to the United States after an absence of four years, Barton's financial situation was secure, but her mental health was still fragile. She sought treatment at a sanitarium in the small upstate New York town of Dansville. As her emotional health grew stronger, her interest in founding an American Red Cross was coming into sharper focus and energizing her. The major stumbling block to its formation was that the nation had not approved the Treaty of Geneva, an essential prerequisite in establishing a Red Cross organization. Officials in the federal government, still struggling with Reconstruction and the demands of a postwar economy, saw action on the Geneva Treaty as a low priority.

Summoning her talents of persuasion, marshaling the backing of senior federal and state officials, and employing her indefatigable spirit to achieve positive results, Barton began her campaign to establish an American Red Cross. Senators, congressmen, the press, veterans' organizations, and two presidents of the United States—James A. Garfield and Chester A. Arthur—found themselves a part of Barton's five-year campaign to make the American Red Cross a reality. On March 16, 1882, the U.S. Senate ratified the Treaty of Geneva, and it was immediately signed into law by President Arthur. Now that the treaty was approved, the country could launch its own Red Cross organization. Once again, over seemingly impossible odds, the petite, sixty-year-old woman, often plagued with self-doubts and bouts of crushing depression, had prevailed.

Barton noted the long-awaited success in her diary with a few brief comments preceded by a succinct phrase written in red at the top of the page: "Treaty Ratified."[30]

Sarah Josepha Hale

[T]here seems now some fear lest [a woman] should, in her eagerness to show the world what she can do, aim rather at doing men's work as the best proof of her ability. This would be a serious mistake.

—SARAH JOSEPHA HALE, 1870

Hale's chief responsibility following the Civil War was to build circulation lost when Southern readers dropped their subscriptions from *Godey's Lady's Book*. The publication had outperformed its chief competitor, *Peterson's Magazine*, in its number of pages before the war but fell second to the Peterson publication during the war. Revamping content and introducing enhanced illustrations to bring Southern readers back while retaining current readers, Hale saw *Godey's* circulation steadily rise. Readers found the new content compelling and enjoyed the steel engravings and color fashion plates that illustrated the text in the updated publication.

The rich literary content in the prewar *Godey's Book*—with works by Edgar Allan Poe, Harriet Beecher Stowe, William Cullen Bryant, and a deep bench of other talented, literate men and women writers—was diminished after the war. A so-called Brown Decade or Dreadful Decade followed the conclusion of the Civil War. Critics complained that dime novels and folksy rhymes were displacing serious literature with the public. A new generation of gifted writers with backgrounds in journalism, such as Mark Twain and Bret Harte, were coming on the literary scene out of the West, but these new writers were not being published by *Godey's*. Some of the magazine's standbys continued to write for the publication: Marion Harland, Mary W. Janvrin, Fitz-Greene Halleck, and Catharine M. Sedgwick, called "the most popular American female novelist before Harriet Beecher Stowe." Frances E. Hodgson began writing for *Godey's* in the 1870s. Hodgson, an accomplished and popular writer, later wrote the children's classics *The Secret Garden, Little Lord Fauntleroy,* and *The Little Princess.*[31]

Both Hale and her publisher, Louis Godey, after publishing the *Lady's Book* for forty-two years, were growing older and had neither the energy nor the understanding of how America was changing to revitalize their publication to be relevant for contemporary readers. Biographer Norma R. Fryatt observed: "Sarah Hale's Editor's Table continued to have a lively quality, but for the most part the word 'predictable' best described this magazine, which had weathered the financial and political storms of the nation but seemed now to be settling into a complacent routine."[32] Like its esteemed founder and editor, *Godey's Lady's Book* was growing old and tired. In 1877 Sarah Josepha Hale, age eighty-nine, stepped down after fifty years as an editor.

The following year, publisher Louis A. Godey, who also authored the Arm-Chair column in the magazine, died at home while reading in his armchair.

Hale had well expressed her public views on the work she thought women should take on: telegraph operators, teachers, post mistresses, and a host of occupations in the arts such as writers and artists. For all these occupations that Hale considered appropriate for women, she also strongly believed in their earning equal pay. Hale's advocacy for women's economic, banking, and legal rights for property ownership, however, did not extend into the political realm. Suffrage, reasoned Hale, would not get a woman a job that paid more or help a woman deal with the challenges of raising a family. Rather than cast a ballot, she thought, women would do better to advocate for the positions they believed in and use their influence for change. In 1870 Hale registered her alarm at the "dangerous boon" represented by the suffrage movement. She claimed that the "complainers represent a very small fraction of American women."[33]

In addition to her disapproval of women voting, Hale also was troubled by the growing practice of women speaking out in public forums on the subject of women's rights. A longtime mentor and friend of Elizabeth Oakes Smith's, Hale found Smith's speaking engagements "indecorous" and "presumptuous," even "indecent." Hale refused to attend a lecture by Smith in Philadelphia and became estranged from her friend over the issue of public speaking. Smith admitted many years later in her journal that the experience of losing an old friend was "painful" and that she "took it to heart rather seriously."[34]

Sarah Josepha Hale who, for fifty years as a widow and single mother, had written extensively and passionately about the role of women and exemplified the life of an independent professional woman, now found herself out of sync with her contemporary feminists. With many reservations, Hale passed the torch of women's rights to a new generation of activists who were preparing the way for achieving women's suffrage in the twentieth century.

12

Concluding Remarkable Lives

Each of the five better angels lived long, productive lives. Two of the women, Tubman and Howe, lived to be ninety-one. And with the exception of Harriet Beecher Stowe, the women retained their mental acuity to the very end. Stowe died at the youngest age (eighty-five years) and showed signs of dementia—according to her children—several years prior to her passing on July 1, 1896. All the other women continued to write or lecture up to their final days even as their physical health grew frail. By twenty-first-century standards, their vitality and longevity are remarkable. By nineteenth-century norms, their life spans were preternatural.

In the mid-nineteenth century, women's life expectancy at birth was forty-two years of age. (Male life expectancy was forty.) By the 1900s the life expectancy for women had risen to forty-eight years of age. Demographers attribute this increase in life expectancy to lower birth rates for women of child-bearing age in the United States. Deaths during and immediately following childbirth took a heavy toll on women before and during the nineteenth century. Improved medical care and better nutrition also had a positive effect on female longevity by the turn of the twentieth century.[1]

Even with this positive increase in life span for the average American woman by the beginning of the twentieth century, the better angels were outliving their average American sisters by four decades. Each of the five was subject to illnesses and maladies— such as severe and chronic headaches—but none seemed to have had a long-term effect on their life spans. If anything, the health problems they did endure seemed to make them even more resilient. Furthermore, their regimens of writing (except for Tubman) and lecturing on a variety of subjects continued to challenge their minds into old age.

The five women, especially Clara Barton, worked hard to keep their ages from being a disqualifier for doing the tasks they thought necessary to advance their causes. Makeup, hair dye, and up-to-date clothing helped convey a more youthful appearance. Many who attended their lectures in their later years or read their books and articles most likely did not know that they were listening to or reading the works of octogenarians. These women had been part of the national scene for so long and had contributed so much that the public may have assumed these five American icons were immune to aging.

Each of the five women would have agreed with the sentiment of twentieth-century poet May Sarton: "Do not deprive me of old age. I have earned it."

Sarah Josepha Hale: October 24, 1788–April 30, 1879

Growing old! Growing old! Do they say it of me?
Do they hint my fine fancies are faded and fled?
That my garden of life, like the winter swept tree,
Is frozen and dying, or fallen and dead?
Is the heart growing old, when each beautiful thing,
Like a landscape at eve, looks more tenderly bright.
And love sweeter seems, as the bird's wand'ring wing
Draws nearer her nest at the coming of night?

—SARAH JOSEPHA HALE, age 90

In her valedictory Editor's Table column in *Godey's Lady's Book*, Hale enumerated those accomplishments of which she was most proud for her readers. At the top she listed her priority of promoting education for women in America. Beginning in her youth when her brother Horatio tutored her using his recently acquired knowledge from Dartmouth College, Hale knew the benefit of higher education for women firsthand. Denied access to higher education because of her gender, she used her power as an editor of one of America's most widely read publications to promote college education for women. Her continuing general appeals for female scholars in *Godey's* and her specific efforts in advocating the establishment of Vassar College were tangible evidence of her commitment. Hale saw Emma Willard, founder of the Troy Female Seminary, as a leader in furthering women's education, and the two enjoyed a long and close friendship. (Both of Hale's daughters attended Willard's school.)

Hale was delighted to see that graduates of women's schools were going into the teaching profession. She found that "woman, as an instructress is, at last, in her rightful place." Hale's daughter Josepha had received her teaching certificate after attending Mrs. Willard's school.

Hale also considered her efforts to establish a national Thanksgiving Day to have been a crucial part of the process of reconciliation as the Civil War drew to a close. As with women's education, she thought that the celebration of thanksgiving on a national scale would have benefits in decades to come. She also took pride in helping establish the Ladies' Medical Missionary Society and in promoting the Female Medical College of Philadelphia, which played an important early role in educating female physicians. Likewise, she felt her work in helping restore George Washington's home at Mount Vernon would have a lasting impact and promote national unity. For each of these projects, she used the considerable power of her pen to motivate people to take action. Hale's ability to persuade rarely failed to achieve results.

Writing her farewell in *Godey's* a year and four months before her death, Hale said goodbye to her readers: "And now, having reached my ninetieth year, I must bid farewell to my country women. . . . New avenues for higher culture and for good works are opening before them which fifty years ago were unknown. That they may improve these opportunities, and be faithful to their high vocation, is my heartfelt prayer."[2]

Harriet Beecher Stowe: June 14, 1811–July 1, 1896

My physical health . . . has been excellent, and I am always cheerful and happy. My mental condition might be called nomadic. I have no fixed thoughts or objects. I wander at will from one subject to another. . . .

And now I rest me, like a moored boat, rising and falling on the water,
with a loosened cordage and flapping sail.

—HARRIET BEECHER STOWE in a letter to Oliver Wendell Holmes,
February 5, 1893

During her twilight years, Stowe's writing slowed to a trickle of
words. Her last book, *Poganuc People*, was published in 1878; it
returns to her early life as a girl living in the parsonage in Litchfield, Connecticut. The book recalls a simpler, nostalgic time unclut-
tered by the demands of the late nineteenth century. According to
Stowe, "Parents were not anxiously watching every dawning idea
of the little mind to set it straight even before it was uttered; and
there were no newspapers or magazines with a special corner for
the bright sayings of children."[3]

At this time in her life, Stowe's other literary activities were
limited to writing plays for Christmas presentations and readings at community events. Her retreat to the cozy world of early
nineteenth-century hearthside memories separated her from a
rising wave of women writers who were advocating women's suffrage and were politically active. In 1885 at the request of Julia
Ward Howe, who was serving as the president of the Bureau of
the Woman's Department of the World's International and Cotton Exposition in New Orleans, Stowe sent a set of her books for
display at the exposition but did not speak at or attend the event.

Other than local travel to visit friends, Stowe limited her major
travels to making the annual November through May Florida
sojourn with her husband. There the couple found a welcome
escape from the cold New England winters. By the mid-1880s, Calvin, who had been diagnosed with Bright's disease, began to decline
rapidly. On August 6, 1886, Calvin died, ending a marriage of fifty
years and leaving his wife alone and struggling with what some
thought were the early stages of dementia. Twin daughters, Eliza
and Hattie, became their mother's caregivers. Hattie, in an 1890
letter to a friend, described her mother: "Intellectually she is not
now above a child of two or three years."[4] In another letter, Hattie
reported her mother's condition in more detail: "Ma is very well

and cheerful, has not had a cold, or anything the matter with her all winter. If her mental facilities were only as sound as her physical health she would be in absolutely perfect condition. But her mind is in a strange state of childishness and forgetfulness with momentary flashes of her old self that come and go like falling stars."[5]

With her son Charles's editorial assistance, Stowe pulled together letters, journals, and other written recollections to produce *The Life of Harriet Beecher Stowe: Compiled from Her Letters and Journals*. The book was published in 1889 by Houghton, Mifflin Company. Two weeks after her eighty-fifth birthday in 1896, Harriet Beecher Stowe died at her home in Hartford—born a Connecticut Yankee and dying a Connecticut Yankee. Among the items she bequeathed to her surviving children was her copy of *The Life of Harriet Beecher Stowe*, which was given to Charles, who had been so instrumental in helping shape the manuscript. On the book's flyleaf she had written: "My sword I give to him that shall succeed me in my pilgrimage and my courage and skill to him that can get it. Harriet Beecher Stowe."[6]

Julia Ward Howe: May 27, 1819–October 17, 1910

My own views on this subject [equality of women] are colored by the sunset light of a life which has long passed the meridian.

—JULIA WARD HOWE, 1888

After the death of Samuel Gridley "Chev" Howe, the sluice gate of her husband was removed and opportunities for creative expression flowed in Julia Ward Howe's life. Her nonfiction work, including a biography of Margaret Fuller and her own autobiography, were released. Her essays that analyzed American society (e.g., *Modern Society* and *Is Polite Society Polite?*) were also published. She continued to write and publish her poetry as well. In addition to her creative output, she had numerous requests to play a leadership role in organizations seeking to capitalize on her fame and her ability to mobilize people for action. She served as the chief of the Women's Department of the World's International Industrial and Cotton Exposition in New Orleans and helped found and served as the vice president of the Society of American Friends of Russian Freedom. Her requests to speak ranged from the World Parliament of Religions to the 1893 World's Fair. Her talks on women's suffrage included venues from the Massachusetts State House to the Radical Club and the Concord School of Philosophy in the Bay State.

In addition to the United States, Howe addressed the subject of women in education in Florence, Italy, and she chaired a Paris suffrage convention while conducting her talks and chair duties in Italian and French, respectively. Recognizing her contribution to the nation's culture across her prose, poetry, and public speaking activities, Howe was elected to membership in the American Academy of Arts and Letters in January 1908.[7] She was the first woman elected into the prestigious academy and remained the sole female member until 1926 when four women were inducted into the academy: Edith Wharton, Margaret Deland, Agnes Repplier, and Mary E. Wilkins Freeman.

The petite, fragile-looking woman in her trim, black silk dress and lace cap was a dynamo. In 1900 Howe undertook an extensive lecture tour from January through May in the midwestern states. Each stop on the tour involved an energetic presentation on the subjects of women's suffrage, abolition of the death penalty, protection of immigrants, civil rights for African Americans, pacifism, and a denouncement of anti-Semitism. Most often she concluded by reading or singing "The Battle Hymn of the Republic." Newspapers reported that when "the grand old woman of America" sang the hymn, there was not a dry eye in the house.[8]

The academic world acknowledged Howe's contributions through the granting of honorary degrees. Beginning in 1904, Tufts University presented her with a degree, followed in 1908 by Brown University, and then Smith College in 1910.

To assist Howe's mobility in her home on Beacon Street in Boston, her daughters Maud and Laura had an elevator installed. Now their mother could avoid climbing stairs and be transported in comfort between floors. In their biography of Howe, her daughters recalled its use: "Watching her ascent, clad in white, a smile on her lips, her hand waving farewell. One could only think of the 'chariot of Israel.'"[9]

Shortly after receiving her honorary degree from Smith College, Howe contracted pneumonia. On October 17, 1910, the woman who wrote "Battle Hymn" and had sung it many times before adoring audiences died peacefully among family at her summer house in Rhode Island. The "chariot of Israel" had taken Julia Ward Howe on her final journey.

Clara Barton: December 25, 1821–April 12, 1912

Like the old warhorse that has rested long in quiet pastures, I recognize the bugle note that calls me to my place and though I may not do what I once could, I am come to offer what I may.

—CLARA BARTON, 1877

The ratification of the Treaty of Geneva by the U.S. Senate and signed by President Chester A. Arthur marked just the beginning of the work to establish a viable American Red Cross. Barton labored tirelessly to set the mission of the operation, to seek funding, and to begin building an organization that could respond to national and international needs. Barton held that the purpose of the American Red Cross was not limited to providing assistance during military operations; it also had the larger mandate of "disaster relief" across a broad spectrum of cataclysmic events resulting in human suffering. And there was no lack of natural disasters that required Red Cross assistance.

In September 1881 a million and a half acres were destroyed by forest fires in the Michigan, and nearly five hundred lives were lost in five hours. The Red Cross helped by rebuilding dwellings and distributing tons of supplies including food, clothing, and household items. Two major floods in the early 1880s—one along the Mississippi and the other along the Ohio River—received relief help from the Red Cross directed by Barton. In the later 1880s the Red Cross provided relief efforts for fires in Galveston, Texas; an earthquake in Charleston, South Carolina; a drought in Central Texas; and a tornado in Mount Vernon, Illinois. The scope of these natural disasters varied, but each put a severe strain on Red Cross resources. Barton was trying to create a viable national relief structure organized to perform its tasks with professionalism while, at the same time, raising funds to support its work from a network of public and private sources. Understandably during this period, sound administrative procedures often fell victim to the urgency of executing the relief work; the priority was getting the job done.

In the late 1880s two major relief efforts starkly demonstrated the flaws inherent in the fledgling Red Cross that contrasted with the outstanding performance the Red Cross was capable of producing. In August 1888 a yellow fever epidemic was devastating the Jacksonville, Florida, area. Approximately thirty nurses—believed to be immune from yellow fever—were rushed from the Red Cross in New Orleans to help the Florida residents. Led by a former Confederate officer, the Red Cross contingent proved to be an ill-prepared, poorly led group of amateurs. Charges of drunkenness, misuse of Red Cross funds, and questions concerning elicit behavior among the workers, including prostitution, were covered in the press and caused a major black eye both for the organization and for Barton, who had delegated supervision of the relief efforts.

By contrast, the relief efforts of the Red Cross following the Johnstown, Pennsylvania, flood were a textbook example of how a relief organization could make a major contribution in mitigating the effects of a natural disaster. Barton personally directed the relief activities on-site, working virtually around the clock for five months. This time the national press was silent on the success of the Red Cross, but the local press lauded its work and Barton's role in the efforts to build houses and to provide food, clothing, and other essential items to the flood victims. For Barton, it was clear evidence that she needed to provide continuous, personal on-site supervision if a relief effort was to succeed. Delegation of efforts only yielded disastrous consequences for the Red Cross and, by association, her own reputation.

Interspersed in the work on national disasters, Barton also took her international responsibilities seriously. The Red Cross supported Balkan War relief (1885), Russian famine relief (1892), and Armenian famine relief (1896). The Red Cross, following a course of strict neutrality when it came to foreign conflicts, managed to walk a narrow line in avoiding political disputes and sovereignty issues while providing effective relief efforts. In 1898, however, the Red Cross's involvement in relief operations for Cuban people relocated in *reconcentrado* (reconcentration) camps, which were operated by the Spanish administration in Cuba during that country's fight for independence, led to a delicate diplomatic ballet for the Red Cross and Barton.

Efforts to aid the Cuban prisoners were organized in the United States under the auspices of the Central Cuban Relief Committee (CCRC), which would manage the donations that were pouring in and organize an effective use of the funds for relief. The CCRC was to be directed by the editor of the *Christian Herald* newspaper (Louis Klopsch), a prominent New York philanthropist (Charles Schieren), and the Red Cross (Clara Barton). The volatility of the situation in Cuba was apparent when on February 15, 1898, the USS *Maine* blew up and sank in Havana Harbor. Only forty-eight hours before, Barton had lunch on board with the ship's captain. Following this incident, Barton, who had been given operational control of the CCRC, sent a message to President William McKinley: "I am with the wounded." True to her "angel of the battlefield" reputation, Barton was with the USS *Maine*'s casualties at a Spanish hospital. Less admirable was her admission that she had taken souvenirs from the USS *Maine*—"charred and splintered" fragments of the damaged ship. Her souvenir hunting aside, Barton's efforts in Cuba were praised by visiting Sen. Redfield Proctor of Vermont. Proctor told his colleagues in Washington: "The American people may be assured that their bounty will reach the sufferers with the least possible cost and in the best manner in every respect."[10]

Concurring with Proctor's praise was Assistant Secretary of State William R. Day. A contrary opinion of Barton was raised by the editor Klopsch of the *Christian Herald*. The newspaperman attempted to wrest control of the CCRC from Barton, but Barton's appeal to the State Department quickly resulted in Klopsch's departure from Cuba and his resignation from the CCRC. Coming from a profession that was male dominated, Klopsch resented a woman—especially a woman as self-confident as Barton—running a major, highly visible organization. What Klopsch had not taken in account was that this woman had contacts in high places and was not shy about calling on them when circumstances required it.

On April 25, 1898, the United States declared war on Spain. Barton's role in Cuba now became more circumscribed in delivering relief supplies. The navy admiral in charge of operations for the port of Havana restricted Red Cross supplies from entering the country. The U.S. military did not recognize the neutrality of the Red Cross as a relief agency in war zones. Even with the bureaucratic scuffles and organizational jousting during the Cuban relief efforts, President McKinley offered a tribute to Barton in his annual message to Congress in 1899, acknowledging her personal involvement in treating the wounded and serving meals to the U.S. troops.

Despite her publicly acknowledged successes in Cuba, Barton was despondent about her own status. In a letter to a local physician with whom she worked in Cuba, she wrote: "In the last two years I have given to Cuba all my time, my strengths until I have little left of my peace of mind, my friends, much of the hard-earned reputation of a lifetime, and stand literally alone watching the dying embers with none to speak to and none to speak for me."[11]

Activists in the U.S. women's rights movement, meanwhile, urged Barton to use her considerable public visibility and empathy to further the cause of the nation's women, specifically to speak on their right to vote. Barton was sympathetic to the cause, attended a number of meetings of suffrage associations and rallies, and was a featured speaker at the First International Women's Suffrage Conference in Washington DC in 1902. The secretary of the New York Woman Suffrage Association requested: "Give Washington and the Red Cross a month's vacation, if need be . . . you can work all the better when you are enfranchised."[12]

Barton's lukewarm involvement in the suffrage movement may have been based on three complicating factors. First, she did not want to link a controversial political campaign such as suffrage to a delicate and complex effort to establish the apolitical disaster relief organization of the Red Cross. It may also have been Barton's personal style of getting things accomplished. Biographer Elizabeth Brown Pryor has characterized Barton's way of working: "Her own interests also leaned more toward practical, social benefits for women, rather than the ability to vote."[13] Finally, Barton was focused on getting the American Red Cross operational. Her own style of accomplishing tasks—based on her experience over the years—was a singular, unwavering attention on her goal to the exclusion of other things that could distract or be digressive. (There were some exceptions. In 1883 she spent eight months as the superintendent of the Massachusetts Reformatory Prison for Women, and she always made time to address the Grand Army of the Republic conventions and gatherings.)

While her time spent on suffrage activities displeased some women in the movement, Barton's commitment to the cause was clear and unequivocal: "This country is to know woman suffrage, and it will be grateful for it. The change is not far away. This country is to know woman suffrage, and it will be a glad and proud day when it comes."[14]

By the turn of the twentieth century, Barton's grip on the Red Cross began to weaken. A growing number of those associated with the organization's leadership and who wanted the Red Cross to be ready for the new century questioned whether a seventy-nine-year-old was fit for the task. Barton's administrative short cuts and lack of interest in organizational processes began to exact a price. Personal charisma aside, was Barton capable of managing a complex, centralized institution? Her inability to delegate responsibility, take constructive criticism, or adhere to a rigorous accounting system irked those who had taken on the cause of reforming the two-decade-old organization. Led by an imperious socialite, Mabel T. Boardman, a group started a campaign to oust Barton from her leadership role. Initially looking at organizational shortcomings in Barton's management of the Red Cross, Boardman expanded the scope to include a personal vendetta against Barton, accusing her of living an extravagant lifestyle at the Red Cross's expense. Boardman's numerous and high-level connections—including Theodore Roosevelt and William Howard Taft—kept the accusations against Barton alive until the duplicity and false statements of key witnesses caused a complete collapse of the investigation into Barton's work.

On May 14, 1904, weary of defending her actions at the organization she had created almost single-handedly, Clara Barton resigned as president of the American Red Cross. It was a wrenching decision, but having spent almost sixty years of her life in service to others, she knew the risks for those who led efforts of good works: "The paths of charity are over roadways of ashes; and he who would tread them must be prepared to meet opposition, misconstruction, jealousy and calumny. Let his work be that of angels, still it will not satisfy all."[15]

For the next eight years, Barton lived quietly at her home in Glen Echo, Maryland, writing and serving as the honorary president of the National First Aid Association of America, an organization she established to serve the growing need for first aid training and advocacy. The American Red Cross rejected that role during Barton's tenure but later adopted it when first aid was proven to be an important skill.

On April 10, 1912, Clara Barton reported to Dr. Julian Hubbell, who was monitoring her slow physical decline at her home in Glen Echo that she had a vivid dream the night before. She was back on the battlefield and caring for wounded men. "I crept round once more, trying to give them at least a drink of water to cool their parched lips, and I heard them at last speak of mothers, wives and sweethearts but never a complaint."[16] Her most enduring memories remained "being with her boys." Two days later, on a clear spring morning in Maryland, Clara Barton died.

Harriet Tubman: ca. February/March 1822–March 10, 1913

I'll meet you in the morning,
I'm bound for the promised land,
On the other side of Jordan,
Bound for the promised land.

—HARRIET TUBMAN (as recorded by Sarah D. Bradford)

During the 1880s and '90s, Tubman spoke to suffrage groups, and her message of liberation, personal and compelling, appealed to African American and middle-class white women. In the abstract at least, the early lack of civil rights and denial of the right to vote for blacks resonated with white women, who could relate to their denial of constitutional rights. Tubman's narrative of gaining freedom was a relevant message for women in the forefront of the suffrage movement.

In 1886 Sarah Bradford reissued her Tubman biography. Retitled *Harriet: The Moses of Her People*, the book contained twenty-one additional pages of information on Tubman beyond that covered in *Scenes in the Life of Harriet Tubman*. Issued seventeen years after the original Bradford biography, the book introduced Tubman's life to a new generation of readers. A trickle of royalties, managed by Bradford, helped pay some of Tubman's bills in her old age.

In 1905 Tubman accompanied her great-niece Alida Stewart on a visit to Boston, where she participated in the opening of the Harriet Tubman Christian Temperance Union at Parker Memorial Hall. Tubman was a vocal advocate for the temperance movement, and her appearance was reported by the *Boston Journal*: "For a woman at so great an age she is remarkably erect, her voice is clear, her manner bright and her wit keen."[17]

Remaining active in Auburn, New York, Tubman began putting in place the steps to establish the Harriet Tubman Home for the Aged and Indigent Negroes. She began by deeding twenty-five acres of her land and home to the African Methodist Episcopal Zion Church in Auburn in 1903. The home opened five years later under the auspices of the church. (Tubman initially challenged the church's requirement that applicants pay five hundred dollars to be admitted; she thought there should be no charge for admittance. Eventually she relented, and the entry fee remained.)

By 1910 Tubman required a wheelchair, and the following year she was admitted to the Harriet Tubman Home "ill and penniless," according to a newspaper report. Learning that the woman who had helped so many others in need was requiring help herself, the Empire State Federation of Women's Clubs raised funds to help support Tubman's care.[18]

On March 10, 1913, fifty years after the Emancipation Proclamation, Harriet Tubman, the former slave who was devoted to seeking freedom for herself and other enslaved people, died in Auburn, New York. She was interred in the city's Fort Hill Cemetery. Buried with Tubman were a crucifix and the medal from Queen Victoria. An American flag covered her casket.

13

The Angels among Us Still

educed to the simplest and most enduring expressions of the contributions the five better angels left us in the early twenty-first century, we have:

A book that inspired action to free enslaved people—Harriet Beecher Stowe's *Uncle Tom's Cabin.*

A song that motivated an army and expressed a noble purpose for its cause—Julia Ward Howe's "The Battle Hymn of the Republic."

An organization that provided relief support for those in need—Clara Barton's American Red Cross.

A manifestation of liberty and freedom through sustained actions to free enslaved people—Harriet Tubman's activities with the Underground Railroad.

A commemoration of a day of thanksgiving that played an important role in national reconciliation after the Civil War and continues to this day—Sarah Josepha Hale's advocacy for a national Thanksgiving Day.

Simplicity and longevity aside, we also know from the preceding narrative that the five better angels forged their legacies during a time and within circumstances that make them truly exceptional, even now over a century and a half later. The outcomes belie the complexities and the extraordinary efforts that contributed to these women's successes. Even so, the five women have not enjoyed sustained fame with the American public since the nineteenth century. Harriet Tubman, for example, languished in obscurity in the late nineteenth and early twentieth centuries before she regained her important position in the public eye in the 1960s. The Thanksgiving holiday is now part of virtually every American's experience and understanding, but Sarah Josepha Hale's role in helping achieve the necessary government approvals and proclamations to give the day national prominence has been largely lost to most Americans in the twenty-first century.

When considering their legacies, each of the five women has often been reduced to mythical status in the past by being subjects of children's books. By its very nature, children's literature needs to condense narrations and minimize the complexities that were inherent in each of the five women's lives. Detailed, well-researched narratives of most of the five women have been produced for adult readers starting in the 1970s and continuing into the twenty-first century. Recent biographies have presented nuanced, more human stories freed from the taint of hagiography and still provide vivid portraits of accomplished, admirable lives. Now we see the women who not only achieved extraordinary and important successes but still struggled with obdurate husbands, poor money management skills, sensitivity to criticism, and rebellious children. Understanding that these five women made such significant contributions while coping with their own personal impediments makes them more exceptional as a result, not less.

For each of the five women, the United States during the Civil War and Reconstruction presented a platform where exceptional deeds would be noticed, valued, and remembered. The door was open for women who were courageous and persistent to realize consequential achievements. To be sure, the legacies of the five better angels were helped along by biographies from doting children, a largely positive contemporary press, and America's hunger for female patriots; but, in fact, their life stories continue to stand up well after the passage of considerable time. Even when their human blemishes are revealed in modern biographies, their accomplishments more than outweigh their shortcomings.

Writing about the Founding Fathers and eighteenth-century America, historian Joseph Ellis admonishes us in the twenty-first century America: "They lived in a premodern world that is forever lost to us. That world was . . . pre-Freud, pre-Einstein, pre-Keynes, and pre–Martin Luther King, Jr. . . . . Viewing and judging the founding generation through the lens of our own values is inherently presumptive and presentistic."[1] The same caution is relevant regarding the five women of the nineteenth century.

Even when we adjust what we know about the five better angels to avoid presumption and presentism, we can acknowledge that their legacies—their gifts from the past to us—have a value undiminished by the passage of over a century and a half.

Harriet Beecher Stowe

Much less a book than a state of feeling.

—HENRY JAMES

Henry James's comment on *Uncle Tom's Cabin*'s being "a state of feeling" is borne out by the breadth of the book's reach in the world and of the inspired plays, poems, songs, souvenirs (plates, figurines, embossed spoons), games, and other assorted memorabilia that twenty-first-century marketing persons would refer to as "cross-marketing" or "promotional tie-ins." Amanda Claybaugh, a professor at Columbia University, has written about *Uncle Tom's Cabin*: "The result was a novel more popular, and more influential, than anyone would have imagined."[2]

Thirty years after the appearance of *Uncle Tom's Cabin* in book form, a handsome illustrated copy of the book was published in 1885 by Houghton Mifflin. This version further boosted sales of the now-classic novel. By the late nineteenth century, *Uncle Tom's Cabin* had been translated into seventy-two languages.

The plays that were created from *Uncle Tom's Cabin* were neither written nor approved by Harriet Beecher Stowe. (U.S. copyright laws for authors' works during the early half of the nineteenth century were weak. More rigorous protections were put in place in the revised Copyright Act of 1870.) These *Uncle Tom* "spin-off" plays were performed around the world. A prominent example is *Anna and the King of Siam* by Margaret Landon (1944), along with the 1951 Richard Rodgers and Oscar Hammerstein musical *The King and I* based on the book. One of the most memorable scenes in the musical is the rendition of a narrated dance "The Small House of Uncle Tom" performed in the king's palace.

The popularity of the book and *Uncle Tom*–based plays in Great Britain also helped foster a growing abolitionist sentiment in Great Britain and may have been a major factor in that nation's decision not to support the Southern cause during the war (despite Britain's close economic ties with the cotton-producing South).

As new media for telling stories became available, versions of Uncle Tom's story were also told in films: *The Littlest Rebel* with Bill "Bojangles" Robinson (1935); *Dimples*, featuring Shirley Temple (1936); *Everybody Sing*, starring Judy Garland (1938); *The Dolly Sisters*, featuring Betty Grable and June Haver (1945); and *The Naughty Nineties* with Bud Abbott and Lou Costello (1945).[3]

Lost in the popularity of *Uncle Tom's Cabin* is the fact that Stowe wrote sixteen other books. While none ever achieved the acceptance or acclaim of her signature novel, they were successful when they were published and are evidence of Stowe's prolific literary talent. She was a best-selling author with a large public following by any measure.

Today those interested in the life of Harriet Beecher Stowe can visit two homes where she lived. One house operates as a museum in Walnut Hills, Ohio, a neighborhood of Cincinnati (State Route 3 and U.S. Route 22). Her home in Hartford, Connecticut, is also a museum in the Nook Farm neighborhood with a visitor center at 77 Forrest Street. Also open to visitors is the rented house where she wrote *Uncle Tom's Cabin* at 63 Federal Street in Brunswick, Maine, on the campus of Bowdoin College. (Recall that author Stowe needed a quiet place where she could concentrate away from her growing family.)

In 2014 a home in Brunswick (on College Street) was listed by real estate agents who claimed that this residence—not only the Federal Street location—was a site where Stowe wrote *Uncle Tom's Cabin*. The three-million-dollar asking price was significantly greater than the value of similar homes in the neighborhood. Knowledgeable critics dispute that this College Street home was the site of Stowe's writing. What is not in dispute is the value of the Stowe name even in the twenty-first century.

Harriet Tubman

She was a fighter important for the freedom of her people and the suffrage of her sex.

—PHILIP KENNICOTT

Achieving fame and appreciation during most of her adult life, Tubman's story slipped from public view for a long period. Some historians and biographers attribute racist attitudes and the rise of the Southern "Lost Cause" movement in the late nineteenth and early twentieth centuries for her disappearance from the general public's view. At this time the Lost Cause narrative of the Civil War was gaining traction, and Tubman's stark tale of slavery was an inconvenient truth as Southerners played down its role as a factor in their reasons for taking up arms against the North. This climate, along with a lack of serious biographers to tell Tubman's life story, was further complicated by the absence of a written record from the subject herself. Tubman's illiteracy meant she did not have any letters, diaries, journals, and autobiographical material for biographers.

In the 1930s and '40s, highly fictionalized accounts of Tubman's life were published for children and young adults.[4] These works, while inspiring and admirable attempts to tell an important story about a nineteenth-century African American woman, were filled with inaccuracies and exaggerations that revealed their lack of serious research. In the words of biographer Kate Clifford Larson, Tubman became a "malleable icon."

In the 1940s, Earl Conrad, a Teamsters organizer and reporter for the *Chicago Defender*, began his lengthy quest to tell Tubman's story. His attempts to conduct the kind of in-depth research that had been absent from so many prior Tubman narratives was thwarted by a lack of cooperation from archivists and interview subjects. Following numerous rejections by publishers, Conrad's biography *Harriet Tubman* was published by Associated Publishers in 1943. Conrad's contention that abject racism had hindered his progress to complete the Tubman biography was complicated by his outspoken far left views during a time when the Red Scare was rampant in the United States. Conrad's work was moderately successful with the reading public, but his lack of access to research sources perpetuated some of the Tubman mythology.

Encouraged by the National Council of Negro Women, the U.S. Maritime Commission named a Liberty ship for Harriet Tubman in the spring of 1944. Members of Tubman's family and admirers watched as a bottle of champagne was cracked over the ss *Harriet Tubman*'s bow and the seven-thousand-ton vessel was launched in the Atlantic at South Portland, Maine, on June 3, 1944. In conjunction with the launch, the National Council of Negro Women also sponsored a war bond drive, using the slogan "Buy a Harriet Tubman War Bond for Freedom."[5]

In the early twenty-first century, the fictionalized children's books on Tubman were followed by a number of well-researched biographies that helped correct the myths that had been perpetuated for so many years. Biographer Kate Clifford Larson, one of the new wave of biographers, stated: "Though Harriet Tubman's life is the material of legend, it is more remarkable in its truth than fiction—the essence of a real American hero."[6] Among this new wave of thoroughly researched biographical works are Larson's *Bound for the Promised Land: Harriet Tubman: Portrait of an American Hero* (2004); Jean M. Humez's *Harriet Tubman: The Life and the Life Stories* (2003); Milton C. Sernett's *Harriet Tubman: Myth, Memory, and History* (2007); and Beverly Lowry's *Harriet Tubman: Imagining a Life* (2007).

After over a century of misrepresentation and mythology, Harriet Tubman has the thoughtful, well-researched, and accurate biographies her exceptional life warranted. In addition to these well-documented biographies of Tubman, museums offer visitors a variety of media to learn about where she lived and where she traveled. The Harriet Tubman Museum and Education Center is located in Dorchester County, Maryland, where Tubman was born, raised, and escaped slavery. A Harriet Tubman Underground Railroad Byway offers an opportunity to experience the path Tubman used for her escape from the Eastern Shore to Delaware. The Harriet Tubman Underground Railroad National Monument is located next to the twenty-five-thousand-acre Harriet

Tubman Underground Railroad State Park also located in Dorchester County, Maryland. In New York State, Harriet Tubman's home in Auburn, located at 180 South Street, is open to the public along with a museum covering the key elements of her life.

In 2016 Secretary of the Treasury Jack Lew announced that Harriet Tubman would replace Andrew Jackson on the front of the U.S. twenty-dollar bill. (Jackson would move to the back of the bill.) Commenting on Tubman's inclusion on the currency, *Washington Post* arts critic Philip Kennicott wrote: "She was a fighter important for the freedom of her people and the suffrage of her sex; she repeatedly put her life on the line for what she believed in. And one hopes that's how she appears on the $20 bill."[7]

Julia Ward Howe

In the words of the "Battle Hymn" we hear not only the voice of the Union Army, but an echo of all the aspiring thoughts and noble deeds of the builders of the great Republic.

—FLORENCE HOWE HALL

In the early years of the new century, the Howes' daughters discussed how they could pay tribute to their mother with a biography. Laura Howe Richards, Maud Howe Elliott, and Flossy Howe Hall collaborated to produce *Julia Ward Howe, 1819–1910*. Laura, the most accomplished writer, took the lead. Maud assisted her sister but did little of the writing. Flossy, who insisted that she have a role, was assigned to the peripheral tasks of the project, generally those falling in the administrative area. The book was published in 1916, six years after Julia Ward Howe's death; it received the Pulitzer Prize—the first awarded to a biography—and was commercially successful. Critics, however, in the years that followed called it "a sanitized portrait" of Howe's life. The daughters had removed any hint of discord between their mother and father in the narrative. Letters and diary entries that suggested conflict between the spouses were excised from the published work. No hint of family rivalry between Chev and Julia was permitted to undercut the idealistic (and unrealistic) portrait of the family offered up by the

Howe sisters. Exploring the tension that was pervasive in the couple's relationship that was such an important backdrop to Julia Ward Howe's work as a writer and an advocate of women's rights had to wait for later biographers who were interested in writing about the compelling dynamics of the Howe household and the effect they had, not in offering a paean to domestic harmony.

The martial cadence and florid Victorian lyrics of "Battle Hymn" were frequently at the center of Civil War commemorations. It was sung in New York City after Richmond was taken in April 1865. During Memorial Day services in Boston in 1899 and in San Francisco during the same period, the music and lyrics of "Battle Hymn" filled the air. When Augustus Saint-Gauden's monument of Robert Gould Shaw and the black troops of the Fifty-Fourth Massachusetts Volunteer Regiment was unveiled, the "Battle Hymn" was performed. Both British writers Rudyard Kipling and Sir Arthur Conan Doyle referred to the anthem favorably in their works (*The Light That Failed* and *Through the Magic Door*). Theodore Roosevelt dedicated his book *Fear God and Take Your Own Part* to Julia Ward Howe, and the lyrics to "Battle Hymn" preface the book. Roosevelt thought that Howe's anthem should be the national anthem. Others thought the "Battle Hymn" was every bit as stirring a national song as "The Marseillaise" and the British national anthem.[8] In a Young Men's Christian Association (YMCA) pamphlet containing the anthem, the accompanying text proclaimed: "[The 'Battle Hymn'] is said to have done more to awaken the spirit of patriotism and to have inspired more deeds and heroism than any other event of the American Civil War."[9]

Julia Ward Howe's reputation continued to flourish even after her death, while her husband's fame declined. Samuel Gridley Howe, once the shooting star of the family with his sterling credentials and national reputation, sank into oblivion. Julia Ward Howe's biographer Elaine Showalter concludes: Chev was prince consort to Julia's queen, but after Julia's death, Chev's reputation continued to fade. The *Boston Evening Transcript* in 1917 said, "Her achievements . . . and her *Battle Hymn of the Republic*, have given off such a blaze of glory around her name that that of her husband is rather lost in the dazzle."[10]

Julia Ward Howe's fame and her "Battle Hymn" continued undimmed into the twentieth century. In the 1940s, Howe was named one of the "Wonder Women of History" in Wonder Woman comic books. On a more propitious level, "The Battle Hymn of the Republic" was sung at the funerals of Winston Churchill, Robert Kennedy, Richard Nixon, and Ronald Reagan. Dr. Martin Luther King quoted from the "Battle Hymn" in his last sermon in Memphis in 1968. Following the attack on the World Trade Center on September 11, 2001, the hymn was performed at numerous memorial concerts. Regardless of its martial cadence and Victorian lyrics, the hymn continues to evoke a sense of majesty and purpose, even in modern times, over 150 years after it was written.

Howe's home of Oak Glen, where she died in Portsmouth, Rhode Island, still stands. It is on the National Register of Historic Places but is not open to the public. The Glessner House in Chicago on Prairie Avenue, where Julia Ward Howe once visited, contains displays of Howe family history but primarily focuses on Maud Howe Elliott, not her mother. The museum is open to visitors.

Clara Barton

Use of volunteers, use of donations, use of press in drumming up support for relief efforts. These were the things that she put in place, and it's still the same practice today.

—AARON LA ROCCA, National Park Service ranger, Clara Barton Historic Site, quoted in *Wings of an Angel*

Clara Barton's most salient contribution and legacy is inarguably her founding of the American Red Cross. Today's organization is the U.S. affiliate of the International Federation of Red Cross and Red Crescent Societies. From its initial start by Barton in 1881, the American Red Cross has grown to 650 chapters supported by 500,000 volunteers and 30,000 employees across the country.[11]

The organization has traditionally ranked at the top of the "most popular charity/non-profit in America," according to *The Chronicle of Philanthropy*.[12] Despite Barton's difficult tenure at the conclusion of her leadership of the Red Cross and her resignation in May

1904, she is regarded universally as the driving force behind one of the nation's most successful humanitarian relief organizations.

While the organization she founded dominates any narrative about Barton's legacy, a more personal legacy surrounded her following the Civil War. Men who had received care from Barton on the battlefield many times expressed their appreciation and honored her by naming their daughters after her. Historian and biographer Stephen B. Oates has chronicled eight women who were named Clara by their appreciative fathers after Barton saved their lives during the Civil War. They include Clara Barton Leggett (daughter of Lt. Col. Robert Leggett), Clara Barton Whitaker, Clara Barton Thompson, Clara Barton Hoffman, Clara Barton Clausson, Clara Barton Bergh, Clara Horace Gardner, and Clara Barton Barnard. "Before long, there were young Clara Bartons all over the United States, from Massachusetts to California."[13] The woman who never married and never bore children had scores of namesakes thanks to grateful soldiers and their spouses.

One touching related story recorded in Clara Barton's war diary tells of her encounter after a lecture at a YMCA. Following her talk, those who were interested in greeting Barton were invited to the stage. One man, in particular, accompanied by a little fair-haired girl, attracted Barton's attention as he made his way to the front of the lecture hall. He walked with a pronounced limp. "Have we met before?" Barton asked as she reached out to shake the man's hand. The man replied, "Yes. Three times." He then described the three encounters: Second Bull Run, where Barton gave the wounded man food; the Battle of Fredericksburg, where his leg was shattered in a charge of Marye's Heights and Barton supplied heated bricks and warm drinks to comfort him; and Petersburg, where again Barton tended to the exhausted soldier with water and bound his head with ice. After acknowledging that she remembered the man on those three occasions, Barton turned to the child. "And this is your little girl?" The man placed his hand on the girl's head and responded, "Yes. She is almost three years old and we call her Clara Barton."[14]

The foundation of the American Red Cross and her indelible experiences on the battlefields of the Civil War were inextricably bound together for Barton. She expressed this lyrically in her poem "The Women Who Went to the Field" written in 1892:

And what would they do if war came again?
The scarlet cross floats where all was blank then.
They would bind on their "brassards" and march to the fray,
And the man liveth not who could say to them nay;
They would stand with you now, as they stood with you then.
The nurses, the consolers, and saviors of men.[15]

Today Clara Barton's work is remembered at her home in Glen Echo, Maryland, a site operated by the National Park Service. Its designation as a national historic landmark was obtained by the Friends of Clara Barton in 1963, and the house was turned over to the park service to administer the site. The home is open to visitors. Through a serendipitous circumstance, Clara Barton's Missing Soldiers Office was discovered at 437 ½ Seventh Street Northwest in Washington DC during a routine inventory of federal properties. The office is now open to the public and operated by the National Museum of Civil War Medicine.

Sarah Josepha Hale

I do therefore invite my fellow-citizens in every part of the United States . . . to set apart and observe the last Thursday of November next as a day of thanksgiving.

—ABRAHAM LINCOLN, Thanksgiving Proclamation, 1863

Those few Americans who today recognize the name Sarah Josepha Hale would consider the signature contribution to her country was her zealous campaign advocating for a national day of thanksgiving. Few American celebrations are as universal and inclusive as Thanksgiving, even if Sarah Josepha Hale remains a lost figure in its derivation. Hale's desire to foster an atmosphere of reconciliation between the North and the South through the observance of the holiday initially proved to be a thwarted hope; most of the South considered Thanksgiving, promulgated by Lincoln, to be a nefarious Yankee plot. References to Puritans of Massachusetts and a date set by the federal (Union) government irritated Southerners. It would be many years after the Civil War and the original Thanksgiving Proclamation before people in the South would embrace the holiday's commemoration.

The North-South enmity was an early barrier to the national observance of Thanksgiving, but another kind of inclusion and national unity—beyond geography and politics—was taking shape in the nation. This growing sense of comity and unification was illustrated by artist Thomas Nast, a young German immigrant who worked for *Harper's Weekly*. Nast provided popular political cartoons for *Harper's*, a publication with a huge circulation across the United States. On November 20, 1869, Nast's drawing "Uncle Sam's Thanksgiving Dinner" appeared in the magazine. Putting aside his usual biting political cartoon format, this time Nast portrayed a diverse group of Americans seated around a Thanksgiving table and facing a centerpiece that reads "Self-Governance" and "Universal Suffrage" while the host, Uncle Sam, carves a large turkey. A group of young people and adults of varying races and ethnicities sits as a family under the portraits of Lincoln, Washington, and Grant. In the corner of the illustration, opposite his name, Nast has, in broad, bold letters, announced "Come One, Come All" on one side and "Free and Equal" on the other. Hale's desire to foster community conciliation had an effect even she had not foreseen.

Following Lincoln's proclamation for a national day of observance, Thanksgiving hit bumpy stretches along the road to the twenty-first century. Southerners slowly began to accept Thanksgiving as an expression of gratitude and appreciation for what the country embodied, not merely as a political ploy by incorrigible, regionally biased Yankees. Then, in August 1939, President Franklin D. Roosevelt shifted the traditional Thanksgiving timing. Responding to requests from large retailers in the United States that wanted a longer Christmas buying season, Roosevelt changed the date to the third Thursday in November rather than the fourth Thursday. The reaction to the changed date was quick and uniformly harsh. The decision promptly took on political dimensions, but in the end, facts trumped fancy. Retail sales did not improve during the two years the new date was in effect, school

schedules were thrown into chaos, and traditional football programs were in disarray. Roosevelt announced in May 1941 that his
short-lived experiment in rescheduling Thanksgiving was over.
Starting Thanksgiving 1942, the date would be—as it had been in
Lincoln's time—the last Thursday in November.

Thanksgiving in the twenty-first-century might be unrecog-
nizable to a Sarah Josepha Hale visiting America today, yet many
of the core attributes of Thanksgiving, as she envisioned them,
remain. She might be appalled at the scenes of Black Friday that
play out following Thanksgiving Day, but she would be cheered by
the acts of families and friends joining around tables across America to express thanks and enjoy the grace of eating a community
meal together. Her wish that Thanksgiving would be a "generous
beneficence to the poor" has been sustained by activities such as
the post-Thanksgiving "Giving Tuesday," which was started by the
Ninety-Second Street YMCA in New York City.

Hale's legacy of Thanksgiving in America overshadows her
more ephemeral, albeit exceptional, literary accomplishments.
Every woman editor in the twentieth and twenty-first centuries
owes a debt of gratitude to the nineteenth-century editor who
demonstrated—over a span of nearly fifty years—that a woman
could be the editor of a highly successful national magazine. And
in the meantime, Hale also produced volumes of poetry (two for
children), fiction, advice, and history. She is also acknowledged
as the author of "Mary Had a Little Lamb," the enduring nursery
rhyme. Hale's literary legacy is substantial.

Today it is remembered and honored at the Richards Free Library
in Newport, New Hampshire, where a memorial statue recognizes
her and an annual literary prize, the Sarah Josepha Hale Award,
is given for a "distinguished body of work in the field of literature
and letters." Recipients have to be born in New England or associated with New England through their works or residence. The
award has been granted since 1956, and recipients are a tribute to
the quality of Hale's work. The winners include Robert Frost, J. P.
Marquand, Archibald MacLeish, Catherine Drinker Bowen, Ogden
Nash, Roger Tory Peterson, David McCullough, Doris Kearns Good-
win, Ken Burns, and similar luminaries in the arts.

14

"Contemplating Their Example"

We live in the past by a knowledge of its history; and in the future, by hope and anticipation. By ascending to an association with our ancestors; by contemplating their example and studying their characters; . . . by accompanying them in their toils, by sympathizing in their sufferings, and rejoicing in their successes and triumphs; . . . we seem to belong to their age, and to mingle our own experience with theirs.

—DANIEL WEBSTER, Founder's Day speech, 1820

Americans—both men and women—faced daunting odds during the Civil War years, but women confronted the additional hurdle of overcoming centuries-old stereotypes. Thousands upon thousands of women experienced the war personally or indirectly during its four-year duration. Loved ones were lost, daily routines turned upside down, and property and worldly goods destroyed. Many women played crucial roles in the war effort in both the North and the South and left records of important accomplishments in their wake. Few, however, achieved the significant and sustained results of the five better angels before, during, and after the war.

While we can acknowledge that being in the right place at the right time can sometimes play a crucial role in achieving success, powerful, defining characteristics set these five women apart from others. In the words of Daniel Webster in discussing the founders of the United States, we would benefit from "contemplating their example and studying their character" by exploring the shared and unique characteristics of the five angels. What are these pivotal characteristics that the five angels demonstrated, and how did their responses lead to success when the odds were stacked so high against them? Ten critical characteristics define the way the five women were able to set themselves apart from their male and female contemporaries in the nineteenth century and helped them successfully navigate through the treacherous waters of the American Civil War.

Persistence: *the quality or state of being persistent; existing for a long or longer than usual time.*[1] When confronted with barriers, serial rejections, and prolonged lack of cooperation from others, the five better angels uniformly kept pressing ahead. Barriers were surmounted (or circumvented), and rejections were considered a learning experience following which a different approach was attempted. Those who did not cooperate with the five women found themselves either sidestepped or the object of unabated persuasion. "No" and "never" were unacceptable responses for the five.

Harriet Beecher Stowe's novel *Uncle Tom's Cabin* was a testament to persistence. The forty-year-old mother of six (one being a small infant) met her publisher's strict deadline of writing and submitting a chapter a month throughout a schedule of over forty chapters. She missed her deadline only twice—once in October and again in December 1851—despite her domestic responsibilities. The publisher, *National Era*, forgave Stowe for her tardiness since the short delay in featuring the ongoing serial only whetted eager readers' appetites for the next installment in the series.

Stowe's persistence was also on display following the publication of *Uncle Tom's Cabin* when she took extraordinary measures to counter each criticism of her book with a well-researched, clearly stated response in *A Key to Uncle Tom's Cabin*. Rather than walk away from conflict, Stowe followed up each challenge to the novel's veracity with specific facts, examples, and corroborating statements from reliable, knowledgeable sources.

Harriet Tubman's persistence in escorting or aiding in the escape of hundreds of enslaved people is legendary. Returning to Maryland some twelve to fourteen times to personally guide blacks out of bondage to freedom in the North put her in danger during each trip. As her work on the Underground Railroad continued, her risks of being caught and severely punished increased exponentially. Slave owners became more skillful in identifying escape routes, while the economic rewards rose for those who became slave hunters. Again and again, Tubman went back to guide people north regardless of the escalating perils involved. Despite adverse weather conditions, aggressive slave hunters, and sometimes reluctant "clients," Tubman modified her approaches to accommodate the challenges she faced and soldiered on in the face great adversity. Giving up was not an option for her. As with her namesake in the Old Testament, "Moses" Tubman was pertinacious.

Julia Ward Howe's persistence was primarily evident within her confining domestic world rather than with external forces. Her husband, Dr. Samuel Gridley Howe, was an omnipresent figure of oppression who sought to restrict his wife to pursuits that he thought appropriate in her domestic sphere. Writing for publication was not among those activities. Generally, she was most productive when the couple was apart—for example, during her unaccompanied time in Europe—and her most successful creative output, "The Battle Hymn of the Republic," was written while she occupied a separate room from Samuel in Washington City's Willard's Hotel. Often conflict between the couple was fueled by Julia Ward Howe's literary successes; thus, her persistence in writing and publishing her works exacerbated the tension between the couple. As her writing increased her fame, she was invited to speak to literary groups throughout the country. If his wife's literary successes annoyed Dr. Howe, her acceptance of speaking opportunities outraged him, especially when the topic was women's suffrage.

Julia Ward Howe's persistence in pursuing her creative aspirations was aided after January 9, 1876, when Samuel Gridley Howe died. She then had unfettered freedom to pursue her dreams wherever they took her. She could then channel her persistence into increasing her creative output, not overcoming spousal resistance.

Clara Barton practiced persistence from the beginning of her professional career. During her tenure as a teacher in Bordentown, New Jersey, she pushed hard to establish and grow a school that met the highest academic standards for its male and female students. At Bordentown she learned that persistence paid off in achieving results, including earning equal pay as a woman. Later, while clerking in the U.S. Patent Office and collecting supplies for the soldiers on the front line, Barton drew upon her reservoir of persistence again. For example, after assembling three warehouses of supplies, she appealed to the head of the Quartermaster Depot in Washington DC to arrange delivery of the collected materials using army transportation—wagons and boats to move the freight—but the officer in charge rebuffed her request. Barton persisted. She pleaded, detailed the amount of the supplies, and demonstrated the value of the goods she had collected for the army. She appealed to the quartermaster's head and heart. The indefatigable Barton prevailed. The quartermaster provided her with a wagon, a teamster, a space on a government packet boat, and a signed pass with permission to travel to the front lines so she could deliver the goods.

Barton's tenacity, honed during wartime, became crucial again when she began working to establish an American affiliate of the International Red Cross. Over a four-year period, she lobbied legislators, met with government leaders, and revealed to the public how an American relief organization would work and why it was important. Countless meetings, written pleas, and public presentations during this time were undergirded by her seemingly infinite determination and dedication to her cause.

Sarah Josepha Hale's four decades of serving as an editor of a national magazine required persistence each day of her career so she could attract the best writers to *Godey's Lady's Book*, keep the content fresh and appealing to readers, and compete successfully with other magazines also vying for subscribers. Yet nothing called on Hale's persistence more than her campaign for a national day of thanksgiving in the United States. In her comprehensive efforts, she reached out to her readers of *Godey's Lady's Book*, to governors of states, and to chief executives of the United States. Columns in the *Lady's Book*, meetings with officials, and letters to the nation's leaders—including the president of the United States—were part of her approach. Starting with President Zachery Taylor, she wrote to every American president who followed, but each ignored her letter. Rejection (or silence) from four presidents did not dampen her will to write another personal, elegant appeal to advocate for her cause. Her resolve paid off on November 26, 1863, the day of national thanksgiving promulgated by President Abraham Lincoln.

Faith: *belief and trust in and loyalty to God.* All of the five better angels were women of faith who professed their beliefs in their writings and/or lectures. Each was a member of a Protestant denomination: Clara Barton, Sarah Josepha Hale, and Julia Ward Howe were Unitarian-Universalists; Harriet Beecher Stowe was a Congregationalist; and Harriet Tubman was a member of the African Methodist Episcopal Church and had connections to the Presbyterian Church in Auburn, New York, where she married her second husband, Nelson Davis. Faith played an important role in each of the five women's lives, but it was most pronounced in two: Harriet Tubman and Julia Ward Howe.

Tubman frequently attributed her success in freeing enslaved people to God. "I tell the Lord what I need," she told her biographer Sarah Bradford, "and he provides." Tubman's life was replete with Christian teachings from the time she was a young girl. She knew and recited biblical scriptures, sang hymns, and had an abiding faith in God throughout her life.

Julia Ward Howe drew on biblical imagery as she wrote "The Battle Hymn of the Republic." Asked in her later years about how many drafts of the hymn she wrote, her response was that it was a single draft. Howe explained that she was God's instrument in writing down what He had directed her to write; therefore, no other alterations or enhancements were required for such a divinely inspired work.[2]

Courage: *mental or moral strength to resist opposition, danger, or hardship.* The better angels demonstrated, in varying degrees, the quality of courage. They exhibited strength in pursuing their objectives and were brave in overcoming difficulties in spite of the opposition, danger, or hardship they faced. Two of the women showed extraordinary courage when facing both difficult challenges and danger as they performed their duties on the battlefield during the Civil War. Both Harriet Tubman and Clara Barton risked their lives and exhibited courage in the midst of perilous situations and enemy fire.

During her time as a "conductor" on the Underground Railroad, Tubman exposed herself to capture and punishment time and time again. Later she participated in combat during the Union's Combahee River attack in South Carolina. Again, she risked capture and certain death at the hands of Confederate forces or being struck by enemy fire during the assault. Often someone who shows such bravery is called fearless, but this term minimizes the extraordinary courage that Tubman displayed. We know from her comments to others that she was not without fear, but she called on a deep reservoir of valor and a providential trust to overcome her fears.

Clara Barton encountered enemy fire on the field of battle, even experiencing a minié ball passing through the sleeve of her dress at the Battle of Antietam. Barton returned to the front lines on numerous occasions. Neither the soldiers who received her care nor the physicians who worked with her would have characterized her as anything less than undaunted. As with Tubman, we know from her letters and journals that Barton knew fear as she went about her work but that she was able to overcome it as she willingly performed her work on or near the fields of fire. In addition to courage on the battlefield, Barton was exposed to the brutal hardships of weather, unsanitary surroundings, and harsh living conditions, often working to the point of exhaustion or illness as she performed her duties. She and Tubman shared similar experiences, laboring in inhospitable climates under the most onerous conditions. Their safety, their health, and their well-being were constantly in jeopardy. Courage was their antidote.

Self-assurance: *self-confidence; sure of oneself.* Each of the five better angels had the shared characteristic of self-assurance. Facing many obstacles as women, the five built incremental levels of successes that helped fuel their self-assurance. Stowe wrote and was published even before her magnum opus, *Uncle Tom's Cabin*, appeared. Each successive published work gave her the confidence—and reputation—that sustained her ambition and self-assurance. Harriet Tubman also built upon a series of successful operations to guide enslaved people to freedom. She honed her guiding skills and increased her confidence with each escape. Her self-assurance was extraordinary.

Julia Ward Howe, among the five, was the one whose self-assurance was the longest in forming. Her husband's hindrance of her creative efforts made her progress in self-fulfillment and self-confidence a long, slow process. Even so, she achieved gains only when she kept her writing a secret from her husband. She completed and submitted for publication *Passion-Flowers*, her first book published, and "The Battle Hymn of the Republic" without her husband's knowledge. After these works were published and she gained recognition, Julia Ward Howe's self-assurance began its slow, steady growth. Following Samuel's death in 1876, Howe's freedom to create and her self-assurance were set free like the release of caged birds.

From the time she began working as a young teacher, Clara Barton's self-assurance grew and was tested in a series of positions. No parents, spouse, or employer held Barton back in achieving her goals and increasing her self-confidence. Once the Civil War started and she began exploring ways to contribute to the war effort, the stakes were higher, the obstacles more daunting, and the resistance stronger as she attempted to fulfill her plans to support the Union. Numerous times government officials, bureaucrats, and army leadership put roadblocks in her way, but Barton prevailed, sometimes questioning her own abilities but always overcoming doubts and uncertainty as she achieved what she had set out to accomplish. Her self-assurance occasionally caused male coworkers or leaders with whom she had to collaborate to resent her bold self-confidence. However, for most, they might have questioned her style of accomplishing her work, but they never doubted her competence and confidence to get the job done. They could count on Clara Barton.

Sarah Josepha Hale's self-assurance sprang from the reality of becoming a thirty-four-year-old widow and the sole support for her five young children. With some initial modest financial backing from family and friends, Hale set to work. She began writing and publishing poems and works of fiction, winning a prize from a Boston publication. These preliminary successes increased her self-confidence that she could provide for the family with her writing skills. Her novel *Northwood* further increased her confidence and exposed her to a broad audience that recognized her literary talent. Demonstrated writing and editing abilities and her self-assurance soon brought her to the attention of publisher Louis Godey, who installed her as the editor of his *Lady's Book*. Hale's long and successful career in editing a national magazine was a testament to her competence as a literary person and her profound self-assurance. Competence, confidence, and an omnipresent awareness of the need to survive on her own blended together to result in an extraordinary career for the widow Hale.

Persuasiveness: *the ability to persuade, move by argument.* Because they were women of significant achievements who made a place for themselves in the nation's history, if not always in the public eye, the five better angels all had as part of their character the ability to persuade others—of their literary abilities, of their commitment to liberty, of their ability to gather supplies and transport them to where they were needed on a battlefield, and of their belief in reconciliation and patriotism. They were called on to persuasively communicate their convictions: to convince someone to take—or not take—action, or to elicit funds, or to build support for a cause they believed in. This persuasion took the form of written and spoken words, and deeds performed.

Stowe convinced citizens in the North that slavery was an evil that needed to be abolished. Tubman was able to persuade enslaved people that she could guide them safely to freedom in the North. Howe's lyrics in "The Battle Hymn of the Republic" helped inspire Union soldiers that their cause was just and worth fighting (and dying) for. Barton induced recalcitrant army officers to help her transport needed supplies—which she had gathered—to the war's front lines. Hale was able to win over senators, governors, and eventually the president of the United States to accept the value of a national day of thanksgiving. Relying on facts, clarity of intent, and a dash of emotion, the women presented their cases and convinced decision makers of the need for decisive action.

Assertiveness: *disposed to or characterized by bold or self-confident assertion.* The five better angels all exercised this behavior early in their lives and continued to be assertive throughout their adult years until the physical frailty of age intervened. Harriet Beecher Stowe harnessed her assertiveness when she was named the editor of her school paper at Hartford Female Seminary and later when she successfully took on duties as the acting superintendent at her sister Catharine's school. These early opportunities to demonstrate her leadership abilities showed her confidence and willingness to take charge when decisions had to be made and communicated. These qualities that she developed as a young girl then became essential after she wrote *Uncle Tom's Cabin* and the criticisms from proslavery forces poured in. Her assertive trait is the underpinning of *A Key to Uncle Tom's Cabin*. In this response to her critics, Stowe took bold steps to counter their arguments with facts and logic. The critics—mostly Southern men—were not used to a woman rebuking them with such vehemence and skill.

Harriet Tubman exhibited assertiveness throughout her service with the Underground Railroad and with the Union Army in South Carolina. Typical are the accounts of Tubman's carrying a pistol during her escape efforts and her claims that she would use it against slave catchers *and* any runaway slave who dared jeopardize the safety of the group by abandoning the escape and turning back. Tubman was unwavering in her commitment to achieve liberty for those whom she led out of slavery.

Julia Ward Howe's assertive nature was challenged most often by her own spouse. Samuel Gridley Howe was a barrier she needed to work around or confront. For both strategies, she had to draw on her reservoir of determination. As her success and fame grew, her self-confidence and willingness to take bold steps—regardless of the consequences meted out by Samuel Gridley Howe—became more important in the way she conducted herself.

When a teacher in Oxford, Massachusetts, and later in Bordentown, New Jersey, Clara Barton learned early in her life that assertiveness was key to achieving her ambitious goals. Speaking up for equal pay and wanting to be evaluated on the same basis as a man, Barton learned quickly that being passive did nothing to further a cause. She applied that same assertive nature when she worked on establishing an American Red Cross in the 1870s. Barton's unstated byword was passion always; passiveness never.

As the editor of *Godey's Lady's Book*, Sarah Josepha Hale displayed assertiveness as she led the magazine, selected authors, and upgraded the graphic look of the publication. Her insistence on American authors, women contributors, and original material all drew on her assertive character. Editing a highly successful national magazine required nothing less. The area where Hale's resolve may have fallen short was the lack of coverage of the Civil War in the pages of *Godey's Lady's Book*. Could Hale have been more assertive with publisher Louis Godey to open the magazine to some Civil War coverage? Did Godey rebuff Hale's assertiveness, or was Hale against the coverage and the change it might have made in the magazine's tone? Hale's writing and her position on having only nonpolitical content for the publication since the beginning suggest the latter reason. Hale's assertiveness did not include stretching the content of *Godey's Lady's Book* beyond hearth and home.

Resourcefulness: *ability to meet situations; capability to devise ways and means.* Three of the better angels relied on their resourcefulness in numerous situations to accomplish their goals. Harriet Beecher Stowe and Julia Ward Howe exhibited resourcefulness in some of their activities, but Harriet Tubman, Clara Barton, and Sarah Josepha Hale surpassed them in the amount and scope of their enterprising endeavors. Tubman, Barton, and Hale would not have achieved the results that history attributes to them without their astute and creative engagement of people, resources, and ideas. For Tubman, it was her use of trails, waterways, and guidance from the stars for navigation coupled with a network of safe houses and sympathetic cohorts that helped lead enslaved people to freedom.

Barton tapped senior-level leaders to break through the bureaucracy of the federal government and employed a widespread system of local contributors to accumulate the medical supplies she needed to support the troops. Through her ingenuity, during the Civil War Barton could fill warehouses with supplies, engage the army's transportation resources, and ensure that medical materials needed by the troops would arrive when and where they were required. She then transferred this extraordinary aptitude to her work with the American Red Cross.

Sarah Josepha Hale's resourcefulness did not free enslaved people or save men's lives on the battlefield, but her ability to apply the necessary means to operate two national magazines successfully for nearly fifty years was exceptional. She assembled a group of talented American writers, continuously updated the graphics of her publication, and built a robust circulation base, even in the midst of an economic depression and then a war. Her sustained efforts to orchestrate myriad assets to make *Godey's Lady's Book* a success for four decades make Hale the long-distance runner in resourcefulness.

Compassion: *sympathetic consciousness of others' distress with a desire to alleviate it.* Of all the characteristics that can be attributed to the five better angels, compassion is the sine qua non for guiding their actions throughout their long lives. Each demonstrated compassionate behavior as they performed their work: writing a novel that movingly exposed the suffering of the enslaved; guiding men, women, and children out of bondage to freedom; creating a hymn to uplift those charged with serving in a war to end slavery; providing nursing and medical supplies to wounded soldiers; and advocating for a national day of thanksgiving to begin healing a nation suffering from the devastation of war. Many in the nation could express their empathy through thoughts and words for those affected by the Civil War, but the five better angels turned their compassionate inclinations into compassionate deeds. For the five women, feeling compassion was an important starting point, only a beginning; their true humanity became the basis for action that yielded results. Stowe, Tubman, Howe, Barton, and Hale were not merely compassionate spectators; they were women of action and accomplishment.

Discipline: *control gained by enforcing obedience or order.* The discipline exhibited by the five better angels is more accurately characterized as "self-discipline." Their individual successes were the result of their determination to set ambitious goals and then follow a prescribed path to completion. They were guided primarily by their own self-identified goals. Seldom did external forces impose detailed requirements on them. The women faced some outside constraints—publishers' deadlines, laws on enslavement and the disposition of escaped slaves, bureaucratic red tape, gender inequality, and indifferent government leadership—but they did not find them insurmountable. Discipline carried the day in most cases as they found alternative paths to achieve their goals. Temporary setbacks only strengthened their resolve and fueled their determination to find new avenues to succeed. Giving up was never an option.

Sovereignty: *freedom from external control, autonomy.* Elizabeth Cady Stanton's biographer Elisabeth Griffith has characterized Stanton's essence of feminist theory as "self-sovereignty." For Stanton this meant that a woman needed to be "physically, emotionally, intellectually, and financially independent."[3] As we examine the five better angels as sovereign women, all exhibit this characteristic in varying degrees during their lifetimes. Harriet Beecher Stowe gained her sovereignty as she achieved her reputation as an accomplished writer. In the early years, her family and her husband, Calvin, did impede some of her freedom, but they never derailed her progress. Keeping in mind the nineteenth-century social climate in which she lived and operated, Stowe achieved autonomy and was widely recognized as an independent entity by the public.

Harriet Tubman was the archetypical sovereign woman once she escaped slavery and found freedom in the North. Her two spouses did not restrain her, and she had no children to compete for her time as a participant in the Underground Railroad and later as a guide for the Union Army. Tubman was autonomous as she returned again and again to guide enslaved people to liberation from bondage in the South. Rejecting the conventional wisdom of zealous abolitionists, she also decided not to join John Brown during his ill-fated raid on Harpers Ferry. Tubman made up her own mind based on her own intuition. She was an emancipated woman in all respects.

Of the five better angels, Julia Ward Howe struggled most to achieve and maintain her sovereignty. Her husband, Samuel Gridley Howe, was an unrelenting impediment to her autonomy until his death. Howe's children also were frequently a complication in her achieving independence. As biographer Valarie Ziegler wrote: "The duties of marriage and motherhood thus intruded on the study opportunities of a woman who still defined herself in terms of her intellectual accomplishments."[4] The road to self-sovereignty for Julia Ward Howe was long and arduous, but in later years, she achieved the physical, emotional, intellectual, and financial independence that she struggled to achieve for so many years.

Clara Barton, meanwhile, was a sovereign woman from her early adult years. No spouse or children hampered her independence. During her service on the Civil War battlefields, her work to engage the federal government in delivering medical supplies to the army and in helping families find their missing fathers and sons, and later her drive to establish an American Red Cross, Barton was a paragon of sovereignty. She was skilled in enlisting the support of others for her projects, but in the end it was Barton's self-sufficiency and independence that contributed to her success.

Sarah Joseph Hale was a widow at age thirty-four and never remarried for the remaining fifty-seven years of her life. Without a husband and with five children depending on her as their provider, Hale achieved the position as an accomplished editor of national magazines. She was the most diligent editor—man or woman—of the mid-nineteenth century. Her self-sovereignty was an integral part of her life for nearly a half-century. It never wavered.

15

Voce Angeli, or "Voices of the Angels"

These "voices" of the better angels have come from their writing, from their speaking engagements, or from transcripts by those who interviewed them. The vocabulary and tone of these quotations reflect their origins in the nineteenth century, and some of their sentiments may appear out of step with our modern world, but the passion with which they held their beliefs rings true to us in the twenty-first century. Time has burnished, not diminished, the importance of these five accomplished women. Their words are the evidence.

Women

The barbarous custom of wresting from a woman whatever she possesses, whether by inheritance, donation, or her own industry ... and conferring it ... upon the man she marries, to be used at his discretion and will ... without allowing her any control ... [is] a monstrous perversion of justice by law.

In this age of innovation perhaps no experiment will have an influence more important on the character and happiness of our society than the granting to females the advantages of a systematic and thorough education.

There seems now some fear lest [a woman] should, in her eagerness to show the world what she can do, aim rather at doing men's work as the best part of her ability. This would be a serious mistake.

—SARAH JOSEPHA HALE

A house is kingdom in little, and its queen, if she is faithful, gentle and wise, is a sovereign indeed.

I feel that a woman's moral responsibility is lowered by the fact that she must never obey a transcendent command of conscience. Men can give her nothing to take the place of this. It is the divine right of the human soul.

God intended for male and female to live in mutual sympathy, learning from one another, so that each gender aspired to acquire the best characteristics of the other. In this way civilization truly advanced.

In my own youth women were isolated from each other by the very intensity of their personal consciousness. I thought of myself and of other women in this way. We thought that superior women ought to have been born men. A blessed change is that which we have witnessed.

In the name of womanhood and humanity, I earnestly ask that a general congress of women, without limit to nationality, may be appointed and held at someplace deemed most convenient and the earliest period consistent with its objects, to promote the alliance of the different nationalities, the amicable settlement of international questions, the great and general interests of peace.

I think nothing is religion which puts one individual absolutely above others, and surely nothing is religion which puts one sex above another. . . . Any religion which sacrifices woman to this brutality of men is no religion.

—JULIA WARD HOWE

Now the question arises, which is in fault, the Declaration of Independence, or the customs and laws of America as to woman? Is taxation without representation tyranny or not?

Yes, I do believe in Female Suffrage. The more I think of it, the more absurd this whole government of men over women looks.

Most mothers are instinctive philosophers.

In old times, women did not get their lives written, though I don't doubt many of them were much better worth writing than the men's.

So much has been said and sung of beautiful young girls, why doesn't somebody wake up to the beauty of old women?

All places where women are excluded tend downward to barbarism; but the moment she is introduced, there come in with her courtesy, cleanliness, sobriety, and order.

Whatever offices of life are performed by women of culture and refinement are thenceforth elevated; they cease to be mere servile toils, and become expressions of the ideas of superior beings.

I wrote what I did as a woman, as a mother. I was oppressed and broken-hearted with the sorrows and injustices I saw.

A woman's health is her capital.

—HARRIET BEECHER STOWE

I may sometimes be willing to teach for nothing, but if paid at all, I shall never do a man's work for less than a man's pay.

If woman alone had suffered under these mistaken traditions [of women's subordination], if she could have borne the evil by herself, it would have been less pitiful, but her brother man, in the laws he created and ignorantly worshipped, has suffered with her. He has lost her highest help; he has crippled the intelligence he needed; he has belittled the very source of his own being and dwarfed the image of his Maker.

Only an opportunity was wanting for woman to prove to man that she could be in earnest—that she had character and firmness of purpose—that she was good for something in an emergency. The war afforded her this opportunity.

—CLARA BARTON

Education

People should not say that this or that is not worth learning, giving as their reason that it will not be put to use. They can no more know what information they will need in the future than they will know the weather two hundred years from today.

—CLARA BARTON

There can be no education without leisure; and without leisure, education is worthless.

My first object in assuming my new position, was to promote the education of my own sex. I believe that the immense importance of this education had never yet been insisted upon; and I believed, moreover, that women were the appointed teachers of the young.

American women, in general, even those who are most eager in demanding what they deem the "rights" of their sex, have failed to comprehend their duties in regard to the schools in which their sons and daughters are educated.

We need Free National Normal Schools to fit young women for their office as teachers . . . we must express our hope that . . . all the women of the United States will join us in asking aid to found Free National Normal Schools for the daughters of America.

—SARAH JOSEPHA HALE

Liberty

We hear often of the negro servants, on the loss of a kind master; and with good reason, for no creature on God's earth is left more utterly unprotected and desolate than the slave. . . . The law regards him, in every respect, as devoid of rights as a bale of merchandise.

—HARRIET BEECHER STOWE

Democracies have been, and governments called, free, but the spirit of independence and the consciousness of unalienable rights, were never before transfused into the minds of a whole people. . . . The feeling of equality which they proudly cherish does not proceed from an ignorance of their station, but from the knowledge of their rights; and it is this knowledge which will render it so exceedingly difficult for any tyrant ever to triumph over the liberties of our country.

I feel it [slavery] is a stain on our national character, and none could more heartily rejoice to see the evil removed.

—SARAH JOSEPHA HALE

Slavery is the next thing to hell.

I grew up like a neglected weed—ignorant of liberty, having no experience of it. I was not happy or contented.

All that time, in my dreams and visions, I seemed to see a line, and on the other side of that line were green fields, and lovely flowers, and beautiful white ladies, who stretched out their arms to me over the line, but I couldn't reach them. . . . I always fell before I got to the line.

When I found I had crossed that line, I looked at my hands to see if I was the same person. There was such a glory over everything: the sun came like gold through the trees, and over the fields, and I felt like I was in Heaven.

I had crossed the line. I was free, but there was no one to welcome me to the land of freedom. I was a stranger in a strange land; and my home after all, was down in Maryland; because my father, my mother, my brothers, and sisters, and friends were there. But I was free, and they should be free.

There are two things I've got a right to, and these are Death and Liberty—one or the other I mean to have. No one will take me back alive; I shall fight for my liberty, and when the time has come for me to go, the Lord will let them kill me.

Now I've been free, I know what a dreadful condition slavery is. I have seen hundreds of escaped slaves, but I never saw one who was willing to go back and be a slave.

God's time is always near. He set the North Star in the heavens; He gave me the strength in my limbs. He meant I should be free.

> When that old chariot comes,
> I'm going to leave you;
> I'm bound for the Promised Land.
> I'm going to leave you.

—HARRIET TUBMAN

Bravery

There is no impossibility to him who stands prepared to conquer every hazard. The fearful are the failing.

Courage and skill are not to be taught by lectures . . . they must be acquired by practice, and improved by braving danger; and the younger we begin our lessons the better.

—SARAH JOSEPHA HALE

I said to the Lord, I'm going to hold steady on you, and I know you will see me through.

I have heard their groans and sighs, and seen their tears, and I would give every drop of blood in my veins to free them.

—HARRIET TUBMAN

He is coming like the glory of the morning on the wave,
He is wisdom to the mighty, he is succor to the brave,
So the world shall be his footstool, and the soul of Time his slave,
Our God is marching on.

—JULIA WARD HOWE

I am braver than I was because I have lost all; and he who has nothing to lose can afford all risks.

—HARRIET BEECHER STOWE, *Uncle Tom's Cabin*

I may be compelled to face danger, but never fear it, and while our soldiers can stand and fight, I can stand and feed and nurse them.

The conflict is one thing I've been waiting for. I'm well and strong and young—young enough to go to the front. If I can't be a soldier, I'll help soldiers.

If my Countrymen are to suffer, my place is with them, my Northern brothers are here in arms, danger and death staring them in the face and I cannot leave them.

—CLARA BARTON

Success

Riches are always over estimated; the enjoyment they give is more in the pursuit than the possession.

Happiness can never be compelled to be our companion, nor is she oftenest won by those who most eagerly seek her. She most frequently meets us in situations where we never expected her visits; in employments or under privations to which we have become reconciled only by a sense of duty.

—SARAH JOSEPHA HALE

I was the conductor of the Underground Railroad for eight years, and I can say what most conductors can't say—I never ran my train off the track and I never lost a passenger.

... and I prayed to God to make me strong and able to fight, and that's what I've always prayed for ever since.

—HARRIET TUBMAN

When you get into a tight place, and everything goes against you till it seems as if you couldn't hold on a minute longer, never give up then, for that's just the place and time that the tide will turn.

Everyone confesses in the abstract that exertion which brings out all the powers of body and mind is the best thing for us all; but practically most people do all they can to get rid of it, and as a general rule nobody does much more than circumstances drive them to.

To do common things perfectly is far better worth our endeavor than to do uncommon things respectably.

—HARRIET BEECHER STOWE

You must never so much think as whether you like it or not, whether it is bearable or not; you must never think of anything except the need, and how to meet it.

The door that nobody else will go in at, seems always to swing open widely for me.

I have never worked for fame or praise, and shall not feel their loss as I otherwise would. I have never for a moment lost sight of the humble life I was born to, its small environments, and the consequently little right I had to expect much of myself, and shall have the less to censure, or upbraid myself with for the failures I must see myself make.

The surest test of discipline is its absence.

Economy, prudence, and a simple life are the sure masters of need, and will often accomplish that which, their opposites, with a fortune at hand, will fail to do.

—CLARA BARTON

War

The strokes of the pen need deliberation as much as the sword needs swiftness.

> The flag of our stately battles, not struggles of wrath and greed,
> Its stripes were a holy lesson, its spangles a deathless creed;
> 'Twas red with the blood of freemen, and white with the fear of the foe;
> And the stars that fight in their courses 'gainst tyrants its symbols know."

Why do not the mothers of mankind interfere in these matters, to prevent the waste of that human life of which they alone bear and know the cost?

From the bosom of the devastated earth a voice goes up with our own. It says: "Disarm, disarm!" The sword of murder is not the balance of Justice. Blood does not wipe out dishonor, nor violence vindicate possession.

—JULIA WARD HOWE

If I were to speak of war, it would not be to show you the glories of conquering armies but the mischief and misery they strew in their tracks, and how, while they marched on with tread of iron and plumes proudly tossing in the breeze, someone must follow closely in their steps, crouching to the earth, toiling in the rain and darkness, shelter less themselves, with no thought of pride or glory, fame or praise, or reward; hearts breaking with pity, faces bathed in tears and hands in blood. This is the side which history never shows.

I don't know how long it has been since my ear has been free from the roll of a drum. It is the music I sleep by, and I love it. . . . I shall remain here while anyone remains, and do so whatever comes to my hand. I may be compelled to face danger, but never fear it, and while our soldiers can stand and fight, I can stand and feed and nurse them.

What armies and how much of war I have seen, what thousands of marching troops, what fields of slain, what prisons, what hospitals, what ruins, what cities in ashes, what hunger and nakedness, what orphanages, what widowhood, what wrongs and what vengeance.

My business is stanching blood and feeding fainting men; my post the open field between the bullet and the hospital.

My heart sickened and stood still, my brain whirled, and the light of my eyes went out, and I said "surely this [Andersonville Prison] was not the gate of hell, but hell itself."

—CLARA BARTON

Admonitions

Well, good-by, Uncle Tom; keep a stiff upper lip.

Any mind that is capable of a real sorrow is capable of good.

By what strange law of mind is it that an idea long overlooked, and trodden under foot as a useless stone, suddenly sparkles out in new light, as a discovered diamond?

True love ennobles and dignifies the material labor of life; and homely services rendered for love's sake have in them a poetry that is immortal.

The bitterest tears shed over graves are for words left unsaid and deeds left undone.

—HARRIET BEECHER STOWE

I am confirmed in my division of human energies. Ambitious people climb, but faithful people build.

There is no hell like that of a selfish heart, and there is no misfortune so great as that of not being able to make a sacrifice.

—JULIA WARD HOWE

Every great dream begins with a dreamer. Always remember, you have within you the strength, the patience, and the passion to reach for the stars to change the world.

If you hear the dogs, keep going. If you see the torches in the woods, keep going. If there's shouting after you, keep going. Don't ever stop. Keep going. If you want a taste of freedom, keep going.

Never wound a snake; kill it.

—HARRIET TUBMAN

An institution or reform movement that is not selfish, must originate in the recognition of some evil that is adding to the sum of human suffering, or diminishing the sum of happiness.

—CLARA BARTON

And the angels are with them to help their humble efforts, when men are probably relying on their own strength.

—SARAH JOSEPHA HALE

NOTES

1. The Better Angels of Our Nature

1. Howe, "Battle Hymn of the Republic."

2. Dunn to wife, undated clipping, Clara Barton Papers, Library of Congress; and Pryor, *Clara Barton*, 99.

3. African American spiritual describing events in the Old Testament of the Bible; songwriter and date unknown.

4. Attributed to William Gilmore Simms in Gossett, *Uncle Tom's Cabin*, 191.

5. Harriet Beecher Stowe to the editor of *New York Observer*, May 1852, Beecher Family Papers, Sterling Memorial Library, Yale University.

6. Stowe, *Life of Harriet Beecher Stowe*, 145.

7. Stowe, *Life of Harriet Beecher Stowe*, 203.

8. Stowe, *Key to Uncle Tom's Cabin*, iii.

9. Stowe, *Key to Uncle Tom's Cabin*, preface, 1.

10. Stowe, *Key to Uncle Tom's Cabin*, 1.

11. Hedrick, *Harriet Beecher Stowe*, 239.

12. Hall, *Story of the Battle Hymn*, 51.

13. Army song especially popular with Massachusetts regiments. See Showalter, *Civil Wars*, 164.

14. Howe, *Reminiscences, 1810–1899*, 273.

15. Oates, *Woman of Valor*, 84.

16. Pryor, *Clara Barton*, 97.

17. Oates, *Woman of Valor*, 84.

18. Oates, *Woman of Valor*, 85.

19. Oates, *Woman of Valor*, 85.

20. Clara Barton, *Notes and Incidents*, Clara Barton Papers, Sophia Smith Collection.

21. Oates, *Woman of Valor*, 86.

22. Pryor, *Clara Barton*, 99.

23. Dubois, *To My Countrywomen*, 27.

24. Fryatt, *Sarah Josepha Hale*, 113.

25. Rogers, *Sarah Josepha Hale*, 114.

26. Fryatt, *Sarah Josepha Hale*, 117.

27. Dubois, *To My Countrywomen*, 97.

28. Sarah Josepha Hale letter to Abraham Lincoln, September 28, 1863, Abraham Lincoln Papers, Library of Congress.

29. Alexander Hamilton, eulogy on Nathanael Greene, July 4, 1789, to fellow members of the Society of the Cincinnati, National Archives, Washington DC.

30. Showalter, *Civil Wars*, 174.

2. Women in Antebellum America

1. Gordon, "Young Ladies' Academy," 83.

2. Hedrick, *Harriet Beecher Stowe*, 46.

3. Woody, *History of Women's Education*, 492–98.

4. Wood, *Empire of Liberty*, 316, 317.

5. Lerner, "Lady and the Mill Girl," 12.

6. Lerner, "Lady and the Mill Girl," 6.

7. Wood, *Empire of Liberty*, 501.

8. Wood, *Empire of Liberty*, 602, 603.

9. Welter, "Cult of True Womanhood," 152.

10. Douglas, *Feminization of American Culture*.

11. Wood, *Empire of Liberty*, 598.

12. Welter, "Cult of True Womanhood," 153.

13. Welter, "Cult of True Womanhood," 153.

14. Finley, *Lady of Godey's*, 27, 43–47.

15. Massey, *Women in the Civil War*, xix.

3. The Underground Railroad

1. Bradford, *Scenes in the Life*, 24.

2. LaRoche, *Geography of Resistance*, 3.

3. Horton and Horton, *Slavery and the Making*, 29.

4. Foner, *Gateway to Freedom*, 19.

5. Foner, *Gateway to Freedom*, 4.

6. Fehrenbacher, *Dred Scott Case*, 559.

7. Horton and Horton, *Slavery and the Making*, 159.

8. Bradford, *Scenes in the Life*, 6–8.

9. Larson, *Bound for the Promised Land*, 11.

10. Larson, *Bound for the Promised Land*, xvi.

11. Larson, *Bound for the Promised Land*, 43.

12. Larson, *Bound for the Promised Land*, 46.

13. Larson, *Bound for the Promised Land*, 47.

14. Bradford, *Scenes in the Life*, 75–76.

15. Bradford, *Scenes in the Life*, 14–15.

16. Bradford, *Scenes in the Life*, 19, 20.

17. Larson, *Bound for the Promised Land*, 85.

18. "Runaways," *Eastern (MD) Star*, August 14, 1849.

19. Larson, *Bound for the Promised Land*, 91; and Cheney, "Moses," 35.

20. Brown, *Rising Son*, 538.

21. Sernett, *Harriet Tubman*, 321–23.

22. Cheney, "Moses," 36.

23. Larson, *Bound for the Promised Land*, 102.

24. Larson, *Bound for the Promised Land*, 101.

4. Abolitionism in America

1. Otis, *Rights of British Colonies*, 37.

2. Abigail to John Adams, September 22, 1774, in Butterfield, *Adams Family Correspondence*.

3. McPherson, *Battle Cry of Freedom*, 39.

4. Beecher, *Autobiography of Lyman Beecher*, 1:46.

5. Hedrick, *Harriet Beecher Stowe*, 32, 35.

6. Calvin Ellis Stowe to Harriet Beecher Stowe, May 2, 1844, folder 61, Beecher-Stowe Collection, Harvard University.

7. Calvin Ellis Stowe to Harriet Beecher Stowe, April 30, 1842, Harriet Beecher Stowe Center.

8. Harriet Beecher Stowe to Catharine Beecher, 1850, Beecher Family Papers, Sterling Memorial Library.

9. Hale, *Woman's Record*, 837.

10. Hedrick, *Harriet Beecher Stowe*, 218.

11. *National Era*, October 30, 1851.

12. Clayhaugh, introduction, *Uncle Tom's Cabin*, xiv.

13. Joel Parker to Harriet Beecher Stowe, May 19, 1852, Beecher Family Papers, Sterling Memorial Library.

14. McPherson, *Battle Cry of Freedom*, 89.

15. McPherson, *Battle Cry of Freedom*, 90.

16. Villard, *John Brown*.

5. The "Seething Hell of War"

1. McPherson, *Battle Cry of Freedom*, 8.

2. Ward, *Civil War*, 27.

3. McPherson, *Battle Cry of Freedom*, 392.

4. Plumb, *Your Brother in Arms*, 6, 10–12.

5. Basler, *Collected Works*, 4:432.

6. McPherson, *Battle Cry of Freedom*, 480.

7. Adams, *Doctors in Blue*, 68.

8. McPherson, *Battle Cry of Freedom*, 483.

9. McPherson, *Battle Cry of Freedom*, 485, 486.

10. McPherson. *Battle Cry of Freedom*, 483.

11. Pryor, *Clara Barton*, 6.

12. Oates, *Woman of Valor*, 25.

13. Clara Barton Papers, Clara Barton Note to Dr. Foote, c. 1875, Clara Barton Papers, Sophia Smith Collection.

14. L. N. Fowler, noted nineteenth-century phrenologist, examined young Clara and determined that her "distinctive traits" suggested she enter the teaching profession.

15. Pryor, *Clara Barton*, 23.

16. Why Barton chose Bordentown as her next challenge as an educator is not clear. Author Elizabeth Brown Pryor cites historical associations; a signer of the Declaration of Independence (Francis Hopkinson) and Thomas Paine, the revolution's political theorist, had resided in Bordentown. Joseph Bonaparte, the elder brother of Napoleon I, lived there as well. Barton was also taken by the town's location on the scenic Delaware River. Pryor cited yet another plausible but unconfirmed reason for Barton's move: a past beau and friend Charles Norton came to Bordentown to teach school.

17. Oates, *Woman of Valor*, 5.

18. Oates, *Woman of Valor*, 17.

19. Oates, *Woman of Valor*, 19.

20. Pryor, *Clara Barton*, 81.

21. Oates, *Woman of Valor*, 57.

22. Clara Barton to Leander Poor, in Epler, *Life of Clara Barton*, 1:174.

23. McPherson, *Battle Cry of Freedom*, 532.

24. Oates, *Woman of Valor*, 70.

25. Oates, *Woman of Valor*, 80, 81.

26. Oates, *Woman of Valor*, 82.

27. Oates, *Woman of Valor*, 91.

6. Noble Watchwords and Inspiring Ideas

1. Showalter, *Civil Wars*, 3.

2. Howe, *Reminiscences, 1819–1899*, 18.

3. Showalter, *Civil Wars*, 10.

4. Fuller, *Letters of Margaret Fuller*, II:72.

5. Howe, *Reminiscences, 1819–1899*, 49.

6. Howe, *Reminiscences, 1819–1899*, 81.

7. Samuel Gridley Howe to Julia Ward, undated letter, Harriet Beecher Stowe, Yellow House Papers.

8. Ziegler, *Diva Julia*, 30.

9. Ziegler, *Diva Julia*, 42.

10. Howe, *The Hermaphrodite*, 2004.

11. Ziegler, *Diva Julia*, 55.

12. Ziegler, *Diva Julia*, 73n35.

13. Showalter, *Civil Wars*, 101.

14. Showalter, *Civil Wars*, 112.

15. Showalter, *Civil Wars*, 122, 123.

16. Howe, *Reminiscences, 1819–1899*, 254.

17. Howe, *Trip to Cuba*, 81.

18. Howe, *Reminiscences, 1819–1899*, 272.

19. Hall, *Story of the Battle Hymn*, 57.

20. Showalter, *Civil Wars*, 166.

7. Tending to the Wounded and Missing

1. Halstead interview, Clara Barton Papers, Library of Congress.

2. Clara Barton to Mary Norton, September 26, 1862, Mary Norton Papers, Duke University.

3. Oates, *Woman of Valor*, 95.

4. Clara Barton to Mary Norton, October 10, 1862, Mary Norton Papers.

5. Clara Barton Lecture [undated], Clara Barton Papers, Library of Congress.

6. Clara Barton Lecture, Clara Barton Papers, Library of Congress.

7. Clara Barton to T. W. Meighan, June 24, 1863, Clara Barton Papers, Library of Congress.

8. Oates, *Woman of Valor*, 99.

9. Oates, *Woman of Valor*, 101.

10. Clara Barton to Elvira Stone, December 12, 1862, Clara Barton Papers, Library of Congress.

11. Longstreet, *Battle of Fredericksburg*, 3:79.

12. Oates, *Woman of Valor*, 113.

13. Oates, *Woman of Valor*, 117.

14. Oates, *Woman of Valor*, 111.

15. Clara Barton letter to Mary Norton, February 12, 1863, Collection of Dr. A. J. Jack, typescript in Hightstown Memorial Library, Hightstown, New Jersey, and cited in Pryor, *Clara Barton*, 393n5.

16. Letter of Introduction, Maj. Edward Preston, March 23, 1863, Clara Barton Papers, Smith College.

17. Oates, *Woman of Valor*, 123.

18. McPherson, *Battle Cry of Freedom*, 487.

19. Parish, *American Civil War*, 147.

20. McPherson, *Battle Cry of Freedom*, 485.

8. The Prolonged War

1. McPherson, *Battle Cry of Freedom*, 564.

2. McPherson, *Battle Cry of Freedom*, 565.

3. McPherson, *Battle Cry of Freedom*, 566.

4. Horton and Horton, *Slavery and the Making*, 186; and Higginson, *Army Life*, xiii.

5. Wood, *Pension Claim of Harriet Tubman*.

6. Wood, *Pension Claim of Harriet Tubman*.

7. Tubman may have accompanied Colonel Higginson's troops on a raid that captured and occupied Jacksonville, Florida, in March 1863, but according to historian Kate Clifford Larson, this "is not known." Larson, *Bound for the Promised Land*, 211.

8. Larson, *Bound for the Promised Land*, 214.

9. Larson, *Bound for the Promised Land*, 215.

10. Bradford, *Scenes in the Life*, 86.

11. Larson, *Bound for the Promised Land*, 216n7.

12. Larson, *Bound for the Promised Land*, 218n92; and Harriet Tubman letter to Franklin Sanborn, June 30, 1863, in Bradford, *Scenes in the Life*, 86, 87.

13. Larson, *Bound for the Promised Land*, 220, 367n102.

14. Hart, *Slavery and Abolition*, 209.

15. Catton, *Never Call Retreat*, 226.

16. Pryor, *Clara Barton*, 119.

17. Pryor, *Clara Barton*, 121.

18. Oates, *Woman of Valor*, 380.

19. Oates, *Woman of Valor*, 232.

20. Oates, *Woman of Valor*, 233.

21. Clara Barton letter to Mrs. Allen, May 30, 1864, Library of Congress.

9. "With Malice toward None"

1. Agassiz, *Meade's Headquarters*, 147.

2. McPherson, *Battle Cry of Freedom*, 742. Emphasis in original.

3. McPherson, *Battle Cry of Freedom*, 742.

4. McPherson, *Battle Cry of Freedom*, 769.

5. McPherson, *Battle Cry of Freedom*, 772, 773.

6. Lincoln, "Second Inaugural Address," March 4, 1865, Lincoln Papers.

7. Rogers, *Sarah Josepha Hale*, 12.

8. Rogers, *Sarah Josepha Hale*, 12, 13.

9. Rogers, *Sarah Josepha Hale*, 15.

10. Rogers, *Sarah Josepha Hale*, 17.

11. Dubois, *To My Countrywomen*, 15.

12. Dubois, *To My Countrywomen*, 16.

13. Hale, *Northwood*, 323.

14. Fryatt, *Sarah Josepha Hale*, 123.

15. Hale, *Northwood*, 2nd ed., 407.

16. Abraham Lincoln, "Second Inaugural Address."

17. Rogers, *Sarah Josepha Hale*, 27.

18. Rogers, *Sarah Josepha Hale*, 32.

19. Rogers, *Sarah Josepha Hale*, 33, 34.

20. Rogers, *Sarah Josepha Hale*, 98.

21. The governors were Nathaniel P. Banks, former governor of Massachusetts and then a major general in the Union Army, and Edwin D. Morgan, governor of New York.

22. Hale, *Manners*, 336.

10. "Joy My Freedom!"

1. McPherson, *Battle Cry of Freedom*, 854. These numbers have been increased since McPherson's book. One historian believes losses were 650,000–850,000 (Dr. J. David Hacker reported on the Battlefield Trust website, https://www.battlefields.org).

2. Foner, *Reconstruction*, xxv.

3. Williams, Current, and Freidel, *History of the United States*, 651.

4. Williams, Current, and Freidel, *History of the United States*, 667.

5. Foner, *Life and Writings*, 3:293.

6. Foner, *Reconstruction*, 18.

7. Foner, *Reconstruction*, 18.

8. Foner, *Reconstruction*, 25.

9. Stowe, *Life of Harriet Beecher Stowe*, 273, 278.

10. Hedrick, *Harriet Beecher Stowe*, 344.

11. Hedrick, *Harriet Beecher Stowe*, 346.

12. Hedrick, *Harriet Beecher Stowe*, 348.

13. Hedrick, *Harriet Beecher Stowe*, 351.

14. Hedrick, *Harriet Beecher Stowe*, 352.

15. Harriet Beecher Stowe to Sara Willis Parton, October 24, 1868, Parton Papers, Smith College.

16. Elizabeth Cady Stanton, "The Moral of the Byron Case," *Revolution*, September 9, 1869, 152.

17. Hedrick, *Harriet Beecher Stowe*, 369.

18. Larson, *Bound for the Promised Land*, 230.

19. Larson, *Bound for the Promised Land*, 232.

20. Larson, *Bound for the Promised Land*, 242.

21. Larson, *Bound for the Promised Land*, 245.

22. "Five of Clubs, a group of ambitious, intellectual, and convivial young professional men . . ." See Showalter, *Civil Wars*, 35.

23. Howe, *Reminiscences, 1810–1899*, 372, 373.

24. Showalter, *Civil Wars*, 186, 187.

25. Howe, *Reminiscences, 1810–1899*, 374, 375.

26. Oates, *Woman of Valor*, 308.

27. Clara Barton Papers, American Antiquarian Society.

28. Oates, *Woman of Valor*, 311.

29. Okker, *Our Sister Editors*, 1.

30. Sarah Josepha Hale to Mathew Vassar, March 30, 1865, Sarah Joseph Hale Papers, Richards Free Library.

31. Matthew Vassar to Sarah Josepha Hale, June 27, 1965, Sarah Joseph Hale Papers, Richards Free Library.

11. Women in Post–Civil War America

1. Sigerman, *Laborers for Liberty*; and Cott, *No Small Courage*, 312–13.

2. Sigerman, *Laborers for Liberty*, 315.

3. Sigerman, *Laborers for Liberty*, 320.

4. Sigerman, *Laborers for Liberty*, 336, 337.

5. Sigerman, *Laborers for Liberty*, 339–45.

6. Sigerman, *Laborers for Liberty*, 304.

7. Hedrick, *Harriet Beecher Stowe*, 361.

8. Koester, *Harriet Beecher Stowe*, 272.

9. Hedrick, *Harriet Beecher Stowe*, 373–75.

10. Koester, *Harriet Beecher Stowe*, 299.

11. Telford, "Harriet"; and Larson, *Bound for the Promised Land*, 277.

12. Larson, *Bound for the Promised Land*, 280.

13. Larson, *Bound for the Promised Land*, 276.

14. Bradford, *Scenes in the Life*, 35.

15. "The Fight for the Ballot," *Rochester (NY) Democrat and Chronicle*, November 19, 1896.

16. Richards and Elliot, *Julia Ward Howe*, 2:374.

17. Ziegler, *Diva Julia*, 108.

18. Address of Julia Ward Howe at the American Woman Suffrage Association, Minneapolis, October 1885.

19. Howe, *Reminiscences, 1810–1899*, 328.

20. Ziegler, *Diva Julia*, 117.

21. Showalter, *Civil Wars*, 271n25.

22. Showalter, *Civil Wars*, 204.

23. Showalter, *Civil Wars*, 174.

24. Clara Barton lecture on Andersonville (not dated), Library of Congress.

25. Pryor, *Clara Barton*, 143.

26. Pryor, *Clara Barton*, 147.

27. "Miss Barton's Lecture," *Jersey City Evening Journal*, April 3, 1868.

28. Pryor, *Clara Barton*, 152.

29. Pryor, *Clara Barton*, 171.

30. Pryor, *Clara Barton*, 210.

31. Fryatt, *Sarah Josepha Hale*, 136.

32. Fryatt, *Sarah Josepha Hale*, 138.

33. Fryatt, *Sarah Josepha Hale*, 137.

34. Rogers, *Sarah Josepha Hale*, 119.

12. Concluding Remarkable Lives

1. Cott, *No Small Courage*, 369; and Golden and Rockoff, *Strategic Factors*.

2. Sarah Josepha Hale, farewell letter, *Godey's Lady's Book*, December 31, 1877.

3. Stowe, *Poganuc People*, 31.

4. Hedrick, *Harriet Beecher Stowe*, 391.

5. Hedrick, *Harriet Beecher Stowe*, 397.

6. Hedrick, *Harriet Beecher Stowe*, 398.

7. Ziegler, *Diva Julia*, 148.

8. Showalter, *Civil Wars*, 239.

9. Richards and Elliot, *Julia Ward Howe*, 2:350.

10. Senator Redfield Proctor, "The Condition of Cuba: It Is Not Peace, nor Is It War," speech in the U.S. Senate, Washington DC, March 17, 1808, 9, 10.

11. Clara Barton to Julio Carbonell, MD, October 20, 1899, Clara Barton Papers, Library of Congress.

12. J. H. K. Willcox to Clara Barton, August 8, 1881, Clara Barton Papers, Library of Congress.

13. Pryor, *Clara Barton*, 199.

14. Harper, "Life and Work of Clara Barton," 701, 702.

15. Barton, *Peace and War*, 197.

16. Pryor, *Clara Barton*, 372.

17. Larson, *Bound for the Promised Land*, 287.

18. Larson, *Bound for the Promised Land*, 288.

13. The Angels among Us Still

1. Ellis, *The Quartet*, xvii.

2. Claybaugh, introduction, *Uncle Tom's Cabin*, xv.

3. Claybaugh, introduction, *Uncle Tom's Cabin*, xxxiv.

4. Larson, *Bound for the Promised Land*, 290, 291.

5. Larson, *Bound for the Promised Land*, 244.

6. Larson, *Bound for the Promised Land*, 291.

7. Philip Kennicott, "Harriet Tubman Is Perfect for the $20 Bill, but Which Tubman?" *Washington Post*, April 2016.

8. Showalter, *Civil Wars*, 241.

9. Showalter, *Civil Wars*, 101.

10. The Listener, *Boston Evening Transcript*, August 11, 1917.

11. See the American Red Cross website, www.redcross.org.

12. "The Charities Americans Like Most and Least," *The Chronicle of Philanthropy*, December 13, 1996.

13. Oates, *Woman of Valor*, 381.

14. Clara Barton Diary, March 7–27, 1866, Clara Barton Papers, Library of Congress.

15. Clara Barton, "The Women Who Went to the Field," which is printed and distributed by the National Park Service at the Clara Barton National Historic Site, Glen Echo, Maryland. Read during a reception on November 18, 1892, at the Willard Hotel in Washington DC for the Potomac Relief Corps, a unit of the National Woman's Relief Corps.

14. "Contemplating Their Example"

1. All definitions in chapter 14 are from *Merriam-Webster's Collegiate Dictionary*, 11th ed., 2003.

2. Showalter, *Civil Wars*, 166.

3. Griffith, *In Her Own Right*, xviii.

4. Ziegler, *Diva Julia*, 30.

BIBLIOGRAPHY

Archives

Barton, Clara. Papers. American Antiquarian Society, Worcester, Massachusetts; Clara Barton National Historical Site, Glen Echo, Maryland; Library of Congress, Washington DC; Sophia Smith Collection, Smith College Archives, Northampton, Massachusetts; and University of Maryland Special Collections, Hornbake Library, College Park.

Beecher Family. Papers. Sterling Memorial Library, Yale University, New Haven, Connecticut.

Hale, Sarah Josepha. Papers. Richards Free Library, Newport, New Hampshire; University of New Hampshire, Dimond Library, Durham; and Vassar College Library, Poughkeepsie, New York.

Howe, Julia Ward. Papers. Harvard University, Houghton Library, Cambridge, Massachusetts; Radcliffe College, Harvard University, Schlesinger Library, Cambridge, Massachusetts; and Yellow House Papers, Laura E. Richards Collection: An Inventory and Historical Guide, Gardiner Library Association and College, Waterville, Maine.

Lincoln, Abraham. Papers. Library of Congress, Washington DC.

Norton, Mary. Papers. Duke University, Durham, North Carolina.

Parton, Sara Willis. Papers. Sophia Smith Library, Smith College, Northampton, Massachusetts.

Stowe, Harriet Beecher. Beecher-Stowe Collection, Schlesinger Library on the History of Women's History, Radcliffe College, Harvard University, Cambridge, Massachusetts; and Berg Collection, New York Public Library, New York; Harriet Beecher Stowe Center, Hartford, Connecticut.

Tubman, Harriet. Papers. Harriet Tubman Museum, Auburn, New York; and Harriet Tubman Museum and Education Center, Cambridge, Maryland.

Wood, Charles P. *Manuscript History Concerning the Pension Claim of Harriet Tubman.* June 1, 1888. HR 55A-DI, National Archives, Washington DC.

Published Works

Adams, George W. *Doctors in Blue: The Medical History of the Union Army in the Civil War.* Baton Rouge: LSU Press, 1996.

Agassiz, George P., ed. *Meade's Headquarters, 1863–1865: Letters of Colonel Theodore Lyman from the Wilderness to Appomattox*. Boston: Atlantic Monthly Press, 1922.

Allen, Thomas B. *Harriet Tubman, Secret Agent: How Daring Slaves and Free Blacks Spied for the Union during the Civil War*. Washington DC: National Geographic Society, 2009.

Baker, Jean H. *Sisters: The Lives of America's Suffragists*. New York: Hill and Wang, 2005.

Barnes, Surgeon General Joseph K., ed. *The Medical and Surgical History of the War of the Rebellion 1861–1865*. Washington DC: U.S. Government Printing Office, 1870–88.

Barton, Clara. *The Red Cross in Peace and War*. Washington DC: American Historical Press, 1899.

Basler, Roy C., ed. *The Collected Works of Abraham Lincoln*. New Brunswick NJ: Rutgers University Press, 1990.

Bearss, Ed. *Fields of Honor*. Washington DC: National Geographic Society, 2006.

Beecher, Lyman. *Autobiography of Lyman Beecher*. 2 vols. Edited by Barbara M. Cross. Cambridge MA: Belknap Press of Harvard University Press, 1961.

Billings, John D. *Hardtack and Coffee: The Unwritten Story of Army Life*, 1887. Reprint, Bison Books, 1993.

Bradford, Sarah H. *Scenes in the Life of Harriet Tubman*. Auburn NY: W. J. Moses, 1869. Reprint, Forgotten Books, 2012.

Brown, William Wells. *The Rising Son: The Antecedents and Advancement of the Colored Race*. Boston: A. G. Brown, 1882.

Butterfield, Lyman H., ed. *Adams Family Correspondence*. Vol. 1. Cambridge MA: Harvard University Press, 1903.

Catton, Bruce. *The Coming Fury*. Vol. 1, *The Centennial History of the Civil War*. Garden City NY: Doubleday, 1961.

———. *Glory Road: The Bloody Route from Fredericksburg to Gettysburg*. Garden City NY: Doubleday, 1952.

———. *Mr. Lincoln's Army*. Garden City NY: Doubleday, 1951.

———. *Never Call Retreat*. Vol. 3, *The Centennial History of the Civil War*. Garden City NY: Doubleday, 1965.

———. *Terrible Swift Sword*. Vol. 2, *The Centennial History of the Civil War*. Garden City NY: Doubleday, 1963.

———. *This Hallowed Ground: The Story of the Union Side of the Civil War*. Garden City NY: Doubleday, 1956.

Cheney, Ednah Dow. "Moses." *Freedmen's Record*, March 1865.

Conrad, Earl. *Harriet Tubman*. Washington DC: Associated Publishers, 1943.

Cott, Nancy F., ed. *No Small Courage: A History of Women in the United States*. New York: Oxford University Press, 2000.

Douglas, Ann. *The Feminization of American Culture*. New York: Knopf, 1977.

Dubois, Muriel L. *To My Countrywomen: The Life of Sarah Josepha Hale.* Bedford NH: Apprentice Shop Books, 2006.

Ellis, Joseph P. *The Quartet: Orchestrating the Second American Revolution.* New York: Knopf, 2015.

Epler, Percy H. *The Life of Clara Barton.* New York: Macmillan, 1926.

Faust, Drew Gilpin. *The Republic of Suffering: Death and the American Civil War.* New York: Knopf, 2008.

Fehrenbacher, Don Edward. *The Dred Scott Case: Its Significance in American Law and Politics.* New York: Oxford University Press, 2001.

Finley, Ruth. *The Lady of Godey's, Sarah Josepha Hale.* Philadelphia: J. B. Lippincott, 1931.

Floyd, Claudia. *Maryland Women in the Civil War: Unionists, Rebels, Slaves & Spies.* Charleston SC: History Press, 2013.

Foner, Eric. *Gateway to Freedom: The Hidden History of the Underground Railroad.* New York: W. W. Norton, 2015.

——. *Reconstruction: America's Unfinished Revolution: 1863–1877.* New York: HarperCollins, 1988.

Foner, Philip S., ed. *The Life and Writings of Frederick Douglass.* 5 vols. New York: International Publishers, 1950–75.

Foote, Shelby. *The Civil War, a Narrative.* 3 vols. New York: Random House, 1958–74.

Fryatt, Norma R. *Sarah Josepha Hale: The Life and Times of a Nineteenth-Century Career Woman.* New York: Hawthorn Books, 1975.

Fuller, Margaret. *The Letters of Margaret Fuller, 1917–1838.* Edited by Robert Hudspeth. Ithaca NY: Cornell University, 1983.

Garrison, Webb. *Amazing Women of the Civil War.* Nashville: Rutledge Hill Press, Thomas Nelson, 1999.

Golden, Claudia, and Hugh Rockoff, eds. *Strategic Factors in Nineteenth Century American Economic History: A Volume to Honor Robert W. Fogel.* Chicago: University of Chicago Press, 1992.

Gordon, Ann. "The Young Ladies Academy of Philadelphia." In *Women of America: A History,* edited by Carol Ruth Berkin and Mary Beth Norton, 68–91. Boston: Houghton Mifflin, 1979.

Gossett, Thomas F. *Uncle Tom's Cabin and American Culture.* Dallas: Southern Methodist University Press, 1985.

Griffith, Elisabeth. *In Her Own Right: The Life of Elizabeth Cady Stanton.* New York: Oxford University Press, 1984.

Hale, Sarah Josepha. *Manners, or Happy Homes and Good Society All the Year Round.* Boston: J. E. Tilton, 1868.

——. *Northwood, or Life North and South.* Boston: Bowles & Dearborn, 1827.

——. *Northwood.* Rev. ed. New York: H. Long & Brother, 1852.

——. *Woman's Record.* New York: Harper & Brothers, 1860.

Hall, Florence Howe. *The Story of the Battle Hymn of the Republic.* New York: Harper & Brothers, 1916.

Harper, Ida H. "The Live and Work of Clara Barton." *North American Review* 195, no. 5 (May 1912).

Hart, Albert Bushnell. *Slavery and Abolition, 1831–1841.* New York: American Nation Series, 1906.

Hedrick, Joan D. *Harriet Beecher Stowe: A Life.* New York: Oxford University Press, 1994.

Heilbrun, Carolyn G. *Writing a Woman's Life.* New York: W. W. Norton, 1988.

Higginson, Thomas Wentworth. *Army Life in a Black Regiment.* Rev. ed. New York: Penguin Classics, 1997.

Horton, James Oliver, and Lois E. Horton. *Slavery and the Making of America.* New York: Oxford University Press, 2005.

Howe, Julia Ward. "Battle Hymn of the Republic." *The Atlantic Monthly* 9, no. 52 (February 1862): 10.

———. *From the Oak to the Olive: A Plain Record of a Pleasant Journey.* Boston: Lee and Shepard, 1868.

———. *The Hermaphrodite.* Edited by Gary Williams. Lincoln: University of Nebraska Press, 2004.

———. *Passion-Flowers.* Boston: Ticknor, Reed, and Fields, 1854.

———. *Reminiscences, 1819–1899.* Boston: Houghton Mifflin, 1899.

———. *A Trip to Cuba.* Boston: Ticknor and Fields, 1860.

Johnson, Robert Underwood, and Clarence Clough Buel, eds. *Battles and Leaders of the Civil War.* 4 vols. New York: Century, 1887–88.

Kerber, Linda. "The Republican Mother: Women and the Enlightenment—an American Perspective." *American Quarterly* 28, no. 2 (Summer 1976): 187–205.

Koester, Nancy. *Harriet Beecher Stowe: A Spiritual Life.* Grand Rapids MI: William B. Eerdmans, 2014.

LaRoche, Cheryl Janifer. *Free Black Communities and the Underground Railroad: Geography of Resistance.* Champaign: University of Illinois Press, 2013.

Larson, Kate Clifford. *Bound for the Promised Land: Harriet Tubman: Portrait of an American Hero.* New York: Random House, 2004.

Lerner, Gerda. "The Lady and the Mill Girl: Changes in the Status of Women in the Age of Jackson." *American Studies Journal* 10, no. 1 (Spring 1969): 5–15.

Longstreet, James. *The Battle of Fredericksburg.* Battles and Leaders of the Civil War. 3 vols. New York: Thomas Yoseloff, 1956.

Massey, Mary Elizabeth. *Women in the Civil War.* Lincoln NE: Bison Books, 1994.

McPherson, James M. *Battle Cry of Freedom: The Civil War Era.* New York: Oxford University Press, 1988.

———. *Crossroads of Freedom: Antietam: The Battle That Changed the Course of the Civil War.* New York: Crown, 2003.

———. *For Cause and Comrades: Why Men Fought in the Civil War.* New York: Oxford University Press, 1997.

Norton, Mary Beth, and Ruth M. Alexander, eds. *Major Problems in American Women's History: Documents and Essays.* New York: Houghton Mifflin, 2007.

Oates, Stephen B. *A Woman of Valor: Clara Barton and the Civil War.* New York: Free Press, 1994.

Okker, Patricia. *Our Sister Editors: Sarah J. Hale and the Tradition of Nineteenth-Century American Women Editors.* Athens: University of Georgia Press, 1995.

Otis, James. *Rights of British Colonies Asserted and Proved.* Boston, 1765.

Parish, Peter J. *The American Civil War.* New York: Holmes and Meier, 1975.

Petry, Ann. *Harriet Tubman: Conductor on the Underground Railroad.* New York: HarperCollins, 1955.

Plumb, Robert C. *Your Brother in Arms: A Union Soldier's Odyssey.* Columbia: University of Missouri Press, 2011.

Potter, David M. *The Impending Crisis, 1848–1861.* New York: Harper & Row, 1976.

Pryor, Elizabeth Brown. *Clara Barton: Professional Angel.* Philadelphia: University of Pennsylvania Press, 1987.

Richards, Laura, and Maude Howe Elliot. *Julia Ward Howe, 1819–1910.* With Florence Howe Hall. Boston: Houghton Mifflin, 1925.

Rogers, Sherbrooke. *Sarah Josepha Hale: A New England Pioneer, 1788–1879.* Grantham NH: Tompson & Rutter, 1985.

Sears, Stephen. *Gettysburg.* New York: Mariner Books, 2004.

Sernett, Milton G. *Harriet Tubman: Myth, Memory, and History.* Durham NC: Duke University Press, 2007.

Showalter, Elaine. *The Civil Wars of Julia Ward Howe: A Biography.* New York: Simon & Schuster, 2016.

Sigerman, Harriet. *Laborers for Liberty: American Women, 1865–1890.* New York: Oxford University Press, 1994.

Stowe, Charles Edward. *The Life of Harriet Beecher Stowe: Compiled from Her Letters.* New York: Houghton Mifflin, 1889.

Stowe, Harriet Beecher. *A Key to Uncle Tom's Cabin—Presenting the Original Facts and Documents upon Which the Story Is Founded Together with Corroborative Statements—the Truth of the Work.* Boston: John P. Jewett, 1853. Reprint, Applewood Books, 1998.

———. *Lady Byron's Life Vindicated: A History of the Byron Controversy, from Its Beginning in 1816 to the Present Time.* Boston: Fields, Osgood, 1870.

———. *Poganuc People: Their Loves and Lives.* (1878) Reprint, Charleston: BiblioBazaar, 2009.

———. "The True Story of Lady Byron's Life." *Atlantic Monthly* 24 (September 1869): 295–313.

———. *Uncle Tom's Cabin*. Boston: John P. Jewett, 1852. Reprint, Barnes & Noble, with Amanda Claybaugh introduction, 2003.

Telford, Emma P. "Harriet: The Modern Moses of Heroism and Visions." Auburn NY: Cayuga County Museum, 1905.

U.S. Congress. *Report of the Joint Committee on the Conduct of the War*, 37th Congress, 3rd Session, 1862–1863. Report no. 108, 3 vols. Washington DC, 1863.

Villard, Oswald Garrison. *John Brown, 1800–1859: A Biography Fifty Years After*. Cambridge MA: Houghton Mifflin, 1911.

Ward, Geoffrey C. *The Civil War*. New York: Knopf, 1990.

Welter, Barbara. "The Cult of True Womanhood: 1820–1860." *American Quarterly* 18, no. 2, part 1 (Summer 1966): 151–74.

Whitman, Walt. *Drum Taps*. New York: Library of America, 1982.

Williams, T. Harry, Richard N. Current, and Frank Freidel. *A History of the United States (to 1876)*. New York: Knopf, 1961.

Wood, Gordon. *Empire of Liberty: A History of the Early Republic, 1789–1815*. New York: Oxford University Press, 2009.

Woody, Thomas. *A History of Women's Education in the United States*. New York: Science Press, 1929.

Ziegler, Valarie. *Diva Julia: The Public Romance and Private Agony of Julia Ward Howe*. Harrisburg PA: Trinity Press, 2003.

INDEX

Abbott, Bud, 186

abolitionism: approaches to, 127; in
Great Britain, 186; Harriet Tubman's
involvement in, 109; history in U.S.,
51–53; Howes' involvement in, 90–91;
literature about, 60, 63–64; methods
of, 64–65

abolitionists: on African American soldiers, 106; assistance to escaped
slaves, 34–35, 42, 43, 45; avoidance
of discussion about, 29; at Harpers
Ferry, 47–49; manifesto of, 53–54; as
military commanders, 108, 110; postwar need for, 139; punishment of, 36,
45, 59; Stowes as, 57, 203; women as,
18, 19, 137

"An Act for the Gradual Abolition of
Slavery" (1780), 52

Adams, Abigail, 52

Adams, Charles Francis, 115

Adams, John, 52

Africa, 38, 39

African Americans: as abolitionists,
36, 40, 42, 60; education of, 136, 137,
150; effect of Civil War on, xi; as prisoners of war, 107; rights of, 36, 39,
45, 52, 135–37, 139, 142, 145, 146, 153,
158, 165, 175, 181–82; speech patterns
of, 60–61; in Union Army and Navy,
102, 106–8, 120, 142; whites' attitudes
toward, 49, 144. *See also* slavery

African Methodist Episcopal Church,
182, 200

Alabama, 67, 136

Albany NY, 35, 45

Alexander, Edward Porter, 101

Alexandria VA, 77, 96

American Academy of Arts and Letters, 175

American Freedmen's Commission, 136

American Ladies' Magazine, 29, 128,
129, 148

American Red Cross. *See* Red Cross

American Slavery as It Is (Weld), 60

American Woman Suffrage Association
(AWSA), 146, 153, 160

Anderson, Robert, 67

Andersonville Prison, 16, 146, 162–63, 218

Andover MA, 61

Andover Theological Seminary, 61

Andrew, Eliza, 9

Andrew, John, 9, 92, 93, 109

Anna and the King of Siam (Landon), 185

Annapolis MD, 146, 147

Ann Lee, Mother, 28

Anthony, Susan B., 140–41, 152, 153,
155, 158–59, 164, 165

Antietam, Battle of, 2, 13–15, 16, 79, 81,
96, 201

Anti-Slavery Society, 139

Appia, Louis, 165

Appomattox Court House, 120, 132

Aquia Creek, 99, 118

Arkansas, 136

Armenia, 177

Army of Northern Virginia, 79, 119

Army of the Potomac: ambulances for,
104; casualties in, 119; Clara Barton
with, 98; command of, 15; low morale
of, 81; medical director of, 69, 70;